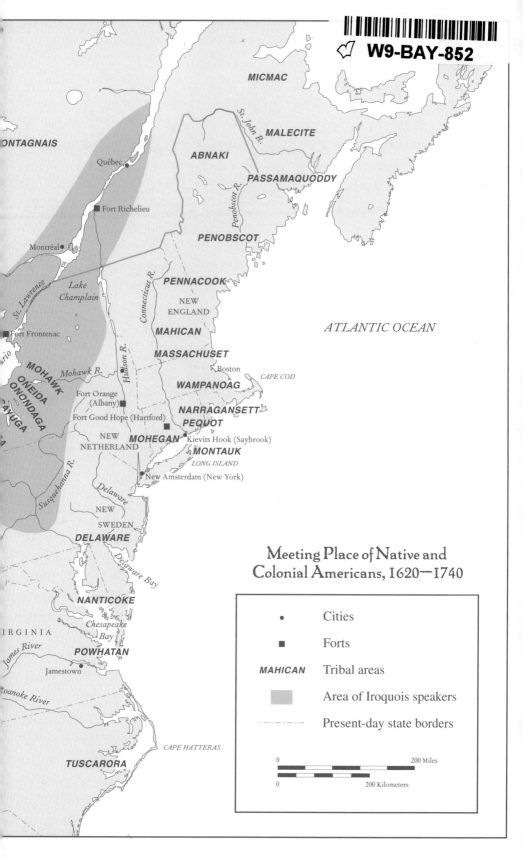

W9-BAY-852

MICMAC

MALECITE

ABNAKI

PASSAMAQUODDY

St. John R.

Penobscot R.

Québec

Fort Richelieu

PENOBSCOT

Montréal

ONTAGNAIS

St. Lawrence

Lake
Champlain

PENNACOOK

Connecticut R.

NEW
ENGLAND

MAHICAN

Fort Frontenac

Hudson R.

MASSACHUSET

Boston

CAPE COD

MOHAWK

Mohawk R.

ONEIDA

WAMPANOAG

ONONDAGA

Fort Orange
(Albany)

NARRAGANSETT

CAYUGA

Fort Good Hope (Hartford)

PEQUOT

NEW
NETHERLAND

MOHEGAN

Kievits Hook (Saybrook)

MONTAUK

LONG ISLAND

New Amsterdam (New York)

Susquehanna R.

Delaware

NEW
SWEDEN

DELAWARE

Delaware Bay

NANTICOKE

Chesapeake
Bay

IRGINIA

POWHATAN

James River

Jamestown

Roanoke River

CAPE HATTERAS

TUSCARORA

ATLANTIC OCEAN

Meeting Place of Native and Colonial Americans, 1620–1740

•	Cities
■	Forts
MAHICAN	Tribal areas
	Area of Iroquois speakers
– · – · –	Present-day state borders

0   200 Miles

0   200 Kilometers

GODS *of* WAR,
GODS *of* PEACE

ALSO BY RUSSELL BOURNE

Floating West:
The Erie and Other American Canals

The Red King's Rebellion:
Racial Politics in New England: 1675–1678

Americans on the Move:
A History of Waterways, Railways, and Highways

Rivers of America:
Birthplaces of Culture, Commerce, and Community

RUSSELL BOURNE

GODS *of* WAR, GODS *of* PEACE

HOW the MEETING *of* NATIVE and COLONIAL RELIGIONS SHAPED EARLY AMERICA

HARCOURT, INC.
New York   San Diego   London

www.HarcourtBooks.com

Library of Congress Cataloging-in-Publication Data
Bourne, Russell.
Gods of war, gods of peace: how the meeting of native and colonial religions
shaped early America/Russell Bourne.
p.   cm.
Includes bibliographical references and index.
ISBN 0-15-100501-X
1. United States—Religion—To 1800.   I. Title
BL252.B685   2002
200'.973'09033—dc21   2001005952

Text set in Fournier
Designed by Linda Lockowitz
First edition
A C E G I K J H F D B

Printed in the United States of America

To Clyde Taylor,

who wanted a history book
about people you could believe,
that is, believe with

For the earth is our mother, nourishing all her children,
bears, birds, fish, and all men. The woods, the streams,
everything on it belongs to everybody and is for the use of all.
How can one man say it belongs to him only?

—MASSASOIT

And then if any one says to you, "Look, here is the Christ!"
or "Look, there he is!" do not believe it. False Christs and
false prophets will arise and show signs and wonders,
to lead astray, if possible, the elect. But take heed . . .

—MARK 13:21–23

CONTENTS

PREFACE

AMERICA'S HISTORY
of CONTENDING FAITHS

THE MEETING OF European civilization with Native American civilization in North America has been called and colored by many words—most popularly, today, by the adjective *invasive*. Yet it seems strange, with religion so often conceded to be at the heart of respective cultures, that this particularly American meeting has so rarely been viewed as a confrontation of two historic and still evolving religious systems, with immense consequences for the different cultures.

If simply and successfully invasive, the clash of two such groups would have resulted in an awful *Götterdämmerung*—the destruction of the native people's divinities. But that did not happen, as Native Americans of today assure us with increasing vigor. Compared to the clashes of religious empires in Europe and Asia (which tended to be matters of wipeout or amalgamation), something quite different occurred in America's northeastern woodlands: As the two peoples encountered each other across the centuries (1620–1830), their religions shuddered, gave good for good and bad for bad, and changed in order to survive. That change through interaction dramatically altered but did not blend the peoples' separate cultures, resulting in a strangely uncombined, uniquely American civilization. It resembles that of no other nation on earth.

The story of that interaction is truly an epic tale, replete with gods of war and peace attended by inspired prophets and thundering apostles. John Stuart Mill, who in his life and works managed to combine spirituality with logic, warned that, "There is no subject in which men's practical belief is more incorrectly indicated by the words they use to express it, than religion." Yes, how difficult it is to square the actual deeds of a group of people with the inspirational words they use to describe those deeds; how difficult also to agree with anyone else's definition of the divine or not divine forces behind our own blessed or cursed history. No wonder that both Native Americans and Euro-Americans tend to balk at the idea of shared religious influences.

Yet in many of the crucial victories and disasters of colonial America and Revolutionary America, Native Americans played key roles, however much we try to forget. They fought for and against the emerging nation, sharing their techniques for life and battle, imparting their codes just as they gave us their place names. Uncounted hundreds of Anglo-American men and women went incorrigibly native, preferring native freedom to Christian regulations. Simultaneously, hundreds of Native Americans went bravely Christian, trusting that the outlandish God might grant survival in this world if not heavenly rest in the one beyond. The evangelical spiritualism of the early American frontier was fueled, in this way, both by Calvinistic visions of hell's fire and by fiery encounters with the aroused Indians. Simultaneously, native cultures evolved, powered by the insights of prophets and the teachings of missionaries who attempted to deal differently with the stresses of changing times.

For millennia, the Native Americans had known sacredness of the land. Gradually, American settlers came to know it, too. Yet, with the exception of Roger Williams and a few others, new Americans chose to ignore or belittle the Native Americans' interpretation of the land's spirits. That interpretation, in the opinion of Vine Deloria (author of the seminal *God Is Red*), "has not been considered by [European and Christian] Westerners." He adds, "Yet it is precisely this consideration that must be made if Western societies are to be released from their religiously ethnocentric universe."

This book, on the other hand, seeks neither to challenge nor to advocate religious concepts but to present the stories of the leaders and followers who shaped early America in images of faith. There on the frontier—the borderland that religious historian Richard Niebuhr called "the rude smithy of the new world"—attitudes of morality and institutions of civilization developed that made America what it is. Two peoples, having called upon their respective gods of peace and war, having been harangued by their prophets and apostles, were battered into becoming Americans of unceasingly, creatively interacting beliefs.

—RUSSELL BOURNE
Ithaca, New York

GODS *of* WAR,
GODS *of* PEACE

CHAPTER I

The DEVILISH INTERACTION
of TWO RELIGIONS

PRESIDENT THOMAS JEFFERSON, having recently hosted and grandly entertained a Seneca prophet in Washington, wrote to him in 1802 that he did, indeed, seem to have been "favored by the Divine spirit." Because Jefferson himself was a rationalist who felt little personal empathy for traditional religionists, it might seem out of character for him to salute a Native American leader in such words and to speak of divinity. But this was no obscure villager to whom Jefferson was writing and certainly no naive shaman; this was the dynamic and articulate Handsome Lake, who, fired by an intense sense of godly purpose, had spent the years after the American Revolution preaching moral reform among the Iroquois peoples. Appropriate and careful words were necessary.

The president, sincerely admiring Handsome Lake's teachings (if only because they stressed his own favorite theme: family farming), praised "the great reformation" that the prophet was undertaking. Yet what made this exchange between two notable Americans of the Republic's early years truly remarkable was the final phrase in Jefferson's letter. He wrote of Handsome

Lake and his people, "You are our brethren of the same land, we wish you your prosperity as brethren should do. Farewell." It was as if the archbishops of two national churches in neighboring countries were nodding genially across a frontier at each other with enduring and mutual respect. How different American history would have been if that fraternal spirituality had actually conditioned the events of the centuries to follow. Congenial brethren of the same continent was not at all what Native Americans and Euro-Americans were destined to be. For neither colonial nor postcolonial Americans would ever extend sufficient respect to the religious beliefs of the Algonquian and Iroquois people whom they encountered on the early frontier—least of all any understanding that Native American religious concepts were evolving in a way closely related to the developments of their own frontier denominations. There was no doubt about one mutual factor among people on each side of the racial barrier: Their religions inspired them, consoled them, united them. Furthermore, in those very, very different American religions there was also a certain commonality: a belief in rituals, even in the imminent reappearance of a messiah, and certainly in men like Handsome Lake who were so charged with godly energy that they seemed nearly gods themselves. No wonder Jefferson felt moved to remark, in the spirit of the Enlightenment, how favored the Seneca prophet was by the "divine spirit."

No wonder, also, that Jefferson, even while focusing on a program of quite secular objectives for his nation, saw the usefulness of religion. Perhaps it would be better to say that Jefferson saw religion—and those who practiced it progressively, like Handsome Lake—as one of the most likely tools for advancement in the United States. In that same letter of November 3, 1802, he referred to the Seneca prophet as an "instrument of so happy a change," and forecast that, in recognition of the advances he had helped make, his "children's children, from generation to generation [would] repeat your name with love and gratitude forever." With what scorn Native Americans today (some of whom, among the Iroquois, remain devoted members of the church founded by Handsome Lake) recall Jefferson's prediction of eternal harmony resulting from cultural change.

CONTACT and CONVERSION

Yet, for all its disappointments and complexities, for all its economic and political aspects, the cultural contact between Anglo-Americans and Native Americans in the past three centuries becomes most understandable when seen as an intrinsically religious encounter. That is the purpose of this book: to assist the reader in entering the time when gods and demons seemed to contend with each other, when prophets and apostles explained the disturbances of the cosmos, and when to be religious was normative. The book's clock starts ticking shortly before the hour in 1635 when the recently arrived Puritans of Massachusetts decreed that church attendance was compulsory for all citizens, under penalty of fines and imprisonment. Though the Puritans would soon become the lesser fraction of their colony's population, they would continue to set the philosophical tone.

It was in religious terms that the early Pilgrims and Puritans evaluated the anxious Algonquian who had greeted them— reaching the peculiar conclusion that the aborigines must be one of the lost tribes of Israel. Otherwise, how would they relate to the Bible, in which all was revealed? Additionally, it seemed probable to the Puritans that the Indians had been corrupted by the Devil, who now worked through them to frustrate the founding of the New Jerusalem.

There were, to be sure, a host of Pilgrims and several Puritans to whom the contacted Native Americans seemed worthy of respect and regard, particularly for their morality and their spiritual qualities. Plymouth's Governor Edward Winslow, for example, expressed admiration for the courage and integrity of the Wampanoag people's *pnieses,* religiously active warrior-counselors. Most outspoken of these open-minded English settlers was the renegade John Morton, known for his remark that the Algonquian of Massachusetts were "more full of humanity" than the stern-backed, parochial English who were then arriving by the shipful.

But it was Roger Williams, Separatist clergyman and founder of Rhode Island, who perceived most accurately the religious nature of his particular neighbors, the Narragansett. As portrayed in chapter 4, those haughty and populous Algonquian had remained untouched by either white men's plagues or other tribes' rivalries, protected they believed by their god Cautantowwit (or Kiehtan), whose ancestral home was thought to have been in the southwestern part of the continent. They welcomed Roger Williams among them, in part because of his natural respectfulness, in part because he proved to be a good trader of goods between them and the English settlements.

For Roger Williams's own purposes—which included gaining a greater sense of God's design by studying the natives and securing land for himself and his followers—he entered upon a methodical analysis of Narragansett religion and language. This occurred at a time when many of the Christians in the settler communities were responding to the New World's opportunities by becoming more interested in how to improve their lots than by how to save their souls. To such backsliders into moralistic individualism and to us in later years Williams wrote, "He that questions whether God made the world, the Indians will teach him."

Here was a European churchman in the distinctly unusual role of studying the character of the Native Americans' religion—a study in which missionaries and other ambassadors of later years were, generally speaking, not successful. The Indians, in their own quite different ways, sought vainly to bring the English settlers into a framework of understanding through the lens of religion. As European-introduced liquors, sugary products, and epidemics decimated the native populations in the Massachusetts villages, these Algonquian suspected there must be a weakening of their old gods—or, at least, of the spiritual powers wielded by their shamans and sorcerers. The prime function of those tribal practitioners was to preserve the health of the villagers; only power from another world, wielded by a well-schooled medicine man, could drive out the demons of ill health. Thus, as the native Massachusetts population declined and the numbers and capacities of the English settlers increased, it seemed manifest that a change of a profoundly religious nature was occurring.

Chief Passaconaway stands forth as one of those early Native Americans who, in the face of religious odds, perceived a change in the heavens and took the course of accommodation. While his Pennacook people had dominated the Merrimack River valley for decades, and while he, as both powwow (sorcerer) and administrative leader of those people, had initially fought against encroachment by the white settlers, he came to see the futility of the fight. This seemed particularly clear to him after his wife and son were taken prisoner by the English forces and after he received heavenly visions suggesting the way of peace. In 1644, he pledged the cessation of hostilities and, upon his deathbed, accepted the invitation to become a Christian that had been offered to him by the Puritan missionary John Eliot.

As further described in chapter 4, this event in New England history was as important in the evolution of Eliot's own spiritual growth as it was climactic in the life and death of Passaconaway. In the broader story of interaction between Native American and Anglo-American cultures, it remains significant as an indication that, while religious-inflamed hatred may be one result of interracial contact, conversion may be another. Yet to many Native American commentators, conversion historically represented not the spiritual breakthrough of an exalted individual but the surrender of an exhausted tribesman to the overweening invaders. When the most effective and most sympathetic missionary of pre-Revolutionary America, Samuel Kirkland, was pressing the Bible upon the Oneida Iroquois, opposed leaders from elsewhere in Iroquoia urged that the magic book be rejected. One Seneca chief warned the Oneida that, if they accepted it, they would become "a miserable and abject people," just like the Pennacook and other humbled tribesmen of the East.

Conversion, it must be said, comes in many surprising guises and is often a two-way affair. One thinks, for example, of the dramatic way in which America's first naturalist, William Bartram, became converted to the astonishingly beautiful and virginal world of the Carolinas, which he explored just before the American Revolution. Not just the land forms and the flora entranced him but also the people, the Muskogee, and their sophisticated variety of worship. Bartram, overcome by the glory of what he had witnessed, wrote of the tribesmen's "cult of the sacred," and described the millenarian theology of their prophets.

Hector St. John de Crèvecoeur, the Americanized French agriculturalist who wrote *Letters from an American Farmer* in 1782, paid special attention to this key issue of who was converting whom in the postcolonial republic. He marveled that "thousands of European [settlers] are [now] Indians; and yet we have no examples of one of those Aborigines having from choice become European."

Yale professor James Axtell, perhaps the most sensitive modern commentator on this phenomenon and author of *The Invasion Within*, urges readers to view the Bartram-type of woodland conversion and the going-native phenomenon described by de Crèvecoeur as vital aspects of American history. He writes that

> the Indians, in the face of incredible odds, managed to convert several hundred English and French colonists not so much to a native religion (which was an individual rather than a national affair) as to the whole native way of life. While wracked by disease, war, and dislocation, the Indians successfully conveyed to large numbers of adversaries, through a remarkable process of education, their own ineluctable pride, social warmth, and cultural integrity.

So here in the early days of contact one can observe accommodation of a peculiarly spiritual sort, not exactly a surrender, not truly a mass movement, but a series of individual commitments on both sides to the other's beliefs. These conversions are obviously different from those forced upon Native Americans by Spanish priests in the wake of the conquistadores. They are also different from the conversions pushed upon weakened Native Americans by the frontier missionaries described in the later chapters of this book. They speak to the whole issue of religion as a meeting ground between people in historic contact—with results both accommodational and otherwise.

The word most often used to describe the spiritual contact opposite from accommodation is nativist. And this word, used by modern scholars to describe the Indians' determination to fight back against cultural takeover, is applied particularly to those Native Americans who responded to the rallying call of certain religious figures. Of these the greatest were Neolin, the Delaware Prophet, who came forth at the time of Pontiac's so-called rebellion in 1763 (chapter 6) and Tenskwatawa, the Shawnee Prophet and brother of Tecumseh, who breathed fire into the Algonquian and Iroquois forces allied against William Henry Harrison on the Indiana frontier before and after the War of 1812 (chapter 8). Yet those visionary and well-remembered spokesmen for the native gods had been preceded by an impressive list of earlier god-struck leaders whose names are honored by nativists today as intuitive founders of an ages-old and never dying movement.

Let us take special note of two of them, Nemattanew and Popé. The former was a charismatic prophet who came forth to aid the people of Powhatan (Wahunsonacock) in present-day Virginia after the death of that great leader in the year 1618.

Though these coastal Algonquian had been discouraged and defeated by the oppressions of John Smith's well-armed colonists, Nemattanew vowed to bring about a return to the ancient order existing before the Englishmen's disruptive arrival. By giving encouragement and inspiration to Wahunsonacock's brother Opechananough, Nemattanew was able to initiate a nearly successful battle plan for freedom before he was assassinated in 1622. It was a close-call struggle for existence that the Virginians never forgot.

The latter nativist leader, a Tewa medicine man in what is now New Mexico, succeeded in carrying out an uprising of some five hundred Pueblo people against the Spanish occupation forces in 1680. Driving the knights and priests of New Spain completely out of the territory, Popé then found himself confronting irresolute tribesmen. They were reluctant to abandon all of the Spanish agricultural improvements and unpersuaded by his preachings of the purity of ancient ways. In response, he himself became something of a tyrant. Finally overcome by a combination of Pueblo people, Popé died in rejection and despair in 1690.

Professor Axtell counts these outbursts led by intensely nativistic and increasingly nationalistic prophets as the second phase of a three-stage progression witnessed among people of the Native American faiths. Preceding the violent era of Nemattanew and Popé had been a time of archaic and tribal beliefs, characterized by an underlying social morality and a burgeoning of nature legends. Following the century of the nationalistic prophets (generally, the seventeenth century) came a time of far more widespread, universal religions, such as the one preached by Handsome Lake. Neolin and Tenskwatawa are seen as existing when the second of these eras was evolving into the third—they are figures in continuum.

In a somewhat similar way, the religious historian Richard Niebuhr sees Anglo-American Protestantism as experiencing its own three-step evolution: first, the sovereignty of God, as so fiercely preached by the orthodox Puritans of the seventeenth century; then, the reign of Jesus Christ, as so emotionally realized by the frontier evangelists of the eighteenth century (particularly those who figured in the so-called Great Awakening of the 1740s); and third, the Kingdom of God, as envisioned by the pluralists of the nineteenth century, who welcomed all to their temples of worship.

Joseph Smith, the apostle of Mormonism, can be understood as belonging among these latter American evangelists, figures who sprang from American soil and preached a form of Christianity replete with wholly indigenous themes. William Apess, the Methodist minister of Pequot ancestry who staged the impressive Mashpee Revolt of 1833 against Jacksonian removal policies, should be recognized as another such leader. He concludes this book as a representative of both nativism and Christian evolution. He and other Americans, whether they knew it or not, were living in a world conditioned by both European and Native American religious factors.

CONVERSIONS for SELF and for COUNTRY

William James, whose *The Varieties of Religious Experience* (1912) continues to give helpful clues to personal spirituality, described religion in one of that book's memorable passages as possessing "a preponderance of loving affections." Indeed, this was the aspect of religion that encouraged President Jefferson to believe he and Handsome Lake could make common cause, eternally. But religion also possesses a dark face—as witnessed during all three phases of the Native Americans' religious evolution and equally during all three phases of Anglo-American religious development. To draw nearer to that contradiction, to that fireplace of light and darkness, is another purpose of this book. Yet it must be remembered that, while religion deals with absolutes, history deals with relative relationships; this book will stick to history.

When it comes to the cause and effect of history and religion, a number of small and large incidents come to mind. One recalls, for example, the church bells that pealed so joyously in Puritan Boston when that city's pelf-hunting soldiers returned victoriously from their bloody slaughters among the Pequot Algonquian during the War of 1637. Or one shudders at the zeal with which God-fearing citizens of that Puritan capital smashed missionary John Eliot's boat when he attempted to sail out to feed and clothe the Christian Indians interned on Deer Island in King Philip's War of 1675. Those incidents helped, one after another in a cultural pattern, to give a weird kind of righteous legitimacy to the later massacres of Indian villages (both Christian and otherwise) at the hands of Bible-thumping frontiersmen during the Revolution. But most of all, in that dreadful connection, one thinks of the white Christian leaders who rejoiced in the racial edicts of Andrew Jackson and cooperated in the annihilistic Indian Removal Act of the 1830s, even as certain other Christians strove to spare the Indians from being forced out on that Trail of Tears to the West.

One answer to the conundrum of religious behavior, good

and ill, is that the prophets and the apostles do not truly control what happens on earth, or even in heaven. Men and women, natives and settlers, are dramatically altered by such traumatic events as wars and earth convulsions. Then the religious leader comes to the fore, to aid or abet his stricken people. The late-nineteenth-century religious historian James Moody (author of *The Ghost Dance Religion*) was but the first of many scholars to recognize the often repeated truth among Native American peoples that when a tribe found its very existence threatened, a prophet would arise who, in Moody's words, would "strive to avert the disaster by molding his people to a common purpose through insistence upon the sacred character of his message."

These were the autochthonous prophets who, along with Anglo-America's own indigenous apostles, uniquely shaped the moral and even political climate of the emerging nation among all its peoples. Richard Niebuhr has referred to this out-of-the-blue appearance of prophets as "the organic movement of those who have been called and sent." Again it should be emphasized that the religious figures tended to arrive on the scene at times when the culture was profoundly threatened. This type of crisis, these disruptions of the cultural norm, had different names and faces—defeats in war, seasons of drought, radical imperial pronouncements, food shortages, or population changes. Whether considered natural or unnatural events, they provided the fiery background for the native and Anglo-American leaders who helped shape American history.

What may be difficult for many Americans to accept is historian Francis Jennings's observation that, between the races, "interaction caused constant transformation *on both sides* [italics added]." So it was in religious matters above all. One small example may be seen in the life of the apostle John Eliot. Because of his personal contact with Passaconaway, Waban, and other native figures of considerable theological comprehension, he transformed himself from an English Puritan with preconditioned views of Native Americans to an American religious leader with the faith and desire to help preserve the native language. This he accomplished through his lifelong mission of translating the scriptures into Algonquian.

A graphic way of expressing such interaction is to imagine the spiritual upheavals that burst upon native villages and white outposts alike after 1620 as a series of firestorms. The first of these paroxysms occurred on the Atlantic coast; it involved the collision of Christian teachings from overseas (introduced by the black-robed Jesuits of Canada and by the wordy theologians of New England) against the resident, native concepts. The second firestorm arose from America's interior settlements and mixed-race communities, swirling upward and outward to excite all people of the borderlands with the fervor of (as it has been called) the Great Awakening. The third storm was witnessed on the more distant, trans-Appalachian territories in the early 1800s, ultimately sweeping up both western land claimants and nativistic tribesmen in a frenzy of nationalistic religiosity. For all the separatism of the two people's religious heritage, the forces that challenged them and called them forth during these times were mutual and interactive.

It was unavoidable that mutuality of experience should result in an influential relationship. As the two peoples harvested during the same seasons and contested for the same woodlands, they exchanged values and spiritual sentiments and goddamning insults in the marketplace, at the treaty tables, and across the battlements. Their divinely inspired prophets and apostles had given them supernatural equipment (rites and prohibitions and admonitions) to defend themselves against the insecurities of an unstable universe. Now they would go forth into the world, expressing their refounded faith in action.

For the Puritans, that meant trying to force the Massachusetts natives into a regularized, short-haired way of life called *civilitie*, even while those perceptive people and their allies sought to employ English arms against the rival Iroquois. For the Quakers and Shakers this meant attempting to teach and deal with the Delaware tribesmen, even while learning from them some forms of meditation and even some dance steps. For certain coastal Algonquian, this meant learning to survive, even at the cost of becoming Christian. For the Iroquois of the interior, it meant putting the torch to hybrid communities founded by the French Jesuits, even while countenancing other interactive communities that accepted Yankee clergy. There was no keeping the other out.

The role of missionaries in this interactive dance of cultures has long been debated. Yet even the most bitter opponents of Christian proselytizing admit that the missionaries of the seventeenth and eighteenth centuries did intend to help Algonquian and Iroquois make a more comfortable transition into the new conditions of the day. James Axtell and others have pointed out, however, that, by their successful inclusion of some hundreds of willingly adopted whites, the Native Americans won "the key victory" in the conversion contest.

At one point in the life of Hector St. John de Crèvecoeur, when overwhelming events threatened his life, conversion seemed to offer the one way to safety. Having arrived in the

New World shortly before Great Britain's 1760 victory in the French and Indian War, de Crèvecoeur, a highly intelligent and sensitive product of France's best Jesuit schools, forsook his French heritage and devoted himself to raising an American family after the war in New York State's Orange County. When the War of Independence burst on the frontier in the next decade, he found himself in a most unfortunate position, for his wife belonged to a Loyalist family. Though his own sentiments favored the patriots, he regarded the war as nothing but a disaster for both the Indians and the whites in the countryside he had come to love. What could he do?

His first thought was to avoid the Revolution in all its guises by fleeing into the wilderness, perhaps finding haven among the Iroquois with whom he and his uncle had traded before the last war. He had been adopted by the Oneida Iroquois during his youth, and he had reason to trust the faithfulness of their hospitality. Reassured by recent messages from his former companions, he made a careful plan of self-exile: He and his family would try to work as basic farmers in the Iroquois villages, where reconciliation had been a cherished principle ever since the people had received the Great Law of Peace and Power from their sixteenth-century native saint, Hiawatha.

Explaining the reasoning behind his plan in the twelfth of his *Letters*, de Crèvecoeur recalled that there, among the Iroquois, "a singular appearance of peace and concord are the first characteristics which strike you." There, he felt sure, he and his family would be able to avoid Old World bellicosities. There he would encounter none of the contemporary European militarists who, as he portrayed them, "for sixpence per day, may be engaged to shed the blood of any people on earth."

De Crèvecoeur fully recognized that he and his family might lose their own civilized ways while living among the Iroquois, saying with deceptive casualness: "Thus shall we metamorphose ourselves." It was in this same letter that he pondered how it happened that, while very few Indians seemed able to adapt themselves to living in the homes and towns of European settlers, no Europeans whom he had heard of, settlers who had been adopted for whatever reason by an Indian family, ever consented willingly to being returned to white civilization. He even considered that Native American culture might be psychologically and ethically "superior":

> Let us say what we will of them, of their inferior organs, of their want of bread, &c. They are as stout and well made as the Europeans. Without temples, priests, without kings, and without laws they are in many instances superior to us; and the proofs of what I advance are, that they live without care, sleep without inquietude, take life as it comes, bearing all its asperities with unparalleled patience, and die without any kind of apprehension for what they have done, or for what they expect to meet with hereafter. What system of philosophy can give us so many necessary qualifications for happiness? They most certainly are much more closely connected with nature than we are; they are her immediate children.

The single fear de Crèvecoeur had for his family in their projected wilderness retreat during the Revolution was that they, or at least his younger children, might get "caught by that singular charm" that Indian "education" possesses. He went on to say that, given the unwillingness of many white captives to return home, "there must be something very bewiching in [the Indians'] manners." And he trusted that two precautions might prevent that bewitchment from occurring. The first of these was that if "we keep ourselves busy in tilling the earth [as opposed to hunting], there is no fear of any of us becoming wild." The second was the hope that he and his wife, having continued to instruct the children in the basics of the Christian religion, would be able to control the wandering of their own souls.

It appears from these ruminations almost as if de Crèvecoeur had already been converted to some of the Iroquois cultural concepts, admiring as he did their communal peacefulness and their nature-based approach to the spiritual world. He even confessed, "As to religion, our mode of worship will not suffer much [negative change] by this removal from a cultivated country, into the bosom of the woods." And he went on to describe the religion his children would possess after their years in the wilderness:

> If they do not fear God according to the tenets of any one seminary, they shall learn to worship him upon the broader scale of nature. The Supreme Being does not reside in peculiar churches or communities; he is equally the great Manitou of the woods and the plains; and even in the gloom, the obscurity of those very woods, his justice may be as well understood and felt as in the most sumptuous temples.

Ultimately de Crèvecoeur thought better of northwestward escape into Indian country and turned eastward with one of his sons, only to be imprisoned and released to France by the British before being returned home after the "unfortunate Revolution" had run its course. Yet his imaginative description of the process of conversion to native ways still has great pertinence, if only as a contrast to conversions forced upon tribesmen by heavy-handed missionaries or excessively zealous (and demeaning) evangelists.

De Crèvecoeur's sincere near conversion to the religious heart of an Indian culture also stands in contrast to a type of false conversion that has been one of the curses of the interaction between Anglo-Americans and Native Americans. This may be called Tontoism or Tammanyism, the former in honor of the early Hollywood image of an all-suffering, noble native sidekick who serves for the greater glory of the heroic Lone Ranger, the latter in recognition of a certain fake saint. This is St. Tammany, a mostly imaginary figure whose name recalled the Lenni Lenape chief who signed the first treaty with William Penn's Quaker colonists at Shackamaxon on the Delaware River in 1682. Inventing their own version of this exemplary chief, a party of activists dubbed him a saint and called themselves "Sons of Tammany" to carry on his supposedly democratic spirit. Their organization, part marching club, part patriotic pressure group, succeeded in making a kind of impression on American politics.

When the Tammany societies became more formally organized in 1786, the very real and much honored Seneca Chief Cornplanter (an ally of Handsome Lake) was among the Native Americans invited to instruct his white friends in appropriate ceremonies. Courteously (and with what kind of inner amusement?) he went along with their charade. Taking as their motto the ugh-like phrase "Freedom our Rock!" the societies held out for reforms on behalf of the common man. And although the societies' pseudo-Indian rites and titles seem ridiculous if not shameful today, they were regarded seriously throughout the

Jeffersonian and Jacksonian eras. Later the movement was taken over by upper-class managers, also known as bosses. The point, however, had been made: Once there was a time of interaction when an Indian saint (real or imagined) could inspire white Americans and could give them an added power in a time of stress, though to Native Americans that bit of fakery could only seem a cultural insult.

RELIGION and NATIONALISM

Alexis de Tocqueville and other European visitors of the early nineteenth century perceived that, in the creation of American democracy, religion was indeed one of the most readily available tools and most curious strengths. He wrote, "On my arrival in the United States [1830], the religious aspect of the country was the first thing that struck my attention, and the longer I stayed there, the more I perceived the great political consequences resulting from this new state of things." In another passage, scratching his head in amazement, he reported that "Religious insanity is very common in the United States."

Insane or otherwise, intermixed or pure, the religion of America has from the earliest colonial times been a driver of the nation's wheels. In the words of colonial historian Edmund S. Morgan,

> The mingling of the sense of national destiny with religious zeal and purpose ... has a complicated history in this country; but it certainly found an impetus in the Puritan effort to set up in the New World a "City upon a Hill" for all the world to behold.

Continuing after the Puritans, in the era of the founding fathers, religion served useful worldly as well as otherworldly purposes—as seen in Jefferson's letter to Handsome Lake.

That same brand of religion definitely helped build a national identity and purpose. Although new ethnic and denominational streams were mixing with the Calvinistic Protestantism and fervid Anglicanism of the original colonists by the late 1700s, historians point out that three-quarters of the men who signed the Declaration of Independence had come from Puritan stock. Their souls still carried that burden; their sons and grandchildren would carry on that tradition in the new century under the watchful eyes of Jonathan Edwards and the Yale faculty (Harvard having lurched off the road into rationalism). Their old religion, as preachers carried it over the Appalachians and into the Ohio valleys, became increasingly evangelical as the settlers faced the perils of aroused and well-armed tribesmen on the frontier. Native American religions simultaneously gained strength and focus in identifying the cause of Indian unification and in helping develop what George Tinker calls "the strategy of alienation" from white society. Nationalism became identified either with the cross (the crusade of Manifest Destiny) or with the totemic red sticks of Tecumseh's allied armies.

Protestant theology turned into something quite different in the United States than in Europe, thanks, in part, to the interaction with American themes and the continuing challenge of the western tribes. The second president's son, John Quincy Adams, asked rhetorically in 1802,

> What is the right of the huntsman to the forest of a thousand miles over which he has accidentally ranged in quest

of prey?... Shall the fields and valleys, which a beneficent God has formed to teem with the life of innumerable multitudes, be condemned to everlasting barrenness?

Obviously God had meant the new Americans to prosper in this great land; that was their divine destiny. Similarly, it was the divine destiny of Tecumseh's forces to hold their land. There they stood, combative forces locked in common purpose, worshiping different gods, abetted by peculiarly American preachers and prophets.

It seems especially ironic, in this connection, to remember one of Cotton Mather's most doom-laden admonitions. The grand old Puritan had warned that as Anglo-Americans pushed farther into the savage wilderness they should defend against becoming, in their habits and in their religious thinking "too like the Indians."

PART I

CHAPTER 2

A WAMPANOAG "SAINT" and a NARRAGANSETT PRINCE

FUR-LADEN SHIPS sailing downriver from Albany for the profit of Dutch colonial merchants and beaver traps on the Maumee in the days of the Old Northwest—they are the stuff of North American history, incidents and artifacts in place and time. Playing significant but overlooked roles in that drama are such figures as the Massachusetts Bay Colony's John Eliot, known as "Apostle to the Indians," and Hobomock, a profoundly spiritual *pniese,* or councillor, of Chief Massasoit's Wampanoag court. Theology apart, the time has come to appreciate what these religious stars and others of perhaps less brightness had to do with the earthy stuff of history. By taking a look at their lives and times—particularly at their inspired handling of crises at the meeting points of Euro-American and Native American cultures—we may gain both a new understanding of who shaped colonial America and also a new regard for the dynamic interactions of early American pluralism.

Admittedly, the religious figures of yesteryear rarely make it easy for us today to make sense of their words or to identify with their actions. Indeed, their words almost immediately seem

to get them into trouble, referring as they do to dogma and supernatural events unknown or distrusted by us. Perhaps it is for
that reason that Algonquian and many other Native American
groups do not have a single word for the practice or the objective of religion. Such holy matters, it must seem to them, cause
misunderstandings and suffer much in translation or expression. When asked by the nineteenth-century ethnologist Charles
Trowbridge whether the Miami people did not have at least one
phrase that made proper reference to things religious, his Algonquian guide replied with the words *Tipeew Eellminanke,* "It
is good to pray."

A further difficulty in trying to understand the proper place
of religious figures in American history is that their words often
do not always conform with their actions. When the Puritan
leaders of Eliot's time urged *civilitie* upon their Algonquian
charges, this appears now to have been merely another word for
exploitation. When the sixteenth-century Iroquois leader Hiawatha welcomed all people to the shelter of the sacred pine tree
in the name of Deganawidah, the great Peace Maker (as narrated in the next chapter), it seemed almost as if he were licens-
ing the widespread wars of aggression that followed. Again the
words of John Stuart Mill, first given in the preface, come to
mind. He wrote, "There is no subject in which men's practical
belief is more incorrectly indicated by the words they use to express it, than religion."

Given such warnings—that the locutions of Anglo-
European and Native American religion may be off-putting,
that the actions of spiritual leaders may have unintended results,
and that we ourselves may be looking at these affairs through
the glass of prejudice—it is nonetheless important to press for

an understanding. Only by bringing these hugely important religious figures out of the shadows where our secular incredulousness has put them will we be able to give them their earned position in the history of a complex and believing people.

THREE ALGONQUIAN FACING CONVERSION

The best way to start watching the intertwining spiritual dance of native prophets and colonial apostles may well be through the intercultural example of Squanto, one of three Native American religious figures who would assist and influence the Pilgrim colony on Cape Cod Bay in southeastern Massachusetts. They were all eastern Algonquian; that is, members of that vast and varied linguistic group that extended along the Atlantic drainage from the Maritime Provinces of Canada to the Carolinas (see endpaper map). They were also, distinctively, members of their own tribes. Their lives of faith, their creative acts among the colonists, and their responses to the stresses then endured by their own people show the changeability of experience at this threshold time of cultural contact.

A decade before 1620, Squanto had been captured by English explorers and sold as a slave in Spain. Escaping to England with the aid of a Franciscan friar, he worked in a merchant's house for several years before returning, finally, to the New England coast as a crewman aboard a fishing vessel. Fond of English ways yet determined to return to his old home at Patuxet (Plymouth's original name), he found there that his family and friends had been wiped out by disease. Then, seeking companionship as well as a livelihood, he took refuge among the neighboring Wampanoag, the people who would greet the Pilgrims soon after their landing.

To the Pilgrims, the clever and English-speaking Squanto became not only an essential teacher of how to survive on that sandy and exposed shore but also an actual "saint" (meaning one who joined and accepted the Pilgrims' Separatist form of Protestantism). In their early writings, the Pilgrims frequently recognized Squanto as their comrade (even though he always seemed to have his own ambitious agenda), calling him "a spetiall instrumente sent of God for their good beyond their expectation." Did his conversion, this easy shift of faiths, indicate that other Algonquian would also, with equal willingness, become devoted to Christ? Or were such conversions viewed by the majority of Indians as odious and corruptive, just as their opposites would to Increase Mather in Boston?

Plymouth's perennial governor, William Bradford, reported in his history of the colony that the religious leaders of "the savages," on learning of the strange ship's arrival and of the Pilgrims' landing on their shores, had first done everything in their spiritual power to exorcise the strangers. According to his account, the Indians had assembled in a "dark and dismal swamp," then had run through every religious rite they could recall for three successive days in an attempt to rout the invaders and their bizarre spirits. Only after failing in that religious maneuver and after recognizing that some other forces were at work here did they devise a diplomatic strategy for meeting with the Pilgrims.

That plan was put into effect after more than six weeks in which the Indians kept cautious watch on the newcomers from behind the dunes—a delay that greatly raised the anxiety level among the sick and hungry Pilgrims. Finally Massasoit's men made their move. As they burst from the forest, a single and virtually naked delegate led the way, striding across the field and through the gates. He marched unhesitatingly down Plymouth's central pathway, halting only when he stood directly in front of the common house, where it happened that an emergency meeting was in session. The tall, shining-skin Indian then raised his hand, and said (to the astonishment of those who came pouring out), "Welcome!"

It's an often told and still remarkable story. Here stood the obliging and flexible Samoset, the dramatically inclined spinner of tales who helped the Pilgrims learn about pastures and rivers beyond their own immediate horizons. He also introduced them to the even more linguistically talented Squanto a few days later.

Samoset began his own embassy to the Pilgrims on that first warm day by asking for some beer; after this was given to him (as well as an overcoat to conceal his nakedness), he explained that he was not a native resident but a visiting Abnaki sagamore, or subchief, from Maine who had learned his English at a fishing station up the coast at Pemaquid. He told the Pilgrims of the terrible plague of 1617 that had wiped out the Patuxet people (including the family of Squanto). Even more important, Samoset explained to the Pilgrims who really commanded affairs in this region: the much-revered Ousamequin (meaning Yellow Feather). Samoset added that in the long-established rulership tradition among the Wampanoag Pokanoket, Ousamequin ruled only with the consent of and by the determination of the people. Yet, as recognized overlord of all the Wampanoag, he bore the exalted title Massasoit. This was the near-king of tremendous religious authority who would grant safety and survival to the Pilgrims by means of the treaty signed with them some weeks later.

Perhaps the arranging of that treaty of peace with Massasoit was the greatest contribution guaranteed by the Anglophilic Squanto to the Pilgrims. By its carefully respected terms, the Plymouth colonists secured tranquillity and harmony with their immediate neighbors for forty years. Massasoit, although personally never as attached to the English settlers as Squanto, greatly preferred an occasionally troublesome alliance with these well-armed strangers to the alternative, which was to deal with the aggressive Narragansett who threatened from the west. Making a treaty with a well-armed European ally seemed far preferable to caving in to a traditional native enemy. The Pilgrims, for their part, wanted a signed and sealed document both because it would give them protection from the unknown and presumably hostile aborigines of greater New England and because, having never received a charter for their colony from the king's ministers, they could base their claims to legitimacy on this freely granted American treaty, blessed by native chants.

In their mutually beneficial and regularly renewed pact, the Pilgrims and Wampanoag pledged themselves not to "doe hurt" to one another in any way. If the peace were broken by an Indian, he was to be sent to Plymouth for punishment; if the offender were a Pilgrim, he was to be sent to Massasoit's capital at Sowams (Warren, Rhode Island). Friendship was sealed, in other words, by the recognition of each nation's equally valid authority. Yet that is not at all the way the treaty was later described by the propagandistic Puritan Cotton Mather, whose *Magnalia Christi Americana* (1698) was a hodgepodge of writings on the ecclesiastic history of New England, designed to show how the development of Massachusetts demonstrated the workings of God's will. By Mather's interpretation, the historic

Plymouth treaty had laid down the law to the natives; in his history, Massasoit and his fellow "Sachims" not only "entered into a firm agreement of peace with the English, but also they declared and submitted themselves to be subjects of the King of England." One searches the original document in vain for any support of that reading.

Not surprisingly, nowhere does Mather's twisted history recognize Squanto either as a saint or as a creative player in the bringing about of the treaty. Instead, Mather portrays him as merely a lucky fluke arranged by the "God who disposeth all." Mather laughs sardonically at Squanto's reported explanation to the Indians of what was foremost on their minds—the plagues that had troubled the land ever since it was first visited by European fishermen in the preceding century. Mather describes the "ridiculous rhodomantado" by which Squanto boasted to the tribesmen that the English, for the destruction of enemies, could use illnesses just as effectively as flintlocks. This was possible because the English "kept the plague in a cellar (where they also kept their powder), and could at their pleasure let it loose to make such havock among them as the distemper had already made among them a few years before."

The Wampanoag Algonquian may indeed have seen the English as technologically capable of great things (though the Europeans were not physically impressive—woefully short of stature); in material affairs at least these newcomers might be helpful allies. Yet Massasoit made not a single move to honor the English king or to accept his religion. Far from it. Near the end of his life, Massasoit tried to insert a clause in the renewed treaty of peace that would guarantee that the English would never attempt to convert his people to their beliefs. Friendship

of a certain sort might be possible, even a working brotherhood, but acceptance of the English settlers' unnatural, biblically ordered life was out of the question. Massasoit's warriors
from his home territory of Pokanoket had seen a man and
woman in Plymouth, two servants, severely punished for having slept together; such moral strictures seemed ridiculous, part
of no religion that might be believed.

Massasoit's suspicions were echoed, but much more loudly,
in the words of the xenophobic colonial leaders who came to
dominate the next group of English settlers, the Puritans. An
almost paranoid distrust of other people's beliefs permeated the
emerging Puritan mind. Soon after their arrival north of Boston
in 1630, they revealed that they were far less tolerant than the
Pilgrims with whom Massasoit negotiated; they decried mixed-
race intercourse (calling it *Creolism*) and pushed aside all attempts of the Indians to establish contact. By the mid-1630s,
they had their superiority myth securely locked in place—a
myth that equated them with the Israelites, carrying out God's
purpose in the wilderness.

The choice of either respecting America's natural landscape
and her native people (as Roger Williams did) or fearing them
(as Increase Mather did) was the critical spiritual issue then
faced by the English colonists. For the Indians the issue was
rather different: Their choice was between hostility toward the
English dominion or assimilation within it. For such free spirits
as Squanto and Samoset, integration was an adventure full of
opportunities; it was a profound worry to Ousamequin. His famous speech to Myles Standish in the 1650s rings forth as a plea
against integration from one wise man's soul—from someone
of a distinctive faith who saw only trouble in a blending of be-

liefs. The speech was precipitated by Standish and two companions' purchase of a fourteen-square-mile tract of land near Bridgewater, Massachusetts. When the Wampanoag learned that their peaceful hunters were being arrested as trespassers within that tract, Massasoit realized the nature of the conflict—it was not just a matter of conflicting property laws but of conflicting views about man and his Maker. His speech rings with godly overtones:

> What is this thing you call property? It cannot be the earth. For the earth is our mother, nourishing all her children, bears, birds, fish, and all men. The woods, the streams, everything on it belongs to everybody and is for the use of all. How can one man say it belongs to him only?

The tensions of one culture working with another—secular concerns and religious principles pushing them together and also pulling them apart—were exemplified in an extraordinary way by the third Algonquian who enters the early settlers' story at this point. He had the curious name of Hobomock or Hobbamock, this being one of the Algonquian words for devil. Several years later, when the Pilgrims proudly showed the Wampanoag their wondrous recently arrived tool, a plow, the natives whispered that it was so devilishly tricky it must have Hobomock in it. Though less well known to history than Squanto or Samoset, Hobomock in fact ranked higher among his people and deserves equal recognition. A nobleman and minister, or *pniese*, of the Wampanoag court, he was called by Bradford "one of their chiefest champions or men of valour." As a religious practitioner, he had been tested in ritualistic ordeals (such as surviving being poisoned by hellebore) and was recognized as being in touch with certain spirits—including the Devil.

Hobomock's name and title signified both his powerful position in Wampanoag society and his spiritual authority. Having served on Massasoit's council, he was appointed soon after 1620 to be that chief's resident minister to the English colony. In a way that the English found especially pleasing, the young man embodied all the characteristics of a knight, including faith, loyalty, and (if the Indians' stories could be believed) divinely granted invulnerability. He seemed a perfect liaison between the English and Wampanoag allies.

His knightly characteristics came to the fore in 1623 when the Pilgrims' military leader, Myles Standish, decided to make an assault on the settlement of Wessagusset (now Weymouth), where Thomas Weston and other English traders were dealing with the Massachusetts Algonquian, much to the Pilgrims' displeasure. The Pilgrims wanted no challenges from other English colonists (particularly those of the Anglican persuasion) in the new and immediately profitable beaver trade. Nor did they want any Indians from their region to enter into trading arrangements outside Plymouth's control. The Pilgrims wished to demonstrate their dominance in the region, and Massasoit's Wampanoag Pokanoket warriors were completely willing to back up, even to lead, such a sudden show of force.

In this allied operation, Hobomock found himself functioning hip and thigh with Standish in a soldierly brotherhood. Built more on manly respect than on religious philosophy, that brotherhood would endure for all of the two warriors' lives. Indeed, when their attack on the Wessagusset Indians raged at its fiercest—several Massachusetts warriors having been slain and all the village risen up to resist the Plymouth attackers—Hobomock stripped off his coat and waded into the fray with the intention of personally slaying all resisters. As Bradford described his action, "being a known Pinese, [Hobomock] chased [the enemy] so fast our people were not able to hold way with him." And of course he suffered not a scratch.

Another side of this knightly figure had been seen a few months earlier when rumors reached Plymouth of Massasoit's severe illness and possible death. Rushing to his lord at the Pokanoket capital at Sowams along with Edward Winslow, Hobomock heard en route that the great chief had already died. *"Neen womasu Sagimus, Neen womasu Sagimus!"* ("My loving sachem, my loving sachem!") he is said to have cried. "Many have I known but never any like thee." By this lament, some scholars—particularly those of today who interpret most Native American actions from the interior, nativist point of view—believe he meant that no other sachems, including those who might succeed him as ruler of the Wampanoag, were or ever would be so adept in their handling of the English.

Fortunately, Massasoit was still alive when Hobomock and Winslow arrived at Sowams. So the knight became a nurse, fulfilling one of his prime duties as a minister of the native religion. Laying his weapons down, he pushed aside the howling medicine men and grieving squaws who were circling about the bed of the stricken leader. In this effort to cure the aging sachem, Winslow cooperated, applying what knowledge of European medicine he possessed—which included washing the old chief's mouth and scraping his tongue.

Massasoit was content to let the young Englishman treat him, accepting the "confection of many comfortable conserves" that Winslow had brought with him. The mixture eased the sachem's internal difficulties and even seemed to restore his failed eyesight. Soon the chief was demanding some of the soup he had enjoyed on a recent visit to Plymouth; within a few days he was "lustie" as ever.

Hobomock pondered the method and the meaning of this apparently miraculous cure: What powers did his English friends really possess? His wonderment deepened the next summer when he witnessed a ceremony held by the Pilgrims' religious leaders to terminate a crop-threatening drought. They had appointed a "solmne day of humiliation" to reverse the weeks of dry weather that had withered their corn and wilted their beans on the stalk. When the Pilgrims gathered in the morning to pray for eight or nine hours under the hot clear sky, Hobomock watched skeptically; at the end of the session it appeared that the dry weather was "as like to continue as ever it was." But then, as Winslow reported, the clouds began to pile up on the horizon and, during the night (and for two weeks thereafter) the clouds shed their rain, dispensing "such soft, sweete, and moderate showers . . . as it was hard to say whether our withered corne or drooping affections were most quickened and revived."

Hobomock must have puzzled over the applicability of Christianity. Was it necessary to accept that strange biblical heaven and that unnatural English way of life in order to make sense of the new order that now reigned in this corner of the earth? But even as Hobomock was considering the dimensions of cultural conversion, Massasoit strengthened his own commitment to the ancient Algonquian beliefs. Although Samoset and Squanto and Hobomock might consider following in the path of the saints, he would remain firmly opposed. Even in his weakened old age, before his much mourned death in 1661, he fought to prevent missionaries from intruding on his people's traditional rites. He died a proud pagan.

As for the peripatetic Samoset, less concerned with things of the spirit than the mighty Ousamequin, this traveler moved on in the challenging new world of colonial America. Returning to the Maine coast, he lived for many years under the name of John Somerset in the mixed-race fishing community at Pemaquid. The knightly Hobomock found yet another way—and this is what makes him exceptionally significant. He stood by and lived with his friend Myles Standish as a kind of guardian spirit. In that old soldier's children-filled household, he died in 1642, always loyal to the English despite the "enticements, scoffs, and scorns" of his own people. As he lay dying, some Pilgrims got the impression that Hobomock was still "seeking after their God, . . . leaving some good hopes in their hearts that his soul went to rest." But the available evidence indicates that this complex man died true enough to his own faith, even while recognizing some virtues in the other, foreign religion.

Remarkably, that was the way Myles Standish lived and died, too—religiously open. Alone of Plymouth's leaders, this lapsed Roman Catholic never joined the Pilgrims' church (though he was happy enough to see his children become conventional church members, even deacons). The conspicuous fact of Standish's declining to be a Protestant in the Separatist mode stands out as worthy of special consideration, for that act violated a decree in Plymouth that no one could be a citizen or officer of the settlement who was not a communicant. Standish simply ignored the decree, although, as commander-in-chief, he was legally an officer of the colony. His whole pattern of life—from the violent attack on Wessagusset to his sorties against the French and Indians elsewhere—demonstrated how individualistically, and aggressively, he had formulated a life for himself in America. Might we conclude that a matter on which Standish and Hobomock would have agreed in their old-soldiers-by-the-fireside conversations was that, in America, a man's religion should be his own business?

Sadly, the concept of letting another person's religion rest with him alone lay beyond the ken of many Pilgrims and most Puritans. Converting the people of another culture—specifically, the "wretched" natives—remained a pressing and disputative issue throughout the Massachusetts Bay Colony, particularly at the highest levels of government (where King James's and King Charles's urgings toward that missionary purpose had some impact). Whereas Plymouth's leadership—the saints who gave American civilization its famous Mayflower Compact with its democratic tendencies—was determinedly anticlerical, the lay leadership of the Massachusetts Bay Colony bowed deeply to the ministerial elite, the university-educated clergy. A consequence of that difference was that, while the Separatist Pilgrims continued to distrust any ecclesiastical figure who told them or their Indian friends what to do and what to believe, the Puritans harkened anxiously to clergy whose judgments determined who might be saved—and who never could be.

Those judgments waxed more and more punishing as it became clearer and clearer that Puritanism was losing its appeal among the swelling masses of immigrants. To gain credibility, Puritanism's leaders needed nameable devils on whom to focus their wrath; they found those devils in the Indians and also in such free spirits as Roger Williams.

ROGER WILLIAMS FINDS FRIENDS in the WILDERNESS

Initially, the Puritans had seen a certain ragged charm in the friendly Massachusetts people who greeted them. The word Massachusetts (Mass-adchu-seuk), meaning "Big Hill People," referred to the gentle undulations north of Weymouth and south of Boston that these Algonquian regarded as their sacred land. Yet now, after the time of first contact, they held expectations as low as the elevation of their hills, having been crushed by the successive plagues that had swept through their villages. Disconsolate, they were in poor condition to oppose the Puritan colonists who, after shifting their location southward from fish-smelling Salem in 1630, set about establishing a trading port at the mouth of the Charles River.

Although forceful John Winthrop held the office of governor in the Massachusetts Bay Colony, the mind and spirit that reigned in the colony belonged to the very learned Reverend John Cotton. His 1633 arrival was warmly greeted by the new settlers, churchly folk who expressed their enthusiasm by naming their raw settlement after the location of his home pulpit— Boston. To that affluent city in England and to Cotton's old St. Botolph's Church had flocked a growing number of middle-class merchants who relished his outspoken brand of Puritanism. But the judges of England's High Court of Commission, affronted by both Cotton's theology and his independence, summoned him to appear before them in 1632. Instead, he resigned and shipped out of the country, to the New World. Following in his wake sailed a steady stream of emigrants—well-to-do, litigious, quite religious Englishmen—eager to enlarge their portions in life and to guarantee their access to heaven.

Addressing them from his new pulpit, John Cotton took time to comment on the apparently hopeless Massachusetts Algonquian. He advised, "Offend not the poor natives!" Echoing the sentiments of the Massachusetts Bay charter—which called upon the Puritans to "wynn and incite the Natives to the knowledge and obedience of the true God and Saviour of Mankind and the Christian Fayth"—Cotton urged his parishioners to make the Indians "partakers of your precious faith." It was in this spirit that a completely false but romantically appealing cliché was devised as the centerpiece of Massachusetts Bay's colonial flag. Depicted on it was an undernourished Indian, with a banner above his head with this pathetic plea: "Come over and Help Us!"

Although the slogan was occasionally useful for the Puritans in raising money for missionary purposes (or, more often, for the clergy's own projects), its Christian sentiment was almost immediately contradicted by the Puritans' actions and inactions. For the Puritans were far more interested in pursuing their own beaver trade and land speculation and fishing and shipping businesses than in spreading the perceived word of God among the Indians. Under the joint authority of John Cotton's tightly restrictive church and John Winthrop's stronghanded government, the Massachusetts Bay Colony set about repressing any radical elements (including Indians) within the "hedge" of their limited, holy community and demonstrating their own special link with God. All people of the world, by lifting their eyes to the Puritans' "Citty upon a Hill," should be able to see how, with these sober Christians at the helm, the prophecies of the Old Testament were finally being fulfilled.

England's and Europe's harassed Protestants, hearing of Boston's vigorous experiment in religious governance (as well as its relative freedom from royal and ecclesiastical interference), were encouraged to come over by the hundreds. The great numbers of successful immigrants and the availability of land (thanks to the cooperation of the peaceful Indians) seemed to confirm the correctness of Boston's brand of Christianity, as preached by John Cotton. So great was his eminence that, a few decades later, Oliver Cromwell, Lord Protector of England, would write to ask him, "What is the Lord a-doing? What prophesies are we [Puritans] now fulfilling?"

But Boston's growth in the mid-1600s was achieved at a tremendous cost. Winthrop and Cotton, whose elitist rule had been unquestioned while the colony was threatened by royal persecution and wilderness terrors, found that new terrors had to be invented if the strictness of Puritan discipline and the structures of society were to be properly maintained within briefly booming Massachusetts Bay. A keen-witted renegade by the name of Samuel Gorton was even so brash as to suggest that sin was invented by the Puritans of Boston to punish the assertive presumptions of the likes of him and of the upstart merchant group (the antiauthoritarians or antinomians).

Punishment unto death at the hands of both cruel monarchs and authoritarian clergy had certainly been the way of life in Stuart England. Before leaving, Winthrop and Cotton had not only seen the beginnings of the great plague that was to decimate London in 1665, they had also seen the burnings and torturings of friend and foe alike in the religious wars of the

Reformation. They had seen so much inhumanity of man to man that they were in no doubt about what kind of Jehovah was rendering judgment. Clearly, the god whom they adored must be as fearful as a tyrannical father. Obedience to his will must be accordingly absolute, even though that obedience gave no guarantee of grace.

The limitations of divine grace were preached ceaselessly from the Bay Colony pulpits. The clerics' shrinking definition of who deserved that grace separated neighbor from neighbor and generation from generation, causing a mortal wound in New England society, separating the recognized elect and those perceived as doomed. In the words of Puritan scholar Andrew Delbanco, New England "ruptured [itself] over the meaning of grace." But, if one can take a sympathetic view of Boston's cruelly determinant Puritan leaders, this was done in the name of salvation by people who had endured much. They were in truth terrified of God's damning judgment, for they believed they had witnessed its inescapable horrors.

Theologians advise that that perception of scanty divine love, as well as being a peculiar feature of the Puritan culture, has been an element of extreme monotheism since the beginnings of the human experience: Very few may kneel at the feet of the single god or make a "covenant" with him. You must strive to be favored, even though—as Puritanism's heir Jonathan Edwards would explicate in the eighteenth century—the fires of hell are stoked for you, and there's not much you can do about it. Meanwhile, the covenanted elect (Cotton, Winthrop, et al.) must struggle to keep the community safe, dealing strongly with such devilish problems as corrupt kings, fractious elements within the colony, and, of course, pagan Indians.

As the Puritan leaders made further (mostly unsuccessful) attempts to control their increasingly trade-oriented and decentralized society, they emphasized the alien nature of the Native Americans. They characterized these once pitied wretches as "the children of Satan." John Cotton, apparently forgetting his formerly sympathetic attitude, said the savages should be "blasted in all their green groves and arbors." Indeed, destruction of the Indians seemed to be merely the other side of the conversion coin. Since paganism was the essential and threatening ill, the Puritans considered as irrelevant the issue of whether it was cured by forcible conversion or by well-delivered death.

Cotton and other scholars among the Puritans who had the godly power to interpret the Bible came up with the exegesis that the Indians, obviously one of the lost tribes of Israel, had been removed by Satan to North America, so he could focus special attention on their instruction. With that understood, the bay colonists must see the difficulties in trying to convert the Massachusetts Algonquian or any other Native Americans. They must recognize those demons of the wilderness as blighted enemies in an unholy land. The old-fashioned Pilgrims, who continued to be relatively tolerant of the Wampanoag in the territories around them, were regarded by their stronger and more numerous English brethren in Boston as dangerously weak in their treatment of the incorrigibly resistant and "uncivil" natives. Such bizarre Indian religious figures as Hobomock, with his devilish name and his admitted contacts with dark as well as light spirits, seemed to the Puritans perfect proof of their popular, satanic theory. Yet the hope of brotherhood glowed in a few breasts on both sides of the religious-racial dividing line.

Among them was Passaconaway. As described earlier, he was the most prominent of all New England powwow sachems (that is, the uniquely powerful sachems who combined religious and administrative roles). Headquartered at the mouth of the Merrimack, he was widely respected among accommodationists as an advocate of peace with the English. What could be more civil and God-pleasing than that? Also hopeful for peaceful relations, John Eliot and Roger Williams eventually made imaginative attempts to construct worlds within which the two people might live harmoniously. Outstanding exceptions to the rule among Puritan contemporaries, these brilliant religious figures from New England history had chosen to integrate themselves with their new homeland—that is, to become Americanized.

On arriving in Boston in 1630 Roger Williams, an unemployed twenty-seven-year-old graduate of England's famous Charterhouse School and Cambridge University, made the risky and fateful decision to decline an offered post as a teacher. This was but the first of many decisions he would make that seemed deliberately calculated to put a stick in the eye of Massachusetts Bay's ruling orthodoxy. Yet, however radical, however independent, however tolerant of other denominations and religions (even the religion of the Native Americans), however universal his spiritual sympathies, Roger Williams was fundamentally a seventeenth-century Puritan. In his many arguments against the Quakers, for example, he found it impossible to credit a faith based on some kind of "inner light" and not on the Bible. And as relations between the Native Americans and the English worsened in the final quarter of his century, he subscribed more and more forcibly to the still current theory of their wicked, devilish origins, trusting that "through the mercie of the Lord ... the Devill and his lying Sorcerers shall be confounded." Even so, Roger Williams—the man, not the theologian—remains a remarkably liberal and congenial spirit for his time. That may be said primarily because he developed such a strong personal connection with the Native Americans in whose territory he located his colony after leaving Boston and Plymouth and Salem behind him; it may also be said because he, as a result of those deep-level contacts, became so fully an independent-minded American.

To the great Narragansett chief Canonicus, Williams was known as "son." In return, Williams constantly and consistently urged the Massachusetts Bay government not to force the Narragansett or other Indians "away from their own religions." Indeed, he referred to forcible conversion at one point as "soul rape." Nevertheless, and despite his brilliant work in figuring out and codifying the Narragansett version of the Algonquian language, Williams remained more abstractly interested in their religion than persuaded that it had much merit. Having deduced that these Native Americans had some thirty-seven divinities, plus many other peculiar spirits, he concluded that, despite certain similarities between their religion and Christianity (such as the strong Messianic strain), there were too many profound differences to hope that the two might be joined.

"My soul's desire was to do the natives good," Williams said of his efforts among the Narragansett. Yet that was not totally true. His desire to keep himself and the colony he founded safe from both English overlordship and native attacks seemed to take precedence over any such mission. Nor did his own Christian ministry seem always to be the most prominent thing on his mind, neither when establishing the colony of Rhode Island (1635) nor originally when he first arrived from England. In those early years, after his rejection of the Boston teaching post, he accepted an invitation to preach and teach at Plymouth. Journeying down to that faithful, if undereducated, colony in a mood of skeptical curiosity, he found the religious spirit among the Pilgrims dull and unexciting. For the ambitious part of him, prospects in Plymouth seemed dim.

Williams was discouraged to find that the Pilgrims, even in their neediest days, had been halting and inept in making profitable trading arrangements with the Wampanoag. Prosperity and self-sufficiency seemed beyond these old-fashioned people. So, after a two-year stay, when an opportunity came for him to take over a pulpit in the more up-and-coming community of Salem, he left Plymouth behind. Yet, as he set off for the bustling northeastern port in 1633, he must have admitted to himself that he would never have much in common with the Salem Puritans or much respect for their management of civic and religious affairs.

All too soon Roger Williams offended the Puritan elect once again, this time by scolding them for taking land illegally (as he saw it) from the Indians. Banished by the hierarchy in the dead of winter, he fled to unsettled southern New England where there was, of course, no chance for him to find clerical employment. But there were many chances for him, in that wild forest, to become something other than the preacher of an established religion—to become a successful operator on the frontier, trading and dealing with the native people. To some biographers and historians, the choice that Williams made—to be sent off, knowingly, into the starving wilderness with his wife and children rather than to be exiled home to England—was an indication of the man's rashness. To others, particularly those who see Williams more as a pioneer than as a minister, the choice was typical of a man ready to meet his Maker in a new and spiritually exciting land.

In fact he had investigated and prepared for this new life with a care that belies the charge of rashness. Back in his months among the Pilgrims, when he had a first chance to investigate the Algonquian landscape, he quickly learned necessary survival skills. Within the course of traveling twenty miles, he found, to his surprise and delight, twenty hospitable native villages. Whereas he had been born to a cloth-merchant father in London and had grown up on cramped city streets (rather than in the comfortable small towns that had produced most other English Puritans), he took easily to the woodland experience. And whereas Dutch and Latin had been the languages he and his fellow Londoners laboriously learned in their youthful years, now he picked up the trading language of the natives with astonishing swiftness (an act of learning in which he was assisted by the equally adept Myles Standish). More importantly, he, as a religiously sensitive intellectual, focused on what the Native Americans really seemed to be about. As he ungraciously put it, he went out and lived "in their filthy smoke holes"; those visits and the perceptions gained there greatly aided his subsequent conversations with Massasoit.

With that benign chief and at that time he apparently made some kind of private land deal, a canny hedge against uncertainty. Later, having learned in Salem how to plant crops and how to handle a canoe, he returned to the welcoming land of the Wampanoag with some confidence not only in his woodland skills but also in the prospects of life as a trader. His decision to deal in goods (including textiles) was a clever one, perhaps not unexpected from a cloth-merchant's son. And a textile trader he would be, not among people so impoverished or downcast as the natives of the Massachusetts Bay Colony, but among Massasoit's economically vibrant Pokanoket and other neighboring Wampanoag. They would surely offer him commercial opportunities, as well as splendid examples for further explorations on foot and in the mind.

Advised, however, by his former friend Edward Winslow that as a disgraced exile from Boston, Williams would pose certain diplomatic difficulties for Plymouth if he chose to remain in Wampanoag territory, he moved just across the Taunton River into Narragansett country. This was despite the fact that he knew the Narragansett to be tough in temperament and mighty in numbers. He had learned firsthand, when located in Plymouth, how brutal Narragansett sorties could be against the neighboring Wampanoag Pokanoket.

No coward, Roger Williams was intrigued by the ferocious arrogance of his new hosts. He admired the inner strengths of the Narragansett, personified by the two co-ruling sachems whom he came to know intimately: Canonicus the seasoned chief, and Miantonomi, his physically awesome nephew. From them he learned that the Narragansett were sufficiently confident in their warriors and secure in their relationships with the gods to feel little need for battle. Even when they were forced to take up arms, the Narragansett fought by well-established codes and for personal scores rather than for total victory. "The Indians' Warres are far less bloudy and devouring," Williams later wrote, "than the cruell warres of Europe."

Still barely touched by the diseases that had punished their Massachusetts and Wampanoag neighbors (reducing those populations to a total of forty thousand from twice that), the Narragansett had reason to believe in the early 1600s that their holy men, usually called powwows, were correctly in touch with the health-giving spirits. At this time the Massachusetts Bay leaders estimated that the Narragansett numbered something like thirty thousand people and feared that they could put six thousand trained warriors into the field—though ethnohistorians downplay those numbers today—while the Bay Colony itself numbered no more than four thousand souls. So it happened that, as he negotiated with Canonicus and Miantonomi about trade and land purchases, Roger Williams recognized that for both diplomatic and business reasons it would be wise to tread delicately with the Narragansett.

His insightful book on their speech patterns, called *A Key into the Language of America* (published in 1643), presumed to open up the whole world of the Native American mind. And in some respects it did that, at least for the author himself, who went on to preach in and to deal in the Algonquian languages with unabashed confidence. For a working frontiersman, this was (it must be pointed out) nothing new. Simultaneously, many gifted Native American linguists were progressing speedily into this lingua franca world of mutual comprehensibility. Many decades had passed since the primitive days when a bright-eyed Algonquian, trying to start an exchange with a foreigner who had wandered or paddled into his forest, would use the strange line, "What cheer, Netop?" The two men would proceed to communicate with hand signs and gestures. But now Williams and other more sophisticated negotiators, red and white, were discovering how much greater the rewards could be if the speaker's language command was more masterful.

Roger Williams pursued a particular interest in the Narragansett religious rites. Central to that study was his identification of their chief deity (Kiehtan or Cautantowwit), a creator god also known and worshiped by the Wampanoag. This enormously important divinity, described in some creation myths as having come to his people from the Southwest along with the gift of corn, stood at the summit of the Algonquian spirits' ranks. Yet Williams perceived correctly that this superior spirit, who was said to have made man and woman and who welcomed the dying to his bosom, was not at all supreme in the Narragansett heaven. He was not at all their Jehovah, a key difference not grasped by Plymouth's equally curious Edward Winslow. Nor did Roger Williams make the error of seeing in the Narragansett's much-loved Wetucks—a figure who supposedly wrought miracles and walked upon the waters but who had no messianic qualities—a Native American Jesus.

Yet Williams was able to appreciate without condescension such creation myths as that of the black crow who flew to Narragansett country from the Great Spirit's garden with the first seeds of corn and beans for man to grow. And he came to respect the ethical, religion-based traditions of the daily life of the Narragansett (which may have had roots in the ancient Mississippian civilizations); Williams saw that moral lessons were so well understood that no laws against theft were needed, and no men or women were outcast from society as criminals. In this appreciation, as much as in making a safe place for himself and his family among the Narragansett, Roger Williams gained a peculiarly American education. He became, along the way, free from the cultural and social strictures and prejudices of his background.

But though his 1636 purchase of land from the Narragansett for the future city of Providence may have made him free from the overlordship of the Boston elect, he could not be totally removed from responsibilities as a colonial citizen. Soon after he had paddled downriver to scout the site for his colony's capital—whose fortunate settlers were all to call each other "neighbor"—Williams received an emergency call for help from Governor Winthrop and his advisors. He had to obey.

The ministers and magistrates of Boston, who had once tried to restrain Williams's freewheeling radicalism, now desperately needed his aid. By their hell-for-leather push for trading monopolies, their agents had so thoroughly stirred up the powerful Pequot (dominating tribesmen of the Connecticut River valley and of the lands between there and the Narragansett) that war with those cosmopolitan people seemed likely. Unless Roger Williams could use his newly gained diplomatic skills to keep the Narragansett on the side of the English colonists, it seemed very likely that all New England would be extinguished in a cataclysmic conquest by the Pequot and their allies.

The CHALLENGE of the PEQUOT PROPHET

Although Cotton Mather and the reigning magistrates in Boston devoutly believed that the events of their lives demonstrated the purposes of God, the frightening situation on the frontier was clearly related to matters economic. Indeed, the economic condition of the Massachusetts Bay Colony in the mid-1630s had to be viewed as desperate. The population boomed, to be sure, but neither the revenues from the fisheries nor the agricultural output was sufficient to fund the colony's government. Over the horizon gleamed the tantalizing golden economy of the Dutch, whose avid pursuit of the beaver trade in (present-day) New York and Connecticut was resulting in the shipment of more than ten thousand pelts a year to the trading houses of Amsterdam. To the Bay Colony's more expansionist and less community-fixated policy makers, the situation seemed quite clear: The western fur business was where salvation lay, and clearly that was where the Bay Colony must move. They therefore had allowed certain traders to operate beyond the colony's borders and to move up the beaver-rich rivers of Connecticut and into the distant pastures of western New England, not perceiving the hostile reactions those freebooters would provoke.

At the very moment when that expansionist philosophy began to take hold in Boston (over the objection of the more strict and religion-focused preachers like John Cotton), two ambassadors from the Pequot tribe in Connecticut had appeared in the Bay Colony capital, carrying with them lengths of wampum (belts woven of bright, strung-together shells). Wampum, as a visiting Dutch agent had explained to the English colonists, signaled wealth. It stood both as the diplomatic symbol of creative trading partnerships and as the recognized legal tender of the beaver-trading territories. The Pequot possessed it abundantly.

Yet Europeans of the day were in no position to understand the difficulties that had been assaulting the Pequot—the pressing difficulties that had compelled them to send ambassadors to Boston. In the preceding year, the Pequot had made an unfortunate decision to attack and severely punish certain tribesmen along the Connecticut River who had presumed to trade with the Dutch. Their attack, in part a reaction to the vicious Dutch act of murdering a Pequot chief some years before, had produced nothing but widespread resentment against the Pequot in the region. In council, their chiefs then had to invent a superior strategy for reestablishing control of the area while also dealing with the Europeans on either hand.

The overall solution seemed to lie in gaining mastery of the fur trade as a supply business while allowing the Europeans to function as marketers. The Pequot chiefs, led by Sassacus (son of the very sachem who had been murdered by the Dutch), saw that they had better move swiftly to salvage a situation that they had almost bungled by the recent attack. Though they were far less numerous than the Iroquois-related Mohawk, who had been very successfully outmaneuvering the French and English for control of the fur trade throughout much of the eastern woodlands, the Pequot still had a chance to grab their share of the game. By forming an alliance with Yankees, they might well be able both to counter the Dutch and to bring local tribes into line.

Although the ambassadors' visit thrilled and encouraged the Bostonians, they prudently declined to negotiate and no agreement was reached. But soon thereafter, two highly revered and very senior Pequot sachems hastened to the capital in renewed and rather desperate hopes of signing a pact. Their single purpose was to win command of the Connecticut River valley, taking it away from the Mohawk; in order to accomplish that, they were prepared to sign a treaty with Governor Dudley, whatever its demands might be. Yet the terms they accepted seemed so out of scale and so impossible to bear that many concluded someone (the governor or possibly the Pequot) must be trying to fool someone else. By the treaty's terms, the Pequot would give the Bay Colony an annual gift of four hundred fathoms of wampum plus forty beaver skins and thirty otter skins, which would be valued at approximately £250 ($50,000), half the total levies that the colony was then receiving! A reasonable man could only conclude that no people could be entering into such an exploitative arrangement with their eyes open; this diplomatic activity on behalf of the Pequot could only be a cover for war and not a negotiation for peace.

One of those who objected to the treaty was the young and recently arrived clergyman John Eliot. He had heard in October of 1634 that the Pequot ambassadors had come to demand a conference with the Bay Colony's deputy governor. Eliot, then aged twenty-six, was a mere teacher, not yet a pastor, in Roxbury, a dozen miles southwest of Boston. There were few signs that he would one day earn international fame and the appellation Apostle to the Indians. But he had received rigorous training at Cambridge University (where courses and techniques were still thoroughly medieval and not yet inspired by the Enlightenment), and, like Roger Williams, felt well-enough grounded in contemporary European Protestantism to deliver a protest on solid moral grounds when it seemed called for. Thus, when he learned that Governor Dudley, in the council meeting after the Pequot ambassadors' visit, had arbitrarily set terms for a soon-to-be-signed Treaty of Amity, Eliot forcefully spoke out against the action.

"Plebe inconsulta!" was the young cleric's argument—the people had not been consulted in this matter. By making such an outspoken objection, John Eliot showed that he was naive in his comprehension of how things were run in the Bay Colony but

also that he had a good eye for a faulty contract. It did seem peculiar that the colony's administrators, in considering what Native American groups might make the best commercial allies,
were rushing so headlong into an agreement with the Pequot.
The name of these widely feared Connecticut Algonquian
means "destroyers of men"; they were known for their aggressive attacks on neighboring Algonquian as well as on settlers'
farms. Roger Williams had long regarded them as the most ferocious of the Algonquian, calling them "unscrupulous."

Personal distrust of the Pequot was just one reason why
Williams chose to accept the nearly impossible mission of arranging an alliance with the Narragansett that had been forced
on him by John Winthrop (the recent replacement for Dudley
in the governor's office). Roger Williams understood that the
whole tribal system of New England had been thrown into tur-
moil by the rapidly increasing competition of the fur trade. The
Pequot—an offshoot of the Algonquian Mahican (not to be
confused with the Mohegan) in western Massachusetts and traditional enemies of the Narragansett—now were reaching too
far. Despite their limited numbers, they were unarguably a
major force, having already spread out into the eastern Connecticut River valleys and even to Long Island.

Williams had his own theories about what made the various
Indian nations tick—which tribes were most charged with a
sense of divine power and which leaders best exercised that
divine authority. Yet he saw that only by becoming intimately
acquainted with those people could any European hope to comprehend the ethics or the dreams that underlay Native American
behavior. Whereas the Pilgrims tended to keep the Indians at
arm's length, and the Puritans wanted to consign them to special

areas of perdition, Williams waded into their midst and joined their meals and observed their songs and dances, always learning something new about their beliefs. The commitment of the Indians to their noninstitutionalized religion and to their hierarchy of gods was indeed a wondrous relationship, one that John Eliot would also strive to understand in his place and time. But it was a relationship for which most later Protestant ministers—especially as their form of Christianity became increasingly judgmental and evangelically Bible-based—had little sympathy.

Roger Williams, now called to defend Britain's northeastern colonies, was also aware—and uniquely so—that the world in which he moved was controlled not by European kings or colonial divines but by the dynamisms of North America. One central factor in that world was, obviously, the beautifully furred beaver, the woodland's greatest source of wealth. Yet another equally important factor was the Iroquois Confederation, a league of five nations that contained the northeast territory's most powerful and ambitious people. These nations—from east to west, the Mohawk, Oneida, Onondaga, Cayuga, and Seneca—had already by 1620 asserted themselves as prepared to determine the destiny of North America. Subject to intense study from that early time until today, the Iroquois remain a confederated and religion-centered government of majesty but also of mystery. Significantly, the most recent in a series of volumes about them by the eminent modern scholar Francis Jennings is entitled *The Ambiguous Iroquois Empire*. In Roger Williams's day, the most pressing question about them was not whether the eastward-oriented Mohawk would strike again, but where they would strike next.

It seemed impossible to block their master plan for controlling the river people of New England. Each summer in times
of peace a Mohawk war party headed by two high-ranking
sachems made an appearance on the Connecticut River. Their
purpose in appearing so grandly before the Nipmuck and Mohegan and other Algonquian was not only to gather tribute but
also to remind all players, reds and whites alike, who owned the
table in this high-stakes, international game.

With the escalation of the fur trade and the advent of what
economists call North America's Wampum Revolution—an
important part of England and France's mercantile systems—
a totally new way of life had been forced upon the Indian villages. The women's sanctified responsibilities of raising corn
and measuring the seasons were replaced by the secular tasks
of drilling beads and weaving lengths of wampum. The manly
pursuit of deer and fish and other catch of the season for the
community's self-sufficient well-being was replaced by the tasks
of snaring and selling fur-bearing animals to the white man's
trading posts, for a price determined by some corporation's dictates. In company with these changes, the very spirits seemed to
deviate, with the Algonquian god Kiehtan losing importance
and the fierce spirits of war coming to the fore.

Roger Williams was alarmed to learn from his Narragansett
and Mohegan sources that the Pequot had a new prophet inspir-
ing them in violent rites and counseling them on the strategies of
war. In a way that precisely forecast the pattern of future Native
American efforts to fight for self-determination on the strength
of a religious call, this prophet was preaching that wounds received in battle would cause the fervid Pequot warriors no real

harm. The spirits would protect them. So instructed, and even as their ambassadors returned from Boston, the Pequot began building forts against possible Dutch attacks. These solidly constructed bastions, whose walls stood firm thanks to craftsmen trained in observance of European outposts, were positioned both up the Connecticut River in newly claimed territory and in their home territory on the Pequot (Thames) River.

For the colonists, the immediate placement of an even larger fort at the very mouth of the Connecticut River seemed an obvious strategic move; it would secure all the rich watershed to the north. First to make that move were the English, led by Governor Winthrop's scientifically inclined son, John Winthrop, Jr., acting on behalf of two Protestant English lords named Saye and Brook. The palisades of Saybrook were just being set in place in 1634 when Commander Van Twiller's Dutch amphibious contingent appeared in the harbor, equipped with sections for a preconstructed fort. Seeing that he was too late, the frustrated Dutch commander sailed back to New Amsterdam.

Not so easily turned away from the river mouth were a troop of Iroquois Mohawk warriors, who fiercely if briefly harassed the fort, and a band of Pequot who settled down for a howling siege. Yet if the prophet-inspired Pequot hoped for swift success, they did not include in their reckoning Lion Gardiner, the military engineer who had been retained by Winthrop. Gardiner not only hurled back all assaults on the walls of the fort, but he also conducted such showy maneuvers in the surrounding fields that the Pequot came to believe in the English soldiers' martial skills. Yet they continued to attack, and Gardiner's men continued to die. Pessimistic about his relative position if it was not reinforced, he sent the leg bone of one of his fallen soldiers up to Massachusetts Governor Winthrop in order to make a point: The bone had been completely shot through by an arrow, evidence enough of the firepower of the offense and the difficulties of the defense.

Adding to those difficulties were the taunts of the increasingly eager Pequot, for whom the English language was apparently no problem. Among other shouted threats and boasts, they claimed (according to Lion Gardiner's report) that, "We have one amongst us who [has killed so many of you that] if he could kill but one of you more, he would be equal with your god!" Then, speaking of their prophet again (presumably the shaman of whom Roger Williams had heard), they called, "As the Englishmen's god is, so would he be." Later, as they saw the English numbers diminishing and their chances increasing, the Pequot called the English "all squaws" and their god "no more than an insect." In other words, they recognized that the struggle that came to be called the Pequot War was a religious war—god against god, prophet against prophet. This was the pattern that set the norm for America.

From their own perspective, the theocentric leaders of the Massachusetts Bay Colony came to realize the same thing— that this war was a divine trial, not just a test of arms. Previously, when hearing of the Native Americans' hostilities among each other, the Puritans had dismissed those fracases as (in the words of Cotton Mather) "a division of the kingdom of Satan against itself." But when they learned that the Pequot, enthused by their prophet, were not only winning at Saybrook but had sent a successful ambassadorial delegation to the Narragansett, they at last realized that they faced an alliance of enormous power.

It was then, at that desperate time, that they had been forced to call upon the diplomatic talents of Roger Williams to do what he could to keep the Narragansett on what they saw as the proper side.

The SLAUGHTERS of WAR and PERILS of CONVERSION

The Puritans' feeling that they must, in the name of God and self-preservation, take immediate diplomatic and military action had intensified in desperate step with their suspicions that they were losing control of events. One of their agents, a troublemaking trader by the name of John Oldham, had, they said, been murdered by Pequot-allied Indians on Block Island (off the Rhode Island coast), and two daughters of a Connecticut settler family had been captured by the Pequot themselves. Furthermore, the Puritans saw that they were being torn apart by dissenters in their own communities, as antinomians and Quakers and Separatists of all stripes strove to make the case for broader grace and greater freedom. Harvard's Perry Miller, long known as the dean of American studies, described the Puritans' reaction to this divisiveness as a process of "universalizing their neurasthenia." The only major problem as they whipped up their self-righteous bellicosity was that they had neither the money nor the armed force for war.

A zealous officer named John Endicott, whose particularly savage form of Yankee Protestantism expressed itself when he slashed the cross out of a British flag with his sword, came to the fore at this moment. If ever a warrior had been inspired by

Puritan saints, Endicott was that man. He would lead a force of volunteers against the pagan savages, he told the governor, and in one attack, he would prepare the way to victory. This, unfortunately, he did—inventing a barely acceptable excuse for first attacking the natives of Block Island (where there were thought to be rich stores of corn as well as captives to sell as slaves). Then Endicott and his troopers turned to Connecticut, which he found even more to his men's liking because of superior plundering prospects among the Pequot. On Endicott's return to Boston, some Puritans hailed his self-supported brigandage as a successful demonstration of godly Puritan might; others scoffed that it had been a "bootlesse voyage," which had, in fact, "Incouraged the Indians very much."

In another quarter, Lion Gardiner—the officer who was trying to hold Fort Saybrook as the Pequot assaults grew ever fiercer—complained to Endicott, "You come hither to raise these wasps about my ears; then you will take wing and flee away." Even more importantly, it was Endicott's pelf-inspired raid on Block Island that caused Roger Williams's neighbors, the Narragansett, to consider siding with the wounded Pequot. Perhaps, they thought, the predictions of the Pequot prophet were justified; perhaps all tribesmen should band together against the armor-clad English to defeat their harsh and vengeful religion.

This was the fraught situation early in 1636 when Roger Williams set forth on his thirty-mile expedition to Chief Canonicus's "Great Citty" on the west side of Narragansett Bay in hopes of out-arguing the Pequot ambassadors. The trek would be a challenge for any frontiersman, and the diplomatic debate an even more formidable test. In his vivid and somewhat self-promoting language, Williams described the event like this:

> Three days & nights my Business forced me to lodge &
> mix with the bloudie Pequot Embassadours, whose Hands
> & Arms (me thought) reaked with the bloud of my coun-
> trymen murthered & massacred by them on Connecticut
> River, & from whom I could not but nightly looke for
> their bloudy knives at my throate also.

Despite such horrors, Williams's eloquence and personal reputation won the day. His main argument to Canonicus and Miantonomi was that the English and their god were not to be blamed for recent outbreak of sicknesses among the Narragansett. In fact, Williams pointed out, the English had been devastated by similar illnesses themselves and had struggled in the same spirit to comprehend God's purposes. The Narragansett were persuaded. So convinced were they that the English intended to support them that they agreed to send a courtly delegation to Boston in October to conclude a formal agreement.

By this Williams-devised alliance, the Narragansett joined with the Mohegan (a nation to the west of the Pequot) in military cooperation with the English. Given that assurance, the Boston hierarchy felt confident enough to raise a small army of 160 men and to send the combined force against the Pequot forts on April 18, 1637. Though the language they used to bolster their spirits was unflaggingly religious, their campaign was an effort to gain land and beaver-hunting territories for themselves in (today's) western Massachusetts and Connecticut. Indeed, when the recently arrived English settlers along the

Connecticut River heard of the approaching fleet of Puritan warriors, they were initially opposed to the idea of the acquisitive Bostonians landing in their region. But at length they agreed, for the Pequot seemed a "common enemie"; they even sent a contingent of men to join the Puritans' war party. Plymouth, for its part, would have none of it, saying rudely that the war, if war it was to be, had been brought on by Endicott's misbegotten raid, and furthermore, they were too poor to participate in any such aggression.

Guided by native scouts who had learned the secret location of the Pequot settlement at Fort Mystic, the combined force of Massachusetts and Connecticut soldiers was able to breach the walls from both sides simultaneously and to prevent the escape of all but a few warriors. The bold attack led to a bloody, blazing firestorm of a victory of the sort that left the victors more shocked and abashed than triumphant and eager for more. When news of the Fort Mystic victory reached Plymouth, Governor Bradford was quick to assert that the burning of the women and the children there surely must have seemed a "sweet sacrifice" to the Christian god. To the allied, participating Indians, the unappeasable fury of the English warriors had not seemed so sweet, however. *"Mach it! Mach it!"* they had cried to the torch-wielding soldiers, meaning, "Enough! Enough!"

When the Pequot warriors at a nearby base first learned of the surprise attack on their home fort, they chose not to flee for safety. Instead, they rushed en masse to die by the dozens in a nearly successful effort to catch the exhausted English and make them pay for their invasion. They were just too late to prevent their proud tribe from being subjected to a memorable defeat.

The Pequot War of 1637 remains on American history books as a vicious and extirpatory act of aggression by English and native forces against a nonneighboring and thus nonthreatening Native American people. It also stands as a model for many other, similar campaigns to follow. Marked by excessive slaughter in the name of a Christian god and by cleanup actions of the most cowardly character, the war's neurotic hatefulness is well portrayed in Alfred Cave's *The Pequot War*. Cave sharply disagrees with that grand New England historian of the mid-twentieth century, Samuel Eliot Morison, who had concluded that the Pequot War gave the region "forty years of peace." On the contrary, Cave sees the war as a factor in setting New England's native people (particularly the Narragansett and the Mohegan) against each other and against the English, a disharmony that would not be resolved until King Philip's War of 1675.

Furthermore, the war caused something murderous to happen in the Puritan mind. Linked with the hierarchy's desperate clampdown on perceived heresies, the elite's leadership of the war seemed a successful reaction to some test set by God. Having diverted God's wrath away from the Puritans' own sins and onto the backs of others—that is, onto the Indians and the unorthodox—the Puritans had claimed their destiny of righteousness. They had raised the sword in triumph, and by that act had contributed to the myth of victorious America. When the Puritan army's battered ships returned to Boston, they were met with an outpouring of unstinted joy: church bells rang and poets spun verse laurels for New England's new heroes.

Perhaps the most shocking event of the Pequot War was the slaughter, near New Haven, of a huddled mass of refugee Pequot women and children driven by defeat from the land of their birth. Firing round after round into the swampland hideaway until there seemed to be no further movement, the heavily armored Puritan forces annihilated the defenseless civilians.

Shortly before that atrocity, Sassacus, the young Pequot chief, nearly lost his life to rivals within his council who objected to his generalship and who mocked the prophet who had inspired the war. Then, fleeing farther west, Sassacus had the not particularly bright idea of seeking refuge (perhaps even finding new forces) among his former rivals, the Iroquois Mohawk. But the Mohawk, now impressed by the importance of negotiating carefully with the English, killed him upon his entry to their camp. Though the Mohawk, in their strategies with the English, would certainly avoid such craven pacts as the one that would soon be forged by the opportunistic Mohegan chief, Uncas, they would bide their time and see when and how to form a much more significant alliance, under the most beneficial terms.

The Pequot War had the unintended effect of reversing the religious allegiance of one of New England's most eloquent Native American spokesmen. This was the Narragansett prince Miantonomi who, before the war, had backed his uncle Canonicus in supporting Roger Williams's efforts to found the colony of Rhode Island. Upon the death of his uncle, Miantonomi had become principal chief of the Narragansett about 1632. Increasingly impressed by Williams, Miantonomi became his convinced friend; he was even persuaded by Williams's fellow colonists to attend their Baptist* church for a session or two. There he saw the peaceful and constructive side of the Christian religion.

But, after the war, it became clear to him that the English colonists were more interested in claiming the land of the Pequot for themselves—with the aid of the Mohegan chief Uncas, who had served with them during the war—than in fulfilling their promises of aid to the Narragansett. Leaving his allegiance to the Rhode Island Baptists behind him, Miantonomi entered into a premature, poorly mounted, but nonetheless remarkable campaign to unite all Indian nations in a confederation against the English. He based his appeal to other tribes on the commonality of the Native American religions and, in that faith, he felt fully armored to meet the Europeans squarely on the field of battle.

Finally captured in a 1634 battle against the Mohegan, Miantonomi was led to Hartford for trial by his sympathetic but no longer helpful friend Roger Williams. Subsequently, after being taken to Boston for further hearings and back to Hartford—all in search of a judicial rubric that would allow the Puritans at either capital to grant Uncas's request to have Miantonomi executed—the Narragansett nobleman was turned over to his bloody-minded captor. The result, along the trail home, was murder of the most brutal sort—after Miantonomi's head had been bashed in, Uncas consumed a portion of the young prince's

---

*Roger Williams's Calvinistic branch of the Baptist denomination, called Particular Baptists, dated back to the group's split from other English Separatists in 1608 and 1611. His first Baptist church in Rhode Island was formally established in 1639.

shoulder. The site of the deed was marked at first by a heap of stones, subsequently knocked down, and now by a granite pile commemorating the native prince turned revolutionary.

Something of even greater value than Miantonomi's monument could never be knocked down: his words uttered upon commencement of his pan-Indian campaign after the Pequot War. When addressing the Montauk of Long Island, he had cried:

> For so we are all Indians, as the English are [English], and say brother to one another, so must we be one as they are; otherwise we shall be all gone shortly. For you know your fathers had plenty of deer and skins, our plains were full of deer, as also our woods, and full of turkies, and our coves full of fish and fowl.

What lingers in the mind on reading Miantonomi's words is not so much his eloquent description of the abundance that had formerly characterized his woodlands and meadows and coves, but the spiritual basis of that wealth. Like Massasoit, he spoke of a human inheritance, all brothers and sisters as heirs of divine bounty. And like Massasoit, he saw, as Squanto and Passaconaway had not, what profound values might be lost as the price of accommodation. That spiritual realization would have earthshaking consequences among subsequent Native Americans.

CHAPTER 3

TWO MEN of OPPOSED GODS on the NORTHERN FRONTIER

A T THE TIME OF the first English settlers' arrival in North America in the late sixteenth century, there were something like 250,000 tribesmen and women in the strategically positioned northern woodlands. This well-watered, undulating stretch of what would become the United States extended from Maine south through Virginia and from the Atlantic west to Pennsylvania and Ohio. It embraced a great variety of Native Americans who spoke dialects from one of three major language groups: Algonquian, Iroquois, and (in the westernmost cases) Sioux. It would be more than two hundred years before the number of Native Americans would rise to the original height again.

By contrast, the number of English and other settlers increased from a few hundred in the 1620s to 2.5 million by the time of independence from Britain. Of those mixed millions, only fifty thousand were Native Americans (ten times that were African Americans). Perhaps enough has been written about the causes of these Native Americans' destruction—the wars, epidemics, and betrayals. Indeed, a favorite form of sentimental American literature concerns the *Last of the* _____ (name of noble tribe to be inserted), as if crocodile tears could make up for centuries of morally ignorant persecution. But little has been written about the equally important story of how the Indian peoples survived, based on their remarkable religious traditions, and where that legacy of survival situates them in the turnings of American history.

Both of the two very different, god-inspired men on whom this chapter is focused helped provide answers to the survival question for people of the Iroquois nations. One was a warrior turned peacemaker who appeared among the tribes of central New York State in the sixteenth century. The second, a French Jesuit, appeared in the next century to the Iroquois-speaking people (mostly Huron) who dwelled just across today's border in the Canadian Province of Ontario. The two men, from such strongly contrasting backgrounds, touched hands, as it were, across the connected centuries on a blazing, racial frontier where white settlers and native villagers alike prayed for divine help in threatening times.

The story truly begins even more centuries ago, when the first Native Americans moved into the glacier-carved lands of central New York State. This is thought to have occurred shortly after the peaking of pre-Columbian civilization in the New World (A.D. 1200–1400). It was then that a legendary figure named Deganawidah, perhaps representing ageless spiritual traditions from America's Mississippi cultures, appeared as a "heavenly messenger" in the eastern forests. In his earthly form, he was a Huron, a very human individual who possessed supernatural powers but suffered, legend has it, from an impenetrable stammer. This blocked him from presenting his message—the Great Law of Peace and Power (*Kaianerekowa*) and a binding constitution—to the awaiting Iroquois nations. In order to fulfill his purpose, a translator was needed.

As so often happens in spiritual affairs, the man who came uncertainly forth and carried out Deganawidah's purpose was a quite unlikely holy man: a war-wearied, cynical Mohawk named Hiawatha. After an initial, numinous meeting with Deganawidah, Hiawatha went on to create the extraordinary confederation of related states that came to be called the Five Nations of the Iroquois. As mentioned in the preceding chapter, this league would grow to dominate trans-Appalachian America in colonial and early republican times. Given the fact that the political mainspring of Hiawatha's confederation was a system of courteous checks and balances, and that that system influenced the shape of the United States government, his life should be recognized not only as a Native American phenomenon but also as a mission that benefited all Americans.

Strangely, Deganawidah came not from one of the Iroquois tribes that would compose the Five Nations in the east (Mohawk, Oneida, Onondaga, Cayuga, and Seneca) but from Huronia in the abundant, untroubled west. Scholars deduce from fragmentary evidence that the Huron may have been separated from the eastern Iroquois some time shortly before A.D. 1500 and driven from the nurturing St. Lawrence valley to their Ontario location. However the division occurred, a dreadful contradiction remains: Barely a century after Deganawidah's and Hiawatha's missions were completed, the well-organized eastern Five Nations proceeded to demolish the Huron in 1648— one of North America's bloodiest purges.

It was shortly before that national tragedy, in which some ten thousand people were eliminated, that this chapter's second great man of God, the French missionary Père Jean de Brébeuf, was sent to live among the oppressed Huron. Neither warrior nor militant prophet and quite a different man from Hiawatha, it was Père de Brébeuf who helped the Huron survive their changing times and horrendous catastrophe. In doing so, he provided such a telling example of martyrdom on the American frontier that even secular historians have difficulty dismissing it. Nor should de Brébeuf's martyrdom be considered an exclusively Canadian affair, since it occurred roughly halfway between present-day Buffalo and Detroit and had a strong influence on the religious-political character of the entire American frontier.

"HOLY MADNESS" MAKES the FIVE NATIONS ONE

Hiawatha's name in Iroquois was *Aiowantha* (meaning, in one translation, "He Makes the Rivers"); he grew up a member of the Turtle clan. Though a Mohawk, he found himself living among the neighboring Onondaga in the mid-1500s. Like most other male members of his nation, he had to be swift of foot and nimble of tongue. No reliable portrait of him exists, but there is a temptation to see his form in that of the tall and trim Mohawk construction workers who leap with such surefooted agility from high beam to high beam amid the rising frameworks of Manhattan's skyscrapers. Edmund Wilson described those athletes in the *New Yorker* five decades ago, amazed at their "uncanny sense of balance." Three centuries before that, William Penn, impressed by the particular handsomeness of the Mohawk he encountered when passing through New York, wrote, "I found them [all] of like countenance and their children of so lively a resemblance that a man would think himself in Duke's Place or [fashionable] Berry Street in London when he seeth them."

However prepossessing in appearance he may have been, however bold in former combat and proud in forthcoming debate, Hiawatha's outstanding feature was his magnetic, if moody, personality. It was this dark attractiveness, not any princely title or star-studded rank, that drew to him the young warriors who followed in his path. For such was the volunteers'-choice nature of Iroquois military leadership: "Come with me if you will." His attractive, passionate personality also gave him a special place around the longhouse fires. But unfortunately, as is so often the fate of saints, the tales of Hiawatha passed down by tribal historians are relentlessly hagiographic, providing only a few hints of the man's authentic character. His life presents itself therefore as a story—a very important story.

When he came upon the stage of history, Hiawatha seems to have been inwardly disturbed by signs of change all around him. The Edenic forest world in which he had grown up—in which nature ruled and traditional values were shared without question—was not the hostile, uncertain world he now addressed. Extraordinary and foreign stirrings were in the wind. Internecine rivalry for leadership in the new trade networks was marked by tribal feuds followed by deadly counterfeuds, and, as a result, the Iroquois population diminished. An existing Onondaga account of society at this time reports that "the men were ragged with sacrifice and the women scarred with flints; so everywhere there was misery." Traditional spirits and agencies no longer seemed to control the universe.

The Iroquois-speaking people among whom the troubled Hiawatha moved and waged his battles included, in addition to his Mohawk of eastern New York State and the closely related Onondaga (centered around today's Syracuse), the more distant Oneida and Cayuga as well as the Seneca out beyond the Finger Lakes. These were the groups identified by the British as the Five Nations. Yet it was because the nations referred to themselves from time to time as Iriakhoiw, the Rattle Snake People, that the French took that phrase and manufactured the name Iroquois. The people themselves most often used the name Haudenosaunee, People of the Longhouse, when they spoke of their own hearth-based, matriarchal culture. They regarded themselves as living in one immense longhouse, of which the western door was guarded by the Seneca and the eastern by the Mohawk.

That longhouse was now threatened, as Hiawatha could see, not only by the surrounding Algonquian nations (particularly the prosperous Susquehannock and the numerous Delaware or Lenni Lenape, who proudly considered themselves the grandfathers of all other Native Americans) but also by the internal and accelerating blood feuds that threatened the Haudenosaunee's very existence. There was, furthermore, an unwelcome race of white warriors that some years before had had the audacity to march up and down the valleys of the Tennessee and Mississippi Rivers. Now came tales of great, winged canoes on the St. Lawrence, canoes filled with men offering wondrous metal gadgets. These were the splendidly armed Europeans with whom each tribe hurried to establish the most beneficial, exclusive contacts. How, religiously inclined people must have wondered, did those unexpected developments fit into any credible divine order of the cosmos?

In Hiawatha's reflective mood, it seemed to him that his

preceding years on the warpath among the tribes had brought about little more than short-term victories and immediately gratifying moments of revenge. His hands seemed so bloody no water could clean them. Returned from this or that raid, his nights in the Mohawk villages had often been lit by scenes of fiery cannibalism, the new victory celebrated in a blaze of torture. Staring skulls poised on the palisade's posts seemed symbols not of triumph but of more war to come. Most painful of all to Hiawatha were the continuing deaths of family members, including his wife—a pain compounded by the haughty antagonism and mockery heaped on him by shamans of the Onondaga with whom he currently dwelled.

These tribesmen dominated the scene as the elders of the Haudenosaunee. Surpassed in harvests only by the Seneca, the Onondaga had farms of immense yields, glowing fields of corn and grain surrounding each of their hilltop villages. They looked down on the Mohawk as being less at ease with the deities, less inclined to ceremony, more warlike, and more inclined to fret about the Algonquian and the European strangers. Although the Mohawk name meant "man eaters," their Iroquois neighbors now referred to them as "pirates of the fur trade." The Mohawk River, central artery into Iroquoia, was often called *La Rivière des Hollandais* because its native lords had so thoroughly allied themselves with the Dutch.* By contrast, the

---

*The ancient treaty through which the Mohawk and other Iroquois League nations (Haudenosaunee) had allied themselves with the Dutch in 1613 was called the Covenant Chain by the Europeans and was recorded by means of a sacred, mnemonic device known as the Two-row Wampum Belt, or *Guswenta*. Its two parallel pathways of interwoven shells reflect the agree-

Onondaga, secure behind their palisades (with each of their villages containing thirty or more buildings and with some of their villages numbering as many as two thousand inhabitants), felt comfortably isolated from the cultural shocks and international threats that Hiawatha witnessed elsewhere. Ignoring intimations of change, the Onondaga trusted in the eternal order of creation. They concentrated on their ancient rites, including the important Feast of the Dead, which occurred every ten or twelve years.

Elaborate processions and solemn chanting ushered in these feasts, held just before the people of an Iroquois village moved on to a new site. Attendant ceremonies concentrated on the removal of ancient bones from drying platforms to common burial grounds. Only after such rituals had been successfully completed could the villagers transfer to their new site. There they would set up their relocated longhouses and prepare fresh gardens to replace their old, exhausted fields.

The Feasts of the Dead, dedicated to the people's imperishable heroes, were considered fundamental to each village within the Iroquois culture in that they resuscitated the community, bringing forth new life from prior generations. They hymned the departed nobles and invoked the traditional spirits of the

---

ment that the Iroquois should proceed peacefully on one course, the Europeans on the other, "as long as the grass is green, as long as the water flows downhill, and as long as the sun rises in the east and sets in the west." The Iroquois believe that that same concept—the eternally honored separation of the peoples—should be recognized as a condition of all subsequent treaties, including those made with the British and the Americans. The still visible belt attests to the concept's unchanging quality, as opposed to tattered and altered documents in official archives.

natural universe, reconfirming their village's way of life. Also confirmed by these ceremonies was the governing power of the nation's chiefs and shamans. In Onondaga, one of these, a sachem named Tadodaho (Wathatotarho), was notorious during Hiawatha's time for his use of spies and of wizardly tricks to maintain power and to prevent any change in the conventional order.

Yet it seemed to Hiawatha that adjustments must be made—specifically, an end brought to the blood feuds and the hostility within the Five Nations. This was a radical position that Tadodaho naturally opposed and that Hiawatha was determined to put to the test. By his eloquence, physical presence, and battle-won credibility, he tried to sway the council chiefs around the central fire in Onondaga toward less slaughter and more unity within the Haudenosaunee. But he was mocked by the sachem-magician and made to feel an outsider. The clan women, in whose hands lay the real power of command, might possibly have responded to Hiawatha's message. Yet they feared Tadodaho's intimidations and kept their silence. Even when Tadodaho arranged to have one of Hiawatha's daughters murdered, the women obeyed his edicts and refused to back any chiefs who would support the new way advocated by Hiawatha.

The only course for him, it seemed, was to travel elsewhere among the People of the Longhouse and to advance his cause around other council fires. Taking to the trail, he first addressed the chiefs of his own Mohawk nation and then moved on to the Oneida and Cayuga. There his enlightened ideas for ending the revenge raids and abandoning cannibalism won a hearing. The conservative clan mothers pointed out, however, that their traditional rights and perquisites must be respected. They must continue to receive "condolence" in the form of captives taken in war who would replace fallen family members and would thereby "requicken" and repopulate the clan. Hiawatha concurred that the authority of the matriarchal lines, the *ohwachiras,* must always be respected. Could not that be done, he asked, by means of righting wrongs and establishing treaties with neighboring people? Would that not be a way to restore traditional balance and harmony in the longhouse?

The women of the nations heard him, and the chiefs who followed the *ohwachiras'* bidding spoke more and more favorably of ending the feuds. Yet they made a hard bargaining point: Before they would officially assent, Hiawatha would have to go back and persuade the Onondaga to join in the agreement. That meant he would have to win over Tadodaho. Returning to the central fire of the Onondaga, he found the wizard in an increased fury. It may have been at this time that Tadodaho arranged the murder of Hiawatha's daughter. Outmaneuvered at the council fire and frustrated at every turn by Tadodaho's henchmen, Hiawatha saw that his entire campaign was coming to nothing. There seemed to be no way he could break out of the circle of revenge and death that gripped all of Haudenosaunee's tribes and villages.

Like many another frustrated man of action, Hiawatha retired to his longhouse and swore that others could take care of the world. Abandoned by friends and trusting few, deaf to the pleas of his remaining family to accept what religious solace might be had for his personal losses, he abandoned himself totally to bitterness and discouragement. Day became night and

night had no end in the smoky gloom of the longhouse as he
huddled in his robes. One can imagine his old-fashioned, wooden
armor stacked and discarded in the shadows of his assigned corner. He slept and dreamed fitfully, awful dreams of torture and
slaughter. One winter's night he dreamed that he went out into
the snow-covered, black-treed forest beyond the palisades of
his village. Or perhaps he ceased to dream and actually went
out into the cold. Or, most likely, he went out into the frozen
wilderness in search of a dream, possibly a dream of life rather
than of death.

In the image-rich narratives of the Haudenosaunee, a voyage into the wilderness and a dream of encounter with one's
mission or one's special angel are often different dimensions
of the same experience. The voyage may be a dream and the
dream a voyage. There are also the dreams that occur in the
course of a youth's initiation trial: Iroquois lads, leaving hearth
and childhood behind, travel out into the wilderness (which is
to them not that at all) as a personal trial. Equipped with neither
weapons nor food, they risk death by exhaustion or starvation,
searching down the valleys and up the mountainsides to meet
with that terrifying, unforeseeable spirit—a dream encounter
of some profound sort with the divine forces of nature.

The vision typically comes to them deep in the forest after
they have collapsed in a hallucinatory trance caused by hunger
or have fallen, dazed and wounded, from a height to the base of
a fostering tree. In that condition they are found by friends or
family, to whom they haltingly tell their stunning revelation:
what the spirits have commanded them to do with their lives.
From the vivid character of that encounter (the animals seen,
the other worlds glimpsed) they receive the name to be used

within their clan, a personal destiny from which they would not presume to deviate.

Nor would another Iroquois clansman think of challenging that dream or that mission. Instead, he would feel obliged to lend whatever assistance he could to help the young initiate work out whatever instructions the spirits might have given him in the dream. For example, Walter Edmonds (author of *Drums Along the Mohawk* and student of Iroquois ways) repeats the story of a Cayuga lad whose wilderness dream had involved friends coming to greet him through holes in the ice. In fulfillment of the boy's vision, his clansmen felt obliged to wait until the river was frozen, then to break through the ice and dive deep enough into the water to resurface through those dreamed-of holes, ignoring all perils of the flesh.

It was in a trance of that sort that Hiawatha, wearied and near death from his nights and days of winter wandering, first saw Deganawidah. In a blaze of light, the Native American messiah came forth from the wilderness, commanding the attention of the exhausted warrior. There are, of course, several versions of the revelation—who found whom when and where—but all agree that this was the turning point in Hiawatha's life. He could understand the older man, despite that one's difficulties with speech, he could trust the sanctity of the moment, and he could accept the severe and timeless obligations that were being loaded upon him.

Archaeologists in the past few decades have confirmed the relationship between the historic Iroquois societies and the divinely inspired ancestral people who prospered in the Mississippi heartland of North America ages before. Religious ceremonies practiced by several other Native Americans—specifically, by the Creek and their neighbors in the southeast who will be discussed in this book's final chapter—also stem from that hallowed Mississippian heritage. Imposed on all progeny of that ancient culture were certain obligations—expected ways of living, imagining, and believing. These included the following:

1. *Moral standards of individual and communal behavior* upheld by leaders of the matriarchal clans (which were named for such totems as turtle, beaver, and snake);
2. *Social and gender codes* that related to the furthering of an agricultural economy, with game and fish (supplied by the male hunters) as supplements to the corn, beans, and squash (supplied by the women farmers);
3. *A strong belief in the divine,* wondrously varied, and omnipresent powers of nature, as recalled in sacred accounts of godly actions and expressed in dances and other rites.

For many Indians of eastern North America, to participate in that life pattern was to be pious, in step with the heavenly mandates. The union of Hiawatha and the messianic Deganawidah, which emphasized these points, should therefore be seen against that background—in effect, a reconnection with the Native Americans' religious heritage.

Despite Deganawidah's messianic-like role, he was not seen by Hiawatha or other Iroquois as a manifestation of the single God. Indeed, such a concept did not exist in their tradition. For many Iroquois, Deganawidah was the expected savior figure, for others a personification of the Good Twin. That latter personality is an aspect of the Iroquois's beautiful and often told creation myth. It tells of how Sky Mother, having been hurled out of heaven, required some bit of firmament on which to alight in the midst of a watery world.* Turtle provided initial assistance by offering his back for her perch. But none of the animals then created could help her find solid ground, with the exception of dauntless beaver. Taking on the challenge of diving deeper and deeper to reach bottom, he finally came back up holding in his paw a bit of mud. Taking refuge on that first earth, Sky Mother soon gave birth to a daughter who, in turn, produced rival twins from whom she had to choose her favorite.

Unfortunately she chose Evil Twin, with eternal consequences for the human condition. But Good Twin, with the cooperation of his grandmother, was nonetheless able to accomplish some of his purposes down through prehistoric time. And now, here, in the form of Deganawidah, was Good Twin's possible reembodiment—the ethereal figure who, like him, would carry the name of Peace Maker down through the centuries.

Deganawidah, first of all, brought comfort to the severely troubled soul of Hiawatha. He convinced the weary campaigner that the evil powers of Tadodaho could not prevail against him as he strove to unite the peoples and that he could carry out his mission of ending the blood feuds within the Haudenosaunee. Then he instructed Hiawatha in a number of rituals and laws

---

*Cultural anthropologists, fascinated by the analogs between religious myth and the earth sciences, confirm that some twelve thousand years ago, immediately after the recession of the glaciers and the warming of North America, this part of New York State was a sea of water, from horizon to horizon. The land did not take today's form until 7000 B.C.

that were necessary to ensure lasting peace and social harmony. The central figure in the ritualistic imagery of Deganawidah was a giant white pine, reaching to the sky. Its five great roots represented the people of the Haudenosaunee and, springing from them, the tree rose high above a luminous snow-white carpet. The carpet spread over the rock hills on which Hiawatha and Deganawidah stood and extended far beyond them, over the lands of all nations. Indeed, the carpet might reach to the ends of the earth, for this was a religion of universal applicability. The soil that gave life to the tree was composed of three principles, each of which had twin components: (1) *purity*, which combined a stable mind and a healthy body; (2) *equity*, which combined righteousness in conduct and fairness in the adjustment of human rights; and (3) *security*, which combined civil authority and self-defense. Atop the lofty pine tree perched an eagle, watching in all directions for any enemy who might come to disturb the Great Law.

Inspired by this universal vision and its humane concepts, Hiawatha also understood that he could only fulfill his mission as prophet by imbuing his teachings with a binding sense of Deganawidah's holiness. In order to bring all the Iroquois people to an acceptance of the Great Law, he would have to become, in effect, the herald of a religion. Having failed to push through his reforms as political leader, he would now have to convert the Iroquois on the strength of his personal declamations. But could he, essentially warrior and leader, do that? Would he have enough of what has been called the prophet's "holy madness"?

In some versions of his attempted transmutation from warrior to prophet, Hiawatha, still in a trance, then turned to see Deganawidah walking away from him to the edge of a nearby lake. From there, with a gesture of farewell, Deganawidah stepped into a stone canoe and paddled off into the mists. In other versions, he accompanied Hiawatha back to Onondaga and stayed with him until the monstrous Tadodaho had been overcome and had bowed to the principles of the Great Law of Peace and Power. In the gospels of this still living faith—the Iroquois religion of the Longhouse—many vivid scenes describe this good-versus-evil wrestling match between prophet and trickster, some sounding more like a session of psychiatric therapy than a physical combat. In one of them, Hiawatha is portrayed as combing the hair of the defeated and redeemed wizard (i.e., sorting out his thoughts). And perhaps Hiawatha's very name means "He Who Combs the Hair" rather than "He Who Parts the Waters." The Iroquois scholar Paul A. W. Wallace quotes the vanquished and reformed Tadodaho as then saying to Hiawatha, "Thou shalt now strive . . . to make reason and the peaceful mind prevail."

Thus were the Five Nations united. No longer would blood revenge be the rule of the day; no longer would cannibalism be tolerated (except ritually, in times of war). Yet the old wizard did win certain concessions from the Peace Maker and Hiawatha, of which the leading one was that he himself would head the roll of the hereditary chiefs and that the Onondaga would forever be regarded as the "central fire." The Onondaga people were confirmed as the eternal fire keepers of the league and as the custodians of the Five Nations' historical records, in the form of long belts of wampum that were hung over the rafters of the council house. Still today, at the great council fire of the Iroquois Confederacy, the Onondaga maintain that custodial charge.

The PROPHET and the LAWS

Hiawatha came out of warrior-tent retirement in order to become prophet, that is, to effect a spiritual conquest. This was not merely a matter of proclaiming and revering the Great Law, the Kaianerekowa, which the Peace Maker had given—an act that, as revisited in today's rituals, requires eight concentrated days of recitation (with the cantor assisted by a great wampum belt into which the law's mnemonics have been woven). It was also a matter of working out daily details of social behavior and community governance. A comparison can be made between this prophet's program for the Iroquois constitution and the efforts of the Pilgrims and Puritans who attempted not many decades later, not many miles away, to build sin-free societies and civic structures on the foundation of their religion. Those Christians, too, began their New World occupations by laying down remarkable plans for government, the Mayflower Compact and the Cambridge Platform, both of which deserve analysis along with the Great Law for what they mean in terms of everyday morality.

In setting forth the Kaianerekowa, Hiawatha remained constantly aware of the three basic principles represented by the roots of Deganawidah's great pine: purity, equity, and security. Without overlooking the ancient system of matriarchal democracy within the Haudenosaunee, the prophet insisted on a *rule by consensus* of the chiefs gathered in great council. Agreement must cut across all lines of kinship and must be heartily accepted by the voices of all chiefs around the fire. Each man, ulti-mately, would assert, "*Niaona,* thou art in the right, brother; that is well."

A tradition of balanced forces—male versus female, war-rior versus peacemaker, league policy versus local interest—had already existed in the Iroquois governance. Fifty chiefs held sway in the great council, thus had it been since time im-memorial. But the chiefs were nominated by clan mothers of the powerful families—that is, by senior women who held their positions by hereditary right in every key village of the Five Nations. The great council, of itself, could also elect other chiefs from outside the hereditary structure (usually military leaders or great orators). These "pine tree chiefs" represented the people in a broader sense, in that they were not members of the established elite. Thus they represented Deganawidah's more all-inclusive, catholic philosophy. Furthermore, the chiefs (a word pronounced by the Iroquois today as *chieves*) could nei-ther name their successors nor carry their titles to the grave. The Great Law provided a ceremony to "remove the antlers of authority" from a dying chief. It also provided for the removal from office of inept or senescent chiefs who could no longer function adequately in office.

Having spoken to the need for peace and humane behavior among the individuals of the longhouse (Purity), and having strengthened the equity of Haudenosaunee society, Hiawatha then considered the security of its civil government. How could he bind together the Five Nations and maintain that bond despite the nations' deep-lying antagonisms? One way, in honor of tra-dition, was to grant senior status to the three "elder brothers," that is, to the powerful Onondaga as well as to the populous

Seneca and the ambitious Mohawk (the latter of whom guarded the eastern door and handled the European thrust with such tenacity). In recognition of the three tribes' seniority, he determined that all motions before the great council must be initiated by the elder brothers, then tossed "across the fire" to the younger brothers (the Oneida and Cayuga), and finally returned to the elders, with the Onondaga being in the final position of review. The genius of this rather roundabout and time-consuming procedure was that it gave Haudenosaunee government a conservative system of checks and balances without violating ancient privileges.

To the councils, all people of the Haudenosaunee should feel free to bring their perceived injustices to be addressed and corrected by their representatives. In the councils, the outrages and insults of certain clans against other clans would be heard and atoned for or rejected. By the councils, through the incredibly complex process of consensus, the excitable and creative People of the Longhouse would gradually be unified in peace as "one voice, one mind, one heart," rather than torn apart in war. Hiawatha the prophet vigorously reenforced the ancient ideal that the autumnal great councils of the Haudenosaunee should function not just as political or governmental forums but as religious and ceremonial occasions. Like prayer meetings, the occasions should climax with the sound of rejoicing. In the words of ethnologist William Fenn, the process might be characterized as "transforming dysphoria into euphoria."

Yet this is not to say that Hiawatha succeeded in giving to the Iroquois a centralized religion or that he, as an evangelistic prophet, succeeded in establishing a compelling religious system, a national church for his people. In those objectives, so difficult to achieve in a noncentralized culture, he failed. Fortunately, a subsequent Iroquois prophet (Handsome Lake) would have greater success toward those objectives more than two hundred years later.

Taking on another aspect of prophethood, Hiawatha then extended himself to become an international peacemaker, traveling far from the central fire to spread the gospel of Deganawidah. By river and trail he roamed across Huronia (where he found that in an earlier burst of religious inspiration, the people of five western nations had melded themselves into an immense, fully functioning confederation) to the distant shores of Lake Superior. He followed ancient paths down along the Mississippi to reach the southern nations (on which missionary trail he would be followed centuries later by Tecumseh, great hero of the pan-Indian ideal). And he returned home by means of the Susquehanna. But it seemed that, however magnetic Hiawatha's personality may have been, he could not (as missionaries might express it) "speak with the tongues of angels." For although he had some success in the teaching of personal purity and social equity, he failed to secure converts in the form of annexed nations. No real expansion occurred in Iroquoia until the Tuscarora, forced northward out of their North Carolina homelands by the British (and their allied Indian warriors), were adopted by the Oneida early in the eighteenth century, making the Five Nations six.

By that time, the People of the Longhouse had gained recognition as the most powerful Native American force in the northeastern part of the continent. Because of their knowing and flexible diplomacy and their continuing warfare against other Iroquois and Algonquian nations that had refused to join them, they succeeded in dominating a vast territory. This woodland territory stretched east and west, from the waters of the Hudson to the most distant Great Lakes and even to the banks of the Mississippi; north and south, it extended from the French settlements in Canada to the British settlements in the Carolinas. So large was their dominion of dependencies that historian Francis Parkman wrote that the victorious Iroquois were entitled to call themselves "Romans of the New World."

Modern revisionists scoff at Parkman's classical hyperbole, pointing out that the Iroquois areas of influence were truly nothing like Rome's conquered states and that the Six Nations squabbled and failed as much as they cooperated and triumphed. Historians also point out that the warfare practiced in this part of North America was carried out in a way totally different from the warfare waged by Caesar's armies. Indeed, both the ethos and the imperative behind these two fighting forces were dramatically dissimilar. Whereas the Roman soldiers fought under the iron command of officers whose highest ambition was to die for their emperor, the individual Iroquois warrior fought for his own or his mother's family's intentions under chiefs who commanded by persuasion if at all. Contrary to the Roman concept of a slain warrior's special place among the gods in heaven, the defeated brave's soul gained, in the Iroquois view, absolutely no points through deeds on the battlefield.

Yet the Iroquois were by any measure mighty at arms. There was no more powerful nation or alliance on this continent north of Mexico than the confederation that Hiawatha the prophet had brought into being on the basis of his religious preachings. The terrible irony is that, whereas he had set out to promulgate and broadcast the Great Law of Peace from the

People of the Longhouse to the nations of the world, the resultant, militaristic league of the Iroquois won an everlasting reputation for the brutality and cruelty of its conquests. Hiawatha's limited success as a missionary was quite overshadowed by his unintentional success in transforming the Iroquois into one of the strongest and bloodiest players in the seventeenth-century world game—namely, the international contest for North American dominance.

This outward eruption of the militant Iroquois League occurred in the generations following Hiawatha's death (which is thought to have taken place in 1590), generations in which confident Iroquois warrior chiefs defeated or faced down most of the Native American nations they chose to dominate and fought with distinction against the best soldiers of imperial Europe. To rationalize this shift of purpose, from a prophet-inspired awakening and a philosophy of open and peaceful government to a war-chief-dominated rulership and a continent-controlling philosophy, historians most often point to the intertribal rivalries and stresses brought on by the Euro-Indian wampum economy. They emphasize particularly the influence of the Dutch in selling arms to the Mohawk and in stimulating the Iroquois to survive by means of total warfare. But there is also a need to consider the idiosyncrasies of religion—religion as it is known generally around the world and religion as it functioned peculiarly in America—sometimes hideously aggressive, sometimes graciously restoring, definitely related to the psychic needs and fears of people on a land in transition.

In the words of Richard Niebuhr, "Faith is part of the defense mechanism of racial, sectional, and above all economic groups." In this case, there was another aspect to the psychic dimension: The Iroquois, having perceived that their numbers were drastically decreasing as a result of European diseases—and that numbers would be vitally necessary for the forthcoming confrontations with other rivals on the frontier—made the defensive decision to console the reduced families and to augment the populations of the Five Nations by means of captives in war. In that decision, one may see a people's inherent religion (not religious theory) at work. Theologian Maurice Bloch reminds us, further, that conquest tends to be a dynamic part of all the world's religions; the passionate rituals of the religion express themselves in violent acts against other peoples. So with all the energy of their new faith did the Iroquois expand at the end of the seventeenth century, striking both at their Native American neighbors and at New France.

In the Iroquois wars with the French, beginning in 1609 and climaxing with the Beaver Wars of the 1690s, the Haudenosaunee suffered nearly as much as they won. One very precious truth almost lost as the French issued increasingly grisly accounts of Iroquois barbarity was the previously mentioned irony that the Five Nations had been organized on the strength of a remarkable constitution that was perceived from within as a grant from heaven. Dutch traders and explorers did report to their home base at Fort Orange (Albany) in 1635 that, difficult though it might be for some to believe, their allies the Iroquois were not simply savages but had united themselves by means of a civilized system of government. In the next century, Benjamin Franklin, speculating on the basis of very little knowledge, wrote admiringly that the (by then) Six Nations had "subsisted for ages" as a confederation, since long before the coming of the white man.

Franklin had first learned something about the constitution of the Six Nations in delegates' accounts of the proceedings at the Treaty of Lancaster (Pennsylvania) in 1744. Then aged thirty-eight, and passionately interested in making an alliance with the Indians that would frustrate the French on the frontier, he read with fascination reports of the aristocratic demeanor and politically astute behavior of an attendant Onondaga chief. Named Canasatego, he stood forth as "a tall and well-made man, [possessing] a very full chest and brawny limbs, with a good natired [sic] smile." He handled the English language and the formalities of the diplomatic session with complete ease, addressing the purposes and processes of the assembly assuredly. But when the delegates from Maryland, Pennsylvania, and Virginia fell apart in quarrels among themselves about their objectives, this chief (whose home government had by then been resolving internal dilemmas by means of check-and-balance debates for a century and more) ran out of patience. Raising his hand and speaking with the eloquence that would have done credit to Hiawatha, he scolded the colonial delegates for their lack of wisdom and ignorance of good procedures. Making reference to the constitution of the Six Nations, he urged the white representatives to hurry up and find a similar way to unify.

His words rang in Franklin's ears. Although he had certainly known about the military might and diplomatic effectiveness of the Six Nations, he only now, through Canasatego's words, caught an intimation of what made its government work—a religion-based constitution. He was so impressed by the effectiveness of the Iroquois constitution that, even in the face of men trained in English universities, he held it up in a series of pamphlets as the world's only available model for a confederation of thirteen contentious colonies. He also advanced that cause at the intercolonial Albany Conference of 1754. Organized like its predecessor for the construction of a common defense against the ceaseless hostilities on the frontier, the conference almost immediately fell apart as regional delegates bickered about their differences, regarding political unification as a hopeless abstraction. Franklin pointed to the very real, very efficient League of the Iroquois as proof that confederation could work, given the proper spirit.

In effect, Franklin asked this question, "Should not Britain's American colonies be able to accomplish something like unity, given the precedent of the barbarian league?" His exact words:

It would be a strange thing if six nations of ignorant savages should be capable of forming a scheme for such a union and able to execute it in such a manner that it ... appears indissoluble; and yet that a like union should be impracticable for ten or a dozen English colonies to whom it is more necessary and who cannot be supposed to want an equal understanding of their interests.

Three more decades would be required before Anglo-Americans, their revolution completed, could organize themselves constitutionally along lines suggested by Deganawidah's precepts as well as by humanistic principles implicit within the Western Enlightenment. At that founding time of their Republic, America's debt to the Iroquois holy messenger was symbolically acknowledged by the five arrows held in the talons of the eagle initially pictured on the United States seal—five arrows for the Five Nations. Only later, in a confusion of images, did the arrows become thirteen. For, sadly, the memory of that debt

to Deganawidah and Hiawatha and Canasatego faded fast—
along with memories of other religious leaders who had brought
other paradigms of peace to the frontier.

MISSIONARY SAINT in a LAND of TRADERS

Jean de Brébeuf arrived at the wharves of Quebec from
Dieppe, Normandy, on a bright day in June 1623, with little
more than a hulking physique and four years of routine training
in the Jesuit order to his credit. But after six months of appren-
ticeship among the missions to the Montagnais Indians, and
after demonstrating a surprising quickness at learning the Algonquian language, he was selected as qualified for service
among the western tribes. Even that early, his capabilities for
frontier life were becoming evident. Although this big, burly,
and humble priest referred to himself as an ox, "fit only to bear
burdens," it was his mind and his spirit that prompted confidence in what he might accomplish.

The shaping of that mind had involved a strange combination of medieval piety and Renaissance intellectualism. In Père
de Brébeuf's subsequent actions on the frontier, one can see
those conflicting strains at work: the inquisitive mind of a latent
ethnologist and the pragmatic skills of a born administrator
competing with the unquestioned faith and self-sacrificing zeal
of a Christian. In his writings about these years in the wilderness, his style sometimes sounds as witty as Montaigne, sometimes as dutiful as other pietists following St. Ignatius Loyola's
Spiritual Exercises. When Père de Brébeuf was recognized as
patron saint of Canada in 1940, his 1649 martyrdom, the result
of an attack by an Iroquois army upon Christianized Huron,
was hailed as one of the key events in North American history.

This positive viewpoint assumes that martyrdom was desirable or necessary for the American people at that moment in history.

It was the explorer and conqueror Samuel de Champlain who had first seen the merits of introducing missionaries to New France, with the objective of establishing more than superficial ties with the empire's Native American allies. In the name of God, the king, and humanity, he urged the religious establishments of France to come and spread the peace-loving Gospel through the wilderness. First to respond to his call were priests of an extreme branch of the Franciscan order, the Recollects. They proved not particularly effective in their missionary endeavors but did succeed in supplying the colony's first priest martyred by the Indians, Nicolas Viel, in 1625.

As a rather broad-minded Roman Catholic, Champlain trusted that the knights and scapegraces, the bold younger brothers, the adventurers of all descriptions who drifted into his colony (whether to find their own fiefdoms, or simply to evade the formalized strictures of medieval France) would cohabit with the Native Americans and breed new generations of loyal children. This was to be nothing like the pure English conquest that was simultaneously overwhelming the Algonquian in Virginia and Massachusetts Bay, where the natives were regarded as somewhat similar to but even more unruly than the Irish, certainly not to be wedded, bedded, and bred by the colonists. No, here in New France, Christianity would bless and encourage the intermixing of the races. It would be the role of the missionaries to study and assist these woodland people, to instruct them and welcome them into baptism, and to conjoin the native converts with the French immigrants as working partners within King Louis's hybridized empire. How it happened that the

Roman Catholic Church came to play this distinctive role in the history of North America requires a few glances back into the first decades of colonization.

Unsurprisingly, the first group of Native Americans who fell under the shadow of Louis's banner, the Algonquian-speaking Montagnais people of the St. Lawrence Valley, responded without ardor to Champlain's intercultural scheme. Although they quickly seized on the wonderful material offerings of the Europeans—the hatchets and blankets and kettles—they showed little enthusiasm for abandoning their nomadic preagricultural ways or for accepting the Gospel of Christ. Decimated by the white man's diseases and no longer energized by the rigors of their traditional work and life, many of them became dependent vassals of the French economy. Some few made creative careers for themselves as *voyageurs* and soldiers' aides at a time when life in the region was exciting but short. Any allies of the French in these early years were threatened not only by the English colonists on the coast but also by the river-traveling Dutch. The latter imperialists had claimed the territory up the Hudson and along its feeder streams into the west as their particular, fur-rich domain, and they were looking for significant allies.

The Dutch, perhaps the most aggressive of Europe's trading empires in this first century of world conquest, had no doubt about what was the best thing to be gained from North America. While some Europeans, like Spain's Francisco Vásquez de Coronado and England's Captain John Smith, dreamed of the continent's silver and gold, and while others, including Champlain himself, dreamed of its Northwest Passage to China's silk manufactories, the Dutch pushed their ways up the

Mohawk River and kept their eyes on the beaver of the north-lands. Although other animals might produce valuable pelts, the glistening hide of the beaver was the essential ingredient in the manufacturing of hats for gentlemen; fortunes awaited those who could produce beaver skins most unfailingly.

Dutch merchants realized that beavers in the numbers de-manded by industry could only be located in the untouched vastness of the western lakes, and that far-traveling native allies would be required to freight the pelts into Fort Orange (Al-bany). Of the competing Native American peoples only certain ones then had the license, figuratively, to roam those distances without hindrance—and these tended to be the confident heirs of Hiawatha. Dutch administrators therefore sought to make links with those Iroquois by all possible means, not just by treaties sealed in the new medium of wampum but by goods of all possible sorts, even including firearms. As early as 1641, they had released thirty-nine highly prized muskets to their most de-sired trading partners, the Mohawk. By 1643, the number of re-leased muskets had topped three hundred. Emboldened by their previous successes, secure in their government and their reli-gion, and equipped now with weapons from a liberal ally, the Iroquois went on the path of conquest. War by firearms seemed the only sure way to protect themselves from perceived ene-mies, to collect prisoners for population growth, and to secure the fur business.

Nor had the French been slow at this deadly business of in-troducing modern firearms to the people of the north woods. In 1641, authorities in Quebec had given a Huron chief named Charles Tsondatsaa the first musket owned by a Native Ameri-can in New France. What made that gift particularly pertinent to the story of religion on the early frontier was that the musket was awarded by the French to the chief in celebration of his baptism.

Many historians of the frontier concur that the watershed event at the beginning of the war-wracked seventeenth century was the decision of newly arrived French commanders to ally themselves not with Hiawatha's arrogant and Dutch-inclined Five Nations but with the cooperative Huron. Champlain had died in Quebec some six years before the granting of Tsondatsaa's baptismal musket. But he would have seen no discrepancy in this admixture of firearms and religion and military assistance. Back in 1624, when confronted by mounting attacks on the Huron by the Iroquois and by battles of a new and deadlier nature than in previous years, he had specifically requested the Jesuits come to his aid. Perhaps they could supply additional aid to the Iroquois-persecuted Huron whom he was reinforcing with all possible food and weaponry.

In those years, a generation before the arrival of Jean de Brébeuf, the Huron had been as eager as the Mohawk to enter into a trading partnership with the French and the Dutch, their eagerness sharpened by distrust of their newly aggressive eastern Iroquois cousins. Champlain had taken careful note of the Huron's beaver-rich lakes, their huge quantities of stored furs, and their uniquely successful history as navigators upon western rivers (where their superior birch bark canoes moved with impressive dependability). He believed that by establishing ties with these people he had chosen the more affluent, as well as the more easily civilized, of the Native American groups. Through them and the nomadic hunters with whom they dealt as middlemen, he could reach out to the Indians of the even more distant west. Under the imperial flag of New France, he would go on to join the Huron with the Algonquian of the St. Lawrence Valley for military and commercial purposes. And he would, of course, seek to make Christians of them all.

The Huron were initially skeptical. One of their chiefs told the French that they might succeed in Champlain's cross-country, mixed-race settlement plan, but that they should forget about proselytizing. In fact, they should practice their own religion more strenuously among themselves. The chief's put-up or shut-up advice: "If you would do well, you should dwell in our country, and bring women and children, and when you come to these [western] regions, we shall see how you serve this God whom you worship." By his witness and through his death, Jean de Brébeuf would answer that sharp challenge.

Champlain's historic linking of lakeshore Huron with river valley Algonquian committed the French to be masters of empire and all that that implied. They were required to supply the most vigorous sort of leadership and reinforcements: French troopers, with their advanced weapons and iron armor, should always be available to march in company with the native allies. So it happened soon after the forging of the treaty that Champlain and two French officers found themselves joining sixty Huron warriors on the warpath south from Quebec up the Richelieu River. Their objective was to head off an Iroquois force three times their number that was reported on its way north to raid Montreal. The march south along the Richelieu was long but, to the French explorers, fascinating. At length they reached the beautiful lake to which Champlain gave his own name, then continued south to the junction of waterways now known as Fort Ticonderoga. There they surprised and routed the Iroquois, killing two of their chiefs with shots from Champlain's own arquebus.

The next year, in 1625, as if to demonstrate that the nature of war in the northland had changed fundamentally and that new gods reigned, the French and Huron attacked an Iroquois force at the mouth of the Richelieu River in the well-planned, total-war manner of European generals: None of the enemy was allowed to slip away. This slaughter (like that visited upon the Pequot by the English) caused a dramatic shift in the Native American perception of proper male behavior, particularly that of the warrior and what he was about. Traditionally, going to battle had been a ceremonialized, rather aristocratic sport for the more athletically inclined Iroquois or Algonquian, an activity entered into not for a national cause (as mentioned earlier) but for individual or family prestige within the tribal order. But now, apparently, warfare was to become something else, a to-the-death act by the male who functioned as part not of a family but of a militarized nation.

Traditionally, when victorious warriors returned to the Iroquois village followed by strings of captives, women would greet them with shrieks of glee, captives would be stripped of all clothing and possessions, and two lines for the gauntlet would be set up. The captive who survived the gauntlet would then either be released and adopted or tied to a stake for further trials. There the controlling clanswoman would "caress" him; that is, she would probe his wounds, perhaps thrust burning branches in his face or hair, degrade him in any possible way, and judge whether the victim should be burned alive, tortured further, or untied and adopted into the clan. It was all part of death and life in the localities of the frontier, ordained by tradition and the spirits. But now—particularly after a well-planned slaughter of Five Nations warriors by Huron and other Native Americans in subservience to the French—war on the frontier became, as a modern commentator might say, "globalized." Native warriors were to obey orders from European officers, as if they were but cogs in the prevailing system of trade and conquest.

Soon after their defeat at the hands of the French in the early contact year of 1610, the chiefs of the Haudenosaunee met around the central fire at Onondaga and began to consider how to respond to the new armaments and new style of war. They formulated accordingly a number of policy decisions. First of all, their recently slaughtered warriors must be revenged not just by another blood feud against French-allied tribesmen but by a particularly brutal strike at the Huron. To achieve that end, quantities of modern weapons would have to be obtained, since war clubs and wooden armor were obviously no longer effective. And finally, total-war strategies would have to be devised on a centralized basis against the invading Europeans. In order to carry out these binding league decisions made around the central fire, more authority would have to be given to the war chiefs, with the power of the fifty traditional chiefs diminished accordingly.

Having heard stirrings along the frontier—where the Iroquois were making claims to be the exclusive suppliers of beaver skins to eastern cities and were profiting mightily from their alliance with the Dutch (who controlled the beaver business as far south as the Susquehanna River)—Champlain saw that he must win the western waters for France swiftly, by all possible means. Setting off with a dozen of his men in July 1615, he risked the arduous canoe journey up the Ottawa and across the Mattawa–French River traverse to Georgian Bay. From there he moved south into the fertile land of the Huron to round up ancillary forces. Finally, accompanied by five hundred Huron warriors, and having sent out aides to gather other Native American forces, he swung back east to launch an attack on the Five Nations' heart at Lake Onondaga. But the attack on the Iroquois fortress was bungled, Champlain himself wounded. The French cause appeared suddenly to be in the deepest jeopardy.

It was in the wake of this disaster that Champlain's favorite strategy for controlling his Indian allies—the mass conversion of the Huron and of their dependent nations to Christianity— became the formal policy of New France. In 1623 and 1624, the call went out more strongly: send us Jesuits to aid in the securing of the west. Jean de Brébeuf responded.

The eight-hundred-mile, month-long passage west to Huronia that de Brébeuf undertook in 1626, after his missionary training, followed the same water trail Champlain had explored a decade earlier. Paddling up the St. Lawrence and Ottawa Rivers to the Mattawa and the Rivière à la Vase, the thirty-two-year-old missionary went on from there via Lake Nipissing and the French River to Georgian Bay in Lake Huron. Since Champlain's early contacts with them, the Huron—never as militant a people as their Iroquois cousins in the Five Nations—had settled into a rather comfortable way of life. Their well-being resulted not only from the fortunate location and natural richness of their land but also from the security offered by their own age-old confederation. With customary facility they had adapted to the new age, becoming traders between the people of the west and the French. At first glance, it seemed to Jean de

Brébeuf that to become familiar with these sedentary and intelligent people, to learn what was on their minds and their spirits as well as to instruct them in the ways of God, would be much more attainable than had been the job of ministering to the nomadic Montagnais of the St. Lawrence Valley. The anthropologist and the missionary in him quickened to the summons.

Père de Brébeuf's most important accomplishment during this first tour among the Huron was to gain a basic understanding of their language and to observe how their clan system functioned within the communal longhouse. He learned the names and differentiations of the four original Huron nations (Bear and Cord being the seniors and Deer and Rock the juniors); he learned of the matriarchal system that made of Huronia one vast, sister-connected family; and he learned how difficult if not impossible it was to get these people—for whom religion figured in every aspect of their daily lives—to accept the concept of the Christian God or of an apostolic priest. Perhaps with more time, he could have made more progress in this early stage, but the press of events in Canada (where Quebec had fallen to an attack by British irregulars) and in the French court forced him to return home to Normandy after only three years.

When he next paddled back out to the land of the Huron, in 1633, he was no longer the young European scholar of his first excursion. Now aged forty, he sought to do more in the wilderness than observe: This was his chance to establish a significant Christian presence among a powerful group of Native Americans. Indeed, he had been told by his superiors in restored Quebec that they would view his mission as a prototype for future developments on the frontier. At a time when the Five Nations were even more forcibly pressing their case as the continent's major power, the French authorities were pinning their hopes on his vitally important, consolidating efforts in the west.

For his own part, Père de Brébeuf yearned to be more than a visitor among the Huron, more than a foreigner tolerated simply because he represented the European nation with which his hosts were trading successfully. He wanted, in fact, to assist them in the cultural transition from isolated primitivism in the northern woodland to informed participation in a larger, more complex world. In light of Jesuit policies (and in keeping with Champlain's early practices), he strove not to wrench the Huron away from their old beliefs but to translate the Gospel into their language and into their world so that they might see through their own eyes a new face of God. He commenced an eight-year labor to produce a dictionary and a grammar that would allow him and his fellow priests to communicate with the Huron not just about matters of trade but also about matters of the soul.

It was only after familiarizing himself thoroughly with the life ways and religious beliefs of the Huron that he presumed to launch his work of conversion and community building. Recognizing a possible compatibility of Huron spirits and Christian angels, he also set about devising a lively, mixed calendar of feasts and vigils. In recognition of the people's rejection of cannibalism and torture, he wisely emphasized the commemorative rather than the sacrificial aspects of the Eucharist. And, most importantly, he honored the family-centeredness of the Huron around their home fires. He also spoke against abortion among the women and alcoholism among the traders, problems that were regarded with concern by the people themselves.

For these seven rewarding years Père de Brébeuf worked to set in place the foundation stones of his mission, first at Ihontiria (St. Joseph Island, about fifty miles from Port Huron, Michigan), then at other nearby posts. To his joy, he succeeded in winning a number of converts. Although he shuddered at the Huron's adoration of the soul's dreams—indeed, the Huron spoke of two souls, one residing with the body, one wandering afar with the mind—he was heartened to learn that some of his students now dreamed of baptism. Seeking to honor both the women and the men who had chosen the Christian path, he appointed "native exhorters" (catechists) to assist him in the training process. All the while, being nothing like a newcomer in the woods, he was aware that many of the Huron males had a special reason to be ready for conversion: As bargainers for the best fur prices on the wharves of Quebec, they had a better chance of getting the business if a silver cross gleamed around their necks.

Despite the growth of his parishes and the number of Jesuit priests accepted in Huron villages, Père de Brébeuf became aware of an increasing resistance among the people. This he attributed not just to the easygoing "immorality" of the Huron (including their disinclination to accept the idea of only one wife) or to their tendency to backslide into native beliefs, but rather to their fear of the disastrous European-engendered epidemics that were sweeping the country. It almost seemed that wherever de Brébeuf and his Jesuit colleagues chose to live among the Huron, the diseases (smallpox, dysentery, and malignant influenza) struck with special fury. The Jesuits noted with alarm and sorrow that whereas Huronia had recently con-

tained some thirty thousand souls, that number had been reduced to approximately twelve thousand by 1640.

The Huron and their Iroquois neighbors had to face the
odd fact that in the regions where no Jesuit "black robes" lived
among the people—that is, where Dutch or (later) English
traders coursed through the eastern woods, never intending
to dwell among the Native Americans on an equal basis—the
diseases seemed to be less punishing. Hostility against the
French increased in the Jesuit villages, and Père de Brébeuf
suddenly found himself confronted by violent threats. The
Huron shamans, traditionally entrusted with the health of the
people, now used their frightening tricks and grotesque symbols to reclaim from the missionaries the power they had momentarily surrendered.

Yet not even the shamans could deny Père de Brébeuf's loyalty to his disease-stricken villagers. In the final days of an ill
Huron, even as the medicine men howled their imprecations
and rattled their gourds, Father de Brébeuf stayed with him or
her, trying to answer all questions, describing the Christian
heaven, accepting the value of a deathbed confession. It appeared that de Brébeuf's mission had become a ministry to the
dying, a noble ministry as he saw it. Even the most suspicious
detractors noted that his steadying voice and his prayers in the
native language gave comfort to the dying. The Huron had
long understood that death and life were parts of a larger reality; they respected a practitioner who could deal with such terrors and could possibly see beyond them.

Violence against the missionaries swelled to murderous
proportions after a smallpox epidemic in 1637. The next year,

angry tribesmen arose again, tearing down the village crosses, throwing stones at the chapel, and approaching the missionaries with hatchets and flaming embers. In 1640, even more villagers participated in an uprising, wounding one of the missionaries and beating Père de Brébeuf himself and another missionary. Even more serious from de Brébeuf's viewpoint was the desertion from the new faith of many parishioners. After two more years trying to carry on in the face of this disillusionment and antagonism (and after an accidental fall through the ice that left him with a broken clavicle), Père de Brébeuf decided to return to Quebec for consultation with his superiors. He had to face the possibility that his missionary endeavors—even those of the last seven productive years—might have been misdirected. As Hiawatha had found before him, the majesty of the divine idea was but one principle among many other contemporary factors on the frontier.

APOSTLE of the DEVOURED HEART

After becoming reacquainted with Quebec and with the capital's power structure, Père de Brébeuf was appointed procurator of the Jesuits' mission to the Huron. Though a gifted manager and natural-born administrator, he dreamed constantly of being out there, among the distant, threatened frontier villages. As he sweated through the home-base tasks of organizing supplies to missions across the land, and while he suffered the frustration of having his supply trains frequently disrupted by Iroquois war parties, he had a chance to study more objectively the intentions of the major contestants. From France one of his colleagues had received diplomatic letters that revealed much of the big picture, the international game of which Quebec was one small part. The letters reported that "...the design of the Dutch is to have the French harassed by the Iroquois, to such an extent that they may constrain them to give up and abandon everything—even the conversion of the Savages." In those words lay a clue to the Iroquois's extreme behavior: In order to fulfill their alliance with the Dutch against the French, they would have to eliminate the Huron.

Faced with that reality, the French Jesuits realized that they must change their mission. Rather than saving native souls for the sake of God and France, they must save a native culture for its own sake. But unfortunately, the weakened government and inadequate population of New France had neither the resources nor the resolve to support that mission on behalf of the Huron. Recruitment efforts had failed to attract more citizens of high or low degree. The entire colony of New France had now but four hundred inhabitants, with perhaps a hundred soldiers to man its guns. While understanding the consequences of that lack, and while awaiting permission to return to threatened Huronia (finally granted in 1644), Père de Brébeuf entered upon a period of spiritual deepening and toughening. Having seen and felt firsthand the violence that could be let loose on the frontier, he prepared himself to endure the worst that might come along. In his prayers and in his writings, he promised to serve Christ even if that service demanded the sacrifice of his life. In 1639 he vowed, for such is the language of the Jesuits, "never to refuse the grace of martyrdom." In the course of this preparation, his thinking became increasingly mystical—which was, perhaps, not all to the good, given the real needs (weapons, clothing, forts) of warfare in the west.

Yet, along with his mysticism, Jean de Brébeuf had a clear

perception of what he wanted to achieve in his missionary villages and a quite pragmatic attitude about the chances of accomplishing his otherworldly goals in a very secular world. What he addressed was a territory far different from the untapped wilderness once explored by Champlain. By this time, the French traders had established numerous posts along the western route, each with the distinctive, biracial character of New France. But in those bustling, hybridized communities, which the Five Nations regarded as affronts to their culture and to their command of the continent, de Brébeuf saw the corruption of both red and white cultures. He feared that Native Americans in such a careless, materialistic society would neither retain the best of their own traditions nor be allowed to emerge as full-fledged French Christians. By contrast, the missionary communities that de Brébeuf was now planning would be removed from that trade-impelled life and also from the archaic Indian ways of life. The citizens of these between-world communities, so insulated, would be allowed to develop their own melding of Native American and Christian patterns.

The Huron stations of which he dreamed could not, however, by any imagining, be abstract communities in the sky. They would have to be defended against the increasingly powerful incursions of the far-ranging Mohawk and the even more ferocious Seneca Iroquois. De Brébeuf feared for his converts and also for the lives of his priestly colleagues. In the very year of Père de Brébeuf's final mission in Huronia, one of the Jesuits was captured by Iroquois warriors and subjected to the most grotesque tortures imaginable—tortures that also informed the world that, though the Iroquois had once responded to Deganawidah's theme of peace and had sought to spread that genial ideal across the land, that time was now long past. The treaty that the Five Nations entered into with the French in 1645 was, in fact, nothing but a truce to allow the mounting of more attacks. Terrified by these events, the Huron traders who customarily launched their canoes in July for a downriver summer cruise to Quebec chose not to voyage forth in 1646.

The Mohawk and Seneca, having struck into the very heart of Huron country (western Ontario), now also turned their destructive energies to assaults on neighboring people, the so-called Tobacco and Neutral nations. The Iroquois's plan of conquest would brook rivals in no corner of the northern woodland. Then, coming back to the attack on Huronia, a thousand and more massed warriors threw themselves on the villages of Saint-Joseph and Saint-Michel, virtually depopulating them by the seizure of seven hundred prisoners. The conquerors left little behind but the arrow-riddled body of the resident priest. Only a small base of resistance still remained to the Huron, a triangular territory between Lake Huron and southern Georgian Bay encompassing the villages of St. Joseph and La Conception and Ste. Marie, as well as St. Ignace and St. Louis. There de Brébeuf was both attempting to tend to the spiritual needs of his parishioners and trying to rouse the Huron leaders to a more vigorous defense.

He realized all too well that his personal strengths were more prayer centered and mystical than activist and down-to-earth. Though he possessed much robust good sense, he tended toward a kind of supernatural empiricism; he would trust in whatever God might choose to provide. Now, faced with the reality of an Iroquois army on the attack, he tried to take comfort from the fact that there were, by mid-1648, twenty-two Jesuits living in secured villages, assisted by forty-six laymen. In addition, more and more Huron were turning to Christianity and requesting baptism, perhaps moved by the stress of the times. Indeed, hundreds were now coming to make their pledges at the altar each year, increasing to a total of seventeen hundred in 1648—meaning that one out of five Huron were Christians. The prospect of complete Christianization of Huronia could be contemplated.

Traveling frequently among the villages to build a greater sense of unity, Père de Brébeuf would never fail to be warmed by the friendliness with which he was greeted on return to St. Louis. Canada's great writer of historical romances, Thomas Costain, has painted a vivid picture of one such return, with Père de Brébeuf (or Echon, as the Huron called him) breaking out of the forest into the village clearing.

> "Here is Echon come again!" they shouted.
>
> Everyone in the village saluted him, touching his hand and saying over and over, "Echon, my nephew, my brother, my cousin, hast thou come again?"
>
> It is pleasant to think of them flocking about him, the sober brown children fearing to touch so much as the hem of his garment, their elders nodding their heads and throwing their usual taciturnity to the winds as they assailed him with questions. In all the villages where duty took him, they knew the sound of his solid footstep, they loved the deep notes of his voice.

But, much as Père de Brébeuf delighted in the loving attitudes of his flock, he knew that unity among the villages was *not* being achieved. For all his satisfaction at the rising number of

baptisms and the creation of a fractionally Christian community, he realized that many of the tribal elders were forever opposed to this abandonment of ancient principles. There was, for
example, the all-important matter of burial. The traditionalists
were disinclined to have their dead interred with the Christians,
just as the latter had little respect for the traditional Feast of the
Dead. Along with the elders' resentment grew an inclination to
withdraw from community life into a tobacco-smoke haze and
to turn away from participation in the defense of the village.

Despite de Brébeuf's urgings that the winter of 1648-1649
should be spent in building up St. Ignace as an unconquerable
fortress—which seemed quite possible, given its superb location atop an elevated ridge, with a strip of level land no more
than a hundred yards wide forming its one approach—little
seemed to have been accomplished as January turned into February. Although archaeological examinations of the site (called
St. Ignace II, nine miles east of Midland, Ontario) have been
limited, there are indications that foundations for the bastions
at either side of the main entrance had only been roughed in.
No actual construction of embankments or palisades had been
carried out. The great missionary himself, for all his understanding of the dangers, seemed unable to plan alternative and
feasible projects for defense. The Huron, used to spending the
snow months in drowsy hibernation or far afield hunting, found
it hard to believe that anything much would happen before full
spring.

Beyond habitual inertia, an acrimonious and divided mood
prevented anything important from being decided in the Longhouse council. Christians and traditionalists possessed different
views of the reality they now faced. Père de Brébeuf must have

shuddered at the thought that all the good and charitable work of the missionaries had, in fact, sapped the cultural will of the Huron. He left St. Ignace on a brief trip to nearby St. Louis in 1649 with a certain sense of dread, though no immediate attack seemed likely. The winter still held fast, snow lying heavily on the ground and river ice not yet cracking. His fears were fulfilled all too soon.

In the blackness of predawn on March 16, one thousand Mohawk and Seneca warriors stormed out of the woods and burst through the flimsy walls of St. Ignace. They were armed with modern Dutch-supplied muskets as well as with their traditional clubs and knives. Shooting and slashing in a murderous fury, they completed the slaughter with such thoroughness that only three Huron were able to escape. The unsated Iroquois, smearing their heads and faces with the blood of their victims, then prepared to move on to St. Louis to complete their mission of annihilation.

When the three who had escaped from St. Ignace finally reached the safety of St. Louis, they hardly had time to report the disaster before the topknot of the first Mohawk was seen poking up above the clearing's edge. By now the sun was rising, and Père de Brébeuf and his accompanying priest, defended against the six hundred oncoming warriors by only eighty Huron armed with a few French rifles and little ammunition, clearly recognized what the result of the attack would be. They therefore devoted their first efforts to removing the sick and the elderly from the scene, hastening them off to the stone-walled haven of the church at Ste. Marie. Then they consulted among themselves how to face the enemy. The warriors' stoutest chief urged the Jesuits to flee. "My brothers, save yourselves," he is reported to have said. "Go now, while there is time!" But de Brébeuf paid the advice little attention, seeming to withdraw more deeply into his own world of mystical contemplation.

He knew that he was where he needed to be—with his villagers. As the battle burst upon them, the Jesuits bound up the wounded and administered last rites to the dying. The Huron fought back heroically; not until three hours had passed were they overwhelmed. Unfortunately for the two missionaries, they were not killed in the final frenzy when the Iroquois crashed through. The victors, taking the few survivors captive, force marched them (including two Frenchmen) to St. Louis where the final orgy of triumph was to be staged.

What is known of the execution of the two missionaries, Jean de Brébeuf and Gabriel Lalemant, comes down through the pages of the *Rélations des Jesuites*. It tells of how the two men were stripped to the skin for torture, of how Père de Brébeuf, the first to be killed, kissed the stake before they tied him to it, and how Lalemant, the younger man (nephew of the Jesuits' superior in Quebec), quoted to his companion the words of St. Paul: "Truly, this day, Father, we are made a spectacle to the world, and to angels and to men."

Père de Brébeuf's continuing admonitions from the stake, exhorting the Huron to keep the faith, were howled down by the screechings of the mob. He was first scorched from head to foot with blazing torches, all the nails being torn from his fingers, then "baptized" with buckets of boiling water. The most frightful of Iroquois tortures was next applied: the "collar," which consisted of six white-hot hatchets attached to a neck band of green-wood lowered down over the victim's head; when he wrenched himself in agony away from the three hatchets that were burning his chest, the other three burned more deeply into his back. Even after de Brébeuf's flesh had been set aflame by means of applied pitch and resin, the priest's deep voice never faltered. He begged forgiveness for his tormentors and struggled to recite the Lord's Prayer in Iroquois (*"Onaistan de aronhise istare. Sasin tehon…"*). Finally the tormentors could tolerate it no longer and cut off his tongue and lips.

The last sight he saw before he fainted was strips of his own flesh being burned before his eyes. Yet the torture went on, from noon until four o'clock in the afternoon, without letup. He may still have been alive when they cut open his chest and—as a mark of respect for his valor at the stake—ate his heart, each one striving to get a piece, and drank his blood. Then it was the turn of Father Lalemant, who, despite his frailty of stature, resisted death for eleven hours.

How are the details of the atrocities known in such detail? Not long after the martyrdom, and when the Iroquois warriors had withdrawn to the east across the Niagara River, a team of Christian priests and laymen stole back to St. Louis to render appropriate honor to the bodies. One of the company, a boot maker and *donné* named Christophe Rengault, made a movingly simple report of the condition of the remains, as he witnessed them:

> Father de Brébeuf had his legs, thighs, and arms stripped of flesh to the very bone; I saw and touched a large number of great blisters, which he had on several places on his body, from the boiling water which those barbarians had poured over him in mockery of Holy Baptism. I saw and touched the wound from a belt of bark full of pitch and

resin, which roasted his whole body. I saw and touched the marks of burns from the collar of hatchets placed on his shoulders and stomach. I saw and touched his two lips, which they had cut off because he constantly spoke of God while they made him suffer.

I saw and touched all parts of his body, which had received more than two hundred blows from a stick. I saw and touched the top of his scalped head; I saw and touched the opening which these barbarians made to tear out his heart.

In fine, I saw and touched all the wounds of his body, as the savages had told and declared to us.

A terrible death it was, without doubt. Yet, despite the apparent triumph of the new breed of all-conquering warriors who had stormed forth from the Five Nations, the execution of Père de Brébeuf and his companion (and the resultant defeat and dispersion of the Christianized Huron) had certain long-range benefits. Word spread far and wide of the French missionaries who had stayed with their Native American villagers during their times of plague and even during the irresistible attacks; this word was believed even where their gospel was not.

Père de Brébeuf's sacrifice undoubtedly contributed to the credibility of the Christian faith among the nations of the Great Lakes basin, in the hearts of native people who wondered where to turn in this confusing, God-bereft time of war and upheaval. A new respect for the "black robes" extended even among the Iroquois themselves, particularly the Mohawk along their eponymous river and (later) in Canada. Peace, as an ideal, seemed all the more precious after the generations of bloodshed. One might even wonder if, in the belief systems of these religiously alert people, there had not been an integration of prophecies: The message brought forth from the wilderness by Hiawatha that had counseled peace but that had countenanced war fit not uncomfortably with the Christian message that also counseled peace but that involved sacrifice. Both existed as intimations of the workings of America's own gods of peace and war.

But one might also ask whether a martyrdom so vividly described and so heartily advertised by the Roman Catholic Church presents the work of Père de Brébeuf in the most helpful way—a way that leads to broader understanding of the frontier's biracial life. As recorded, the execution at St. Louis was particularly ghastly (and especially worthy of veneration) because of having been committed by "barbarians," perpetrated by "savages." Yet how much grimmer was it, in fact, than the drawings and quarterings, the well-attended stretchings on the rack, the crowd-pleasing burnings carried out by churchmen and visible in Europe's squares at this time and later? It came to be seen as grimmer in part because a well-practiced way of forgetting one own's barbarisms is to write histories about the barbarisms of another culture, particularly a culture regarded as lower.

Regrettably, the sensational descriptions of the way the care-bringing Jesuits were executed has continually served not as an aid but as a hindrance to broader historical understanding. Because of those lurid descriptions, both Catholics and non-Catholics have been blocked from seeing the real contribution of this scholarly priest and his companion to the very real and unsavage people of the frontier and to the always difficult cause of intercultural compassion. Certainly Père de Brébeuf was a martyr, but he was, significantly, a godly man trusted by other men in search of God.

De Brébeuf's visionary yet respectful dedication to the stricken people among whom he served merits admiration from secularists and spiritualists alike. His concept of the progressive, self-sufficient community, removed from both the white and the red cultures, had much merit (it was merciful and intelligent), as well as some obvious drawbacks (it was paternalistic and formulaic). For good or ill, his design of such native-style, Christian communities reflected both his ethnographic and his religious perspectives. The experiment anticipated the work of the Puritans' Apostle to the Indians, John Eliot, and assisted many other ambassadors of various ethnicities and persuasions as they strove, sometimes successfully, to bring two peoples together in the very teeth of international disaster.

CHAPTER 4

The NEW ENGLAND APOSTLE'S NATIVE CHURCHES

WHEN A JESUIT PRIEST named Gabriel Druillettes knocked on the door of John Eliot's home, it was Christmas night 1650, the year after Father de Brébeuf's martyrdom. This was a momentous occasion in all respects: One of the continent's most respected Roman Catholic figures stood rapping on a door of the Puritan establishment.

John Eliot by that time had begun his famous missionary work among the Massachusetts Indians, work that would earn him that famous name (granted by Cotton Mather in a grandiose mood): Apostle to the Indians. Yet Eliot, who had arrived from England in October of 1631, served in a lonely cause. He was the single Puritan clergyman engaged in fulfilling the Bay Colony's original pledge that it would "wynne and incite the Natives to the knowledge and obedience of the only true Son and Savior of Mankind and the Christian Fayth." Laymen in Massachusetts Bay tended to regard his proselytizing efforts as pretty much a waste of time, and the ministerial hierarchy saw his mission as a bothersome sideshow. Nonetheless, his work had succeeded in winning support from the highest levels in England, where enthusiasm for mission work flourished in both pulpit and parlor and the Apostle was renowned and revered. To the far-traveled Jesuit who journeyed to his threshold as a representative of the needy colony of New France, John Eliot's door did, therefore, seem a likely place to knock.

Père Druillettes had come to plead for aid in his colony's urgent war against the Iroquois. In the year since the slaughter at St. Louis, the thousands of Iroquois warriors had completed their bloody campaign against the Huron and were now storming through the northern regions with little or no opposition. To survive, New France (which was a colony not of a few thousand, but a few hundred) needed fresh allies and a new strategy. Despite centuries of warfare with England and fierce antagonism between Catholics and Protestants, French authorities in Quebec were desperate enough to hope that English colonists along the coast, whatever variety of Christianity they professed, would recognize the danger to all civilized humanity posed by the savage Iroquois. Yet only a man of unquestionable character, possessing diplomatic talents of the highest order, could dare try to arrange such an unprecedented cross-cultural connection between Quebec and Boston. Gabriel Druillettes filled the bill.

Since his arrival in New France in 1643, Druillettes had demonstrated a rare ability to honor the Indians' ways of life and to live among them, even in the snow-heavy travails of the woodland winter. Having been nominated to join Père de Brébeuf's western mission, he was barely prevented by the Iroquois blockade of the western territories from going out to share the martyr's death in Huron country. Instead, he became known for his far-ranging journeys among the Montagnais. On one of those hauls, having been blinded by smoke from too many campfires, he allowed a sympathetic native woman to scrape his cornea with a rusty knife. The blindness remained. But a few days later, as he was singing Mass, the sun's light burst anew upon his sight—a miracle, many thought.

Subsequently, having been called back to Quebec from service among Maine's Christianized Abnaki in September of 1650, Druillettes was appointed to be the governor's ambassador to lower New England. His mission began auspiciously: When traveling south on the Kennebec River, the Jesuit met and befriended enterprising colonist John Winslow at Plymouth's trading post on that river's fall line (present-day Augusta). Armed with a favorable letter from Winslow, he trusted he would find support at the Pilgrims' capital. But there he learned that, in fact, Massachusetts Bay and the Puritan elite held the reins among the northeastern English colonies. He was also given the clue that if he wanted to find a sympathetic contact among the Puritans he might well begin with a certain John Eliot, teaching elder of the church in Roxbury and missionary to the local Algonquian.

Although the French priest must have been relieved, on that Christmas night, to reach the Roxbury meetinghouse and parsonage safely, he found meager comfort. A bare and unheated structure, the meetinghouse had only recently been completed; forever unadorned, it would keep rain and snow off that Puritan community for four decades but devoid of a stove, it would never offer them warmth in winter. It served as focus for a particular community, as shelter for the like-minded family members and friends who came to sing psalms (quite beautifully, records indicate), to exchange memories of the Old Country, and to be instructed by their "unfailingly kind" teaching elder.

In the homes and streets of the little town of Roxbury these transplanted English folk carried out their business in a way much removed from that of the earliest English arrivals. Their farms stretched out beyond the town, yielding adequate harvests in response to more than a decade of concentrated labor; besides their meetinghouse, the flour mill and sawmill served as foci of the community. Although reports came through of fractious Indians on the frontier, here neither fort nor armed force seemed necessary. The only Native Americans the townspeople knew were troops of Algonquian passing through, survivors from somewhere looking for a chance to sell a bit of handwork here or to receive a gift of charity there. It bothered the friends and neighbors of John Eliot that these "strolling poor" seemed so constantly on the move, for English tolerance of a shiftless people was slight. One should stay in one place, as they saw it; only by that settling down could a proper community be established, a church instituted, civilization maintained.

Although Druillettes's decision to seek out John Eliot at this Puritan town of Roxbury was soundly conceived, the two missionaries had quite different visions of Christian mission work in America. Whereas the French Jesuit had made many converts among the free and roaming peoples of Maine and Acadia, John Eliot planned to serve as a minister to needy people who had been persuaded to live not in the Devil-stinking wilderness but in a safe and walled town. While the conversation between the two men must have been cordial (a conversation held in Latin, it is assumed, since neither spoke

the other's language), Père Druillettes's descriptions of Iroquois atrocities surely seemed distant and unthreatening from
the perspective of Roxbury.

The following morning, in wishing his guest well on his
way to Boston, John Eliot could not have given him much encouragement about how his petition for an alliance might be received among the Puritan magistrates. In fact it was received
with a special kind of hostile interest. This mixed reaction resulted both from the Puritan leaders' simultaneous antipathy to
anything French or Catholic (having learned in the Old Country to blame many of mankind's ills on the "satanic" character
of the pope) and from their guarded curiosity about those
hugely powerful Native Americans of the north and west.
What feature of God's plan did the Iroquois represent? Might
they even, for all their rapaciousness, be utilized (as the Dutch
had found) for the economic purposes of the westward-inclined
Protestant traders and settlers? On the other hand, Père Druillettes's reports on the burning of French outposts and the tor-
turing of Catholic missionaries, not to mention the threats to
Quebec, while not exactly touching the Puritans' hearts, did
reach their minds.

Père Druillettes, after a swift return to Quebec, voyaged
south the next year to urge his case once again: New France
and New England and the Algonquian all united against the
Iroquois. But his proposal suffered a quick death, and for good
reasons. The Puritan magistrates who rejected the French-
Algonquian alliance had but a dim understanding of what an important part the Iroquois might play on the American continent.
They certainly could not foresee that one day (1678) English authorities would actually recruit Iroquois Mohawk warriors for

their own cause. By then, and having more or less inherited the Iroquois after the 1664 defeat and departure of the Dutch, the British had come to realize that no other Europeans but these confederated Indians held the key to North American conquest.

"The DAY-BREAKING if NOT the SUN-RISING of the GOSPELL"

Despite his later renown, John Eliot, in the years immediately following his 1631 landing at Boston, seemed of insufficient importance ever to command an ambassador's visit or a word of praise from Cotton Mather. Although he would be called an apostle one day, he was never brilliant or charismatic enough to appear transcendent, certainly not in Boston. On reaching these shores, he was twenty-seven years old and possessed little more than twenty-three barrels of books. Having joined his old English friends in new Roxbury as a teacher, and having questioned the governor's spurious Treaty of Amity with the Pequot in a burst of well-remembered impudence, he regained some status by taking an altogether orthodox position in the vexing matter of Anne Hutchinson. Her attempt to broaden the concept of grace on the basis of her personal "revelations" could only be viewed with horror by clerics who were attempting to save the world by defining more and more exactly who was "sealed within the covenant" and who was not. Furthermore, the members of the elect knew that all revelation came from the Bible, certainly not from any individual or female source. Eliot, asked to serve in the judicial process of 1637 against the irrepressible woman, said that her replies to the judges "shake the very foundation of our faith." He also wrote in support of Roger Williams's banishment and participated in the creation of the first volume published in the American colonies, the famous *Bay Psalm Book.*

Yet, however tamed and acceptably orthodox he may have appeared, John Eliot remained disturbed by the vengeful workings out of the Pequot War. He joined others in the sentiment that the English soldiers had betrayed their own moral codes by their murderous conduct toward civilian women and children. He also harbored a "long-felt concern" for the apparently helpless condition of the defeated Algonquian he observed around him, referring to them as "perishing, forlorne outcasts." Massachusetts had no regular place for them. As explained in environmental terms by the modern writer William Cronon, "the material conditions" that had allowed these people "to practice their annual journey through the seasons no longer existed."

In 1644, according to some biographers, Eliot took a first decisive step toward missionary commitment by engaging the Indian servant of an acquaintance, Richard Calicott of Dorchester, to be his tutor and guide in the Algonquian language. Other biographers see this as happening later, after the commencement of his missionary efforts. That young Algonquian tutor was named Cockenoe. Though brought to Boston along with others captured in the war against the Pequot, he had been born a Montauk (for Long Island's Montauk had had much business with the Pequot before the war of 1637 and had rendered them regular tribute). He was able to give Eliot, in two years of study, an adequate introduction—or key, as Roger Williams might say—to the language generally spoken in the New England woods. With a kind of patronizing fondness, Eliot wrote later of the "pregnant-witted" Cockenoe that "he was the first that I made use of to teach me words, and to be my interpreter."

Whether linguistically prepared in 1644 or later, Eliot felt called to action when, in the spring of 1646, the General Court (Massachusetts Bay's legislature) passed a rather vague ordinance to the effect that something should be done to "promote the diffusion of Christianity among the Aboriginal inhabitants" of the colony.

His action took the form of walking to the Neponset River in nearby Dorchester and attempting to preach the Gospel to the native people there. His presentation proved to be an "embarrassment," not only because of the Indians' amusement at his language but also because of the surprising hostility of their sachem, Cutshamekin, a presumed ally. This young chief had fought alongside Endicott in the first phase of the Pequot War and had sent to the Narragansett a Pequot scalp, showing them how solid his connection was with the colonists. Yet Cutshamekin, whose time in office dated only from the time of his brother Chickataubut's recent death, had no desire to see his people lured away by a competitive allegiance.

Undeterred by the Dorchester failure, John Eliot considered where he might have better fortune. Learning that Waban, a petty chief in slightly more distant Nonantum (on today's Newton-Watertown line), had enrolled his son in the English school at Dedham, Eliot deduced that there would be greater tolerance of the church's teachings among that village's people. In the fall of 1646, he therefore took the trail to Nonantum, Bible and fruit basket in hand, accompanied by a few encouraging friends. As he recalled that day, "Upon October 28, four of us (having first sought God) went over to the Indians inhabiting within our bounds, with desire to make known the things of peace to them."

This turned into a far more successful visit. Waban himself became John Eliot's first convert, a key accomplishment in his missionary work. Yet, however much one might admire Eliot's persistence, his proselytizing triumph must be seen in the light of other economic and political factors, including the Massachusetts peoples' dispirited condition. Reduced in numbers from perhaps five thousand to half that by disease and starvation, unable to pursue their usual woodland way of life among the fast-growing English land claims, and harassed by other Indians in the north and west (that is, by the northwoods Micmac and by the Narragansett, who were rumored to be allies of the Iroquois), they had lost confidence in their own culture and its reigning divinities. Why not try to figure out what this compassionate-seeming Englishman had to say? Why not make a canny move toward survival?

It must also be said that John Eliot had a talent for reaching into people's souls. Dressed in woodsman's leather brown rather than in clergy black, Eliot strove to find if there might be any common themes between Christianity as he knew it and the religion of the villagers. Rather to his surprise, he discovered that there were commonalities: The biblical angels might be compared to some of the Algonquian woodland spirits; the villagers practiced family prayer as a respected tradition. Furthermore, there was the concept of *manitowuk*—the holiness that dwells within certain forms and practices. Where there was holiness there might be God. Yet, for all that, John Eliot perceived tremendous and crucial differences between his religion and theirs—most important, by their complete unawareness of sin.

In his later writings, Eliot, the Apostle, described some of the cosmic issues that were most on the minds of the people with whom he held question-and-answer sessions. On one occasion he was asked: (1) What is the cause of thunder? (2) What causes the ebbing and flowing of the sea? and (3) What of the wind? He was even asked whether the English had originally been as ignorant of God and Jesus Christ as they themselves were now. "Yes!" the Apostle replied, glad to explain the ever troubling contention between saints and sinners, that is, between the elect and the unregenerate in his own society. In answer to the question of why, given the good Lord's rule over all, strawberries are sweet and cranberries sour, he referred simply to the "wonderful work of God."

For even the most nimble proselytizer, however, it was difficult to move beyond the essential teachings of Puritan Christianity and to communicate higher concepts to an unlettered group of people. Whereas the French priests had been able to make spiritual connections by symbols and images, the Puritans insisted that their religion be *understood* (meaning that one should be able to pass a test on its tenets); confession should not be accepted and baptism should not be considered until the supplicant could base his case on a theology spelled out in a complex catechism. In the concepts and practices of Puritanism there were absolutely none of the religious expressions to which these Algonquian were accustomed—no dance (the most important feature of all their observances), no crafted images, no private spirits recalled in fetishes. Only the endlessly exegetical biblical lessons.

Obsessed as the Puritans were by the rooting out of evil from mankind, fearful of a vengeful God and of the wilderness beyond their "hedge," they concentrated their intellectual passion on the rules and structure of their holy community. John

Eliot understood this fundamentally—that he would have to bring the Algonquian into English "civilitie" before they could be truly converted. Yet as he strove, in small steps, to enlighten them, the question remained: how to inform them when these nature-worshiping people possessed no connecting cognition systems, no Christ, no abstract concepts like grace or salvation?

His ultimate answer—the answer that gives him a very special place in the chronicle of religious and nonreligious leaders who have built bridges across cultural borders—was to translate increasingly complex prayers (and eventually the whole Bible) into Algonquian. Given these prayer guides, the Massachusetts people would be enabled to name and thus grasp the workings of God; they would remain their own people, with their own preserved language, even as they approached the Christian religion and the church. Perhaps they would not be able to enter the guarded, communal, holy space of the Puritan elect, but at least they would be empowered to consider the word of the Lord.

Eliot's associate Thomas Shepard described the Apostle's first missionary and translation labors in a progress report entitled *The Day-Breaking if Not the Sun-Rising of the Gospell with the Indians in New England* (published in London in 1647). But it was not until 1663, after fourteen years of working with Algonquian verbiage, that Eliot's dutiful translation of the scriptures, the *Up-Biblum God,* was published in Cambridge, Massachusetts, the first Bible in any language to be produced in America. Unlike this one-man effort, the seminal King James Bible, published in 1611, had been the work of fifty-four assembled scholars working collegially for seven years. From the Apostle's point of view, the *Up-Biblum* was more a working tool than a literary feat. As a by-product, it also helped him master the native phrases needed for his style of informal, person-to-person preaching. When local skeptics asked what in the world the Bible of the Hebrews and of the saints could mean to the Massachusetts Indians, he replied (as a true Protestant), "The Bible is the word of life—they must have it!"

An unexpected result of Eliot's successful preaching to Waban's villagers was that more and more Native Americans came to reside there and to join in the thronged weekly services. No beginner in the art of capturing and retaining an audience, Eliot regularly brought apples for the children, tobacco for the men, thread and needles for the women, medical assistance for the sick. One is reminded of Albert Schweitzer's statement from Africa: "I did not come here to civilize but to heal." As the Apostle ministered, his popularity grew; as the village population swelled (and white neighbors complained), Eliot began to fear for the security of his gathered people.

A more directly hoped for result of Eliot's popularity among the Algonquian was that important and highborn figures in England paid attention and opened their purses. They had learned of the missionary's work through the publication in 1643 of a laudatory pamphlet by Shepard entitled *New England's First Fruits*. This prompted Parliament to pass a new bill encouraging the "preaching and propagating of the Gospel of Jesus Christ among the natives" and persuaded a sympathetic noblewoman named Lady Mary Armine to start sending Eliot a series of grants. He also received a regular stipend (£50) from a group of other English benefactors. The Bay Colony had been appalled at the idea of supporting the essentially private work of a peculiarly enthused missionary. Nonetheless, as the monies began to roll in, the authorities took it on themselves to manage much of it for their own purposes—one result being the building of a brick structure at Harvard called Indian College (supposedly a hall for the instruction of natives but actually a home for the first printing press).

The popularity of young John Eliot was neither instant nor universal, however. Just as Cutshamekin had distrusted the effect he might have on the coherence of the Massachusetts community, so the powwows (often called sorcerers) in many villages saw their authority threatened. In his first brushes with them, he thought that they were possessed by devilish spirits, which they called *Hobomock* (only later would he learn the complexity of that connection). Often he was challenged by powwows and sachems alike as he went his missionary rounds, risking the same danger of martyrdom that Jean de Brébeuf had faced. Once an angered sachem confronted him brashly, knife in hand. Eliot's response, "I am about the work of the great God, and he is with me, so that I fear not all the sachems of the country. I'll go on, and do you touch me if you dare."

The strategy that Eliot seemed to have devised for spreading the Gospel and for befriending the Massachusetts Algonquian within his very English church was to work with their leadership—that is, to focus on the sachems and, to a lesser extent, on the powwows. Though now subject to English authority (the most important of them having formally submitted to the Bay Colony in 1644 after more than a decade of dilatory negotiation and weak resistance), the power they retained over their people remained formidable. Most impressive of them all was a previously mentioned chief, the mighty Passaconaway who reigned as both sachem and powwow over the Pennacook of the Merrimack valley. The sharp-eyed English observer and diarist William Wood had used Passaconaway as his prime example when he chose to write of the Algonquian's "Worship, Invocations, and Conjurations." Wood began that chapter of his book with the perceptive words, "As it is natural to all mortals to worship something, so do these people." He went on to write of Passaconaway that this supernaturally endowed man "can make the water burn, the trees dance," and that he can "metamorphose himself into a flaming man." Passaconaway's additional miracles included making "of a dead snake's skin a living snake, both to be seen, felt, and heard." Here was an extraordinary religious leader; John Eliot yearned to meet him, and perhaps to convert him.

Their first appointment, in 1647, was, in today's verbiage, a no-show: Passaconaway decided to be elsewhere when Eliot called. The second attempted meeting, held in the spring of 1648 when numbers of alewife fisherfolk were flocking to the banks of the Merrimack, proved far more fruitful. Changed in mind and spirit as a result of receiving heavenly visions, Passaconaway welcomed the Puritan missionary, asserting that he would worship the Christian God and would "persuade all his sons to do the same." Perhaps this was a truly religious commitment; to contemporaries it seemed totally sincere. On the third visit, Eliot was asked to stay in the sachem's village, "to live and to teach there." But if the revered chief could have spoken from the grave to later ages, it must have been with regret, for his son Wannalancet later suffered the horror of seeing his peaceful, Christianized village burned to the ground by colonial vigilantes during King Philip's War.

On further considering Passaconaway's story, one is impressed by how much of the grand old man's wisdom and progressive spiritualism rubbed off on Eliot the Apostle. Certainly these encounters encouraged Eliot to respect the Algonquian in a way that could not have happened to stay-home clerics of the established church. The preexisting English cleric in John Eliot was being transformed, not into Passaconaway's "flaming man" but nonetheless into an American alive with the additional broadening knowledge of native spirits. Indeed, like Christ himself, he was breaking out of a narrow and restricted religious setting to find in people of another race elements of the divine. Henceforth, his concept of the Christian church would be more universal and inclusive.

As the Apostle developed his rather different ideas of native churchmanship, the orthodox clergy grew more active in opposing him. Most objectionable to them was Eliot's idea of admitting everyone within a given community to the church "so as to keep the whole heape of chaff and corne together, only excluding the ignorant and prophane and scandalous." Thereafter, he felt the elect (the sacred spearhead of Puritanism) might be selected from the whole, and they could then "enjoy together a more strikt and selecte communion without deserting the regular parochial communion." That concept, however, was totally inconsistent with Puritan practices. Such an inclusive design for the church—what might be called the Apostle's evolved American design—struck his contemporaries as dangerously heretical.

REALIZATION of the APOSTLE'S VISION

Tradition-minded Englishmen and women, residents of towns near Nonantum, were also apprehensive, seeing the in-flocking, well-treated Indian population as a threat to their own real-estate programs. Waban himself wanted to remove to another location where his people would be free from the fence-building, cow- and pig-herding English settlers with their constant pressures and changes of rules. John Eliot also came to see the building of a new and centralized missionary village as a highly desirable objective. Earlier, revealing another side of himself, he had stated frankly that, as things stood, Waban and his people were "incapable . . . to be trusted therewith [meaning with Calvinistic Christianity] whilst they were so unfixed, confused, and ungoverned alike, uncivilized and unsubdued to labor and order." Now that the beaver had been extirpated from local streams and the Algonquian faced the collapse of their one and only profitable industry, they needed to reform themselves as producers for an English world.

The Apostle therefore discussed with the General Court (colonial legislature) the possibility of a new site, trusting that it might be "somewhat remote." By this he meant, on one level, that it should be removed from both hostile Indian groups and from jealous English land seekers. On another level, his meaning was that an altogether new kind of space should be established—neither English nor Native American—in which the villagers might be secure, self-reliant, and able to work out their own religious destiny. One cannot but wonder whether Gabriel Druillettes's tales of the otherworldly communities that Père de Brébeuf had planted in Ontario had had some effect on the safely set-apart village of which Eliot now dreamed.

The magistrates and ministers of Boston concurred that the perplexing, irregular Indians should be put out of the way, some place where they might be trained to "live in an orderly way." It happened that a massive amount of land, more than

two hundred square miles, had been given in 1636 to the town
of Dedham as its home territory. Surely, the magistrates thought,
some of that could be made available to the proposed Indian
village. Despite Dedham's arguments to the contrary, a piece of
that grant, two thousand acres on the north side of the Charles
River, was signed over for the Apostle's purposes. The village
was to be called Natick, Algonquian for "My Land." Thomas
Waban signed the deed for it in 1650—the very year when Père
Druillettes visited New England and warned of the Iroquois.

A recent, searching biography of Eliot by Richard W. Cogley focuses on another aspect of the move to Natick, namely,
on its mirroring of the Apostle's deepest religious beliefs and
purposes. The author, citing Eliot's millennialist tendencies (his
faith that certain signs pointed to the predicted coming of Christ
on earth), identifies the building of the new missionary village
with the ideal of an exemplary biblical community. Eliot and all
other New England Puritans were taking special note of recent
reports of Cromwell's victories over the English king, which
ended with the beheading of Charles I. Those events of the late
1640s seemed to confirm the idea that the era of kings was at an
end and that the Second Coming of Christ might well be experienced. "Oh the blessed day in England," Eliot wrote to Edward Winslow, "when the word of God shall be their only
Magna Carta and chief law book!" Extrapolating from Eliot's
thinking, given the fact that America was free of most royal
structures and had originally been inhabited by one of the lost
tribes of Israel, might this not be the land were Christ would
reign again?

Hastening to build the village for their own reasons of survival, Waban's fellow tribesmen followed a plan obviously more

English than indigenous: Natick was laid out with three straight streets (two on one side of the Charles, one on the other), a circular fort palisaded with trees, and a meetinghouse directly in the center of all. The fort's lower level was to be used for public worship on Sundays, for a schoolroom on other days. Connecting the town on both sides of the river was a wooden footbridge, eighty feet long and sustained by four arches rising to a center height of nine feet above the river. Builders began putting up a few wooden houses in the colonial style, devoting special attention to a large structure (fifty feet by twenty-five feet) with a "prophet's chamber," anticipating Eliot's visits. Many of the Indians, however, preferred to live in their own wigwams.

Like the other constructions, the bridge was impressive for having been designed and built by the Indians themselves, with the occasional help of an English carpenter. Its form is recapitulated in the stone bridge that now stands on the site, though the gentle purling of the Charles through its arches gives only the dimmest echo of the noisy industriousness of the community that arose there 350 years ago. Eliot considered the basic town more or less complete by 1651 and invited Governor Endicott to come and see it. Catching a bit of the Apostle's enthusiasm for his millennial community, the governor exclaimed, "The foundation is laid!" Impressed as he was by the villagers' psalm singing and deportment, he was even more won over by their mechanical ingenuity and their productivity.

For by then Eliot had seen to it that the Natick villagers were well supplied with tools and materials (bought with the money that continued to stream in from England). He also saw to it that both men and women accepted their revised gender roles in this community: The men were to be not hunters but farmers, tending to livestock and cultivation of the fields; the women were not to raise their sacred crops and brew medicines but to spin and carry out English-style domestic functions. The hope was that flax cultivation would produce enough fiber for the women to make the necessary clothes for all residents. Despite this Anglicized program, many families continued to prefer their wigwams to the English houses, the latter being drafty and expensive, with unfamiliarly blank walls. The Apostle seems to have tolerated this predilection, just as he permitted the men to take off on their traditional fishing and hunting quests. Increasingly, he was listening to and trusting the Indians' will.

Centrally important to Eliot's concept of the community was its self-determined political character. Though Natick's government could certainly not be called democratic (a theory equivalent to mob rule in Puritan minds), it did reflect the kind of choice given to the Hebrews in the time of Moses. That is, heads of families were allowed to vote for accepted nominees. So it happened that certain Americans, removed from Bay Colony regulations, here commenced their first ever experiment in political self-determination. And so to the list of important, transracial contributions to the United States (right after the constitutional concept of checks and balances) can be added this first self-governed community. The citizens of Natick voted Cutshamekin to be their headman; this once hostile sachem, formerly so cool to the Apostle's preaching, announced that he now accepted Christianity.

Eliot confessed that he was somewhat "doubtful in respect of the thoroughness of [Cutshamekin's] heart," and regretted the sachem's unreformed drinking habits. Yet Cutshamekin seemed to have adopted the now favored strategy of following where his people were going. After his election as "ruler," Natick's population—some thirty families, comprising 145 souls—fasted and on September 24, 1651, held a day of sermons and prayers. The famous Civil Covenant that they then entered upon read, in part, as follows:

> The grace of Christ helping us, we do give ourselves and our children unto God to be his people; he shall rule us in all our affairs, not only in our religion and affairs of the Church...but also in all our works and affairs in this world; God shall rule over us.

Bells rang in accordance with a regularly imposed schedule, the flogger's whip lashed sinful backs, and erring citizens dutifully paid their fines. The ten-article code of "civilitie" that Eliot and Waban had initiated at Nonantum was expanded in Natick. Recent commentators have found unintended humor in the section of the new code that related to hygiene: "if any shall kill their lice between their teeth, they shall pay five shillings." Regarded in their own time as not at all amusing, such regulations controlled domestic relations (ending polygamy), sexuality (the English being excessively concerned with "unchasteness"), and hairstyle. Neighboring white laymen were brought in to train the villagers in what the English considered to be productive tasks. Based on their not always gentle instruction, the Natick Indians started up cottage industries that turned out baskets, brooms, and weirs. They also worked as servants, sold fish and fruit in local markets, and tended English farmers' livestock.

Seeing the new prosperity of Natick, Indians beyond Waban's and Cutshamekin's original groups flocked to the village in increasing numbers. Although access to tools and the availability of clothing may have been main motives for this in-flux, the desire to learn English and to become literate were also strong. Neither conversion as such nor church building were stressed, if only because of the Puritans' rusted-keyhole stipu-lation that a church could only be formed *by Christians who had made an acceptable confession within an existing church.* None-theless, the religious discipline and worship practices in Natick were sufficiently regularized so that it became known as the Apostle's first so-called praying village.

The village having been judged a viable experiment and a feasible solution to the vexing problem of local Indians, the General Court permitted the establishment of additional com-munities. Within the course of twenty-five years between 1650 and 1675, thirteen similar praying villages or towns were es-tablished throughout coastal and interior Massachusetts Bay (including the one at Wamesit or Pennacook, Passaconaway's location on the Merrimack). Some four thousand Native Amer-icans from a variety of tribes eventually inhabited these vil-lages, industriously producing cedar shingles and clapboards, prize hogs and specially branded cattle, as well as a host of other marketable goods for local markets.

The Apostle gave "hints" as to how the new villages might manage themselves but otherwise left them alone. An example of this was Eliot's response to an ill-advised raid against the nettle-some Mohawk that the Massachusetts natives—including some young men from the praying villages, Passaconaway's among them—organized by themselves in 1669. (Ironically, this was the type of attack that Père Druillettes had suggested nearly twenty years earlier, an attack by Algonquian through Iroquoia's eastern door.) Though quite sympathetic to the villagers' desire to defend themselves against their enemies, Eliot considered this strike to be "imprudent." Yet he held his tongue. The force of three hundred men stormed over the Berkshires and up the Mohawk River to besiege a stronghold near present-day Schenectady, unsuccessfully. Straggling home in bad order, the chastened, retreating troops were severely punished by Mohawk waiting in ambush. Bible lessons that counseled peace were then heard with greater attentiveness throughout the villages.

At the highest levels, the praying villages were deemed a providential success. The rulers both of Massachusetts Bay and of England, when boasting of their colonial accomplishments, pointed with unseemly pride to the mounting number of "praying Indians." Could either France or Spain, for all the extent of their colonies, hold up to heaven such a harvest of souls? Overlooked in that proud boast was the issue of how the establishment of the villages—these battle zones of spiritual conquest between the two cultures—benefited the Algonquian themselves. Eliot himself and other observers of the day did stress the *Indianness* of the praying villages. The villages sounded Algonquian in language and laughter, they smelled Algonquian in cookery and curing, they looked Algonquian in their wigwams and their day-to-day leadership. They were neither prison camps nor reform schools; they were a visionary attempt to conserve a culture by helping it to adapt. Furthermore, the Apostle paid the leadership and people of the praying towns the ultimate compliment of leaving them mostly alone, visiting only from time to time.

Even today's revisionistic historians have recognized that the Apostle gave the villagers a determinant voice in the management of their borderland society. But they condemn as "naive"

Eliot's attempt to assist the Indians at all—his personal, charitable reaction to the plight of natives whose misery had struck
him so forcibly. They also question his respect for the ancient
Native American values. Given English interference, these formerly peripatetic people could no longer roam lands that were
once their own and listen to the voices of nature's spirits; no
longer could they, in their unrestricted roamings, come upon and
spontaneously worship in a spirit-blessed and holy space. Their
life-giving mother, nature, was being taken away from them. Yet
as the economy changed and as land expansion became such a
central factor of English colonial policy, perhaps the praying village represented the best possible, short-term salvation.

The Bay Colony's Puritan leaders struggled with the theological consequences of the Apostle's relaxed policies among
the native population, some of them still dreading the possibility that the English colony would become "Indianized." In the
words of biographer Cogley, many feared the prospect of having to "take their eschatology from the Indians." Meanwhile,
Eliot went ahead with his translations: In 1654 he published his
Indian Primer and Catechism, and in 1658 his *Book of Psalms*
(completed in 1653) rolled off the Harvard presses.

His unprecedented effort to bring qualified Indians into the
Church and thus into full Christian membership went on apace.
As he rode over the hills to see how his friends were doing in
one or another of the fourteen praying villages, he was badly
impeded by recurring sciatica, the lonely horseman's curse.
Nonetheless, his controversial attempts to foster Indian church
membership eventually received the backing of the elders of his
own Roxbury congregation: They consented to hear and evalu-
ate the "conversion narratives" that several native proselytes had

rehearsed among their own people and now needed to lay before covenanted members. Even though the confessions of the eight Indians examined were rather formulaic, sounding suspiciously unindividual and very much like memorized phrases from a Puritan catechism, they also contained uniquely Indian elements. These included references to their "wildness" and their "powwowing" (worst deviancy of all!) and their "laziness." The examiners were impressed, and the applicants were deemed admissible to full membership in the Roxbury church.

The significance of this was enormous. Because the "native saints" were now church members, it was possible for them to set up their own church in Natick. This fulfillment of the Apostle's dream in 1660 was accompanied by an invitation for him to move to Natick as the people's regular minister—an invitation he did not accept for fear of overwhelming the town's leadership. He yearned to see Natick's church members develop their own ordained leadership to serve throughout the colony. By 1683, with the ordination of Daniel Tokkohwompait, he must have felt that the Second Coming was that much nearer at hand. In Cogley's words, he saw the Indians as "poised on the brink of the Millennium."

In front of the handsome church that one can visit today in Natick stands a sign with these two sentences, of which the second is the more important:

On this site John Eliot helped his Indian converts to build their first meeting house in 1651, with a "Prophet's Chamber" where he lodged on his fortnightly visits to preach to them in their language. His disciple Daniel Takawambait succeeded to the pastoral office in 1698.

The sign testifies to the Apostle's success in ushering in an era of native discipleship. But it says nothing about an equally fascinating subject: the transformation of John Eliot himself, from an English Puritan to what may be called an "American exceptionalist," a singer of psalms in another tongue.

NATIVE SAINTS for CAPE COD and the ISLANDS

Was New England of the 1650s and 1660s truly a heavenly gateway through which Christian leaders might usher their red and white flocks into a millennialistic kingdom of peace and reconciliation? From one very special viewpoint, at one very special time, it looked that way. For one could see more than a thousand Algonquian dwelling in the praying towns within Massachusetts Bay and spy hundreds more in Plymouth's territory on Cape Cod. Beyond those communities could soon be counted six hundred Christianized Algonquian living in mixed communities on the islands of Martha's Vineyard and Nantucket. On the other side of the racial line, there were crossovers in the reverse direction. These were no longer European colonists who had, in one way or another, chosen the Indian way of life, declaring themselves free from the restraining bonds of Puritanism. Emotionally and spiritually all had been transformed into that wondrous mutant, an American (though a century would pass before they called themselves that).

In the words of historian Francis Jennings, the interaction between the white settlers and the social and material world in which they found themselves "caused constant transformation and evolution." No mere coincidences were the 1660 cessation of persecution of the Quakers and the 1662 cancellation of the Massachusetts Bay requirement that all freemen must be covenanted churchmen. The faltering of Puritanism—indeed the failure of Puritanism to provide a suitable context in which the settlers could respond to the opportunities of seventeenth-century America—continued to alarm the orthodox. John Eliot's plan for the independent governance of the praying villages was regarded as so radical in some quarters that, when published in Boston, the document was burned on the common by the public hangman. But the Apostle's deepest fears, that his radical villages, by becoming more prominent, might cause violent reaction in traditional quarters, now seemed on the point of fulfillment.

The reactionary rulership in Connecticut condemned the Bay Colony for policies that seemed to coddle the natives—self-governing Indian villages indeed! Connecticut was the colony, it will be remembered, whose very opening up by means of the Pequot War had been morally problematic for some Puritans. Generally, however, that war of 1637, with its crushing of the Native Americans, was regarded as the proper guide to racial relations. The General Court in Hartford, still relishing wartime victories and attitudes, sent the following message to former comrades-in-arms in Massachusetts: "We intreat you to consider how incongruous and cross it would have bin [sic] twenty yeares agoe to an English spirit . . . to beare such things as we are now forc't to beare."

Yet, convinced peacemakers like John Eliot and Passaconaway continued to believe that a just society of coexistence could be constructed. Even with the restoration of the monarchy in England and the royal determination to strip the Bay Colony of its fragile but prized independence—an independence symbolized by the absence of any English sign on the coinage issued in Boston in 1652—the peacemakers trusted that liberal interracial policies would prevail. The graduation from Harvard in 1665 of an Indian named Caleb Cheeshahteaumuck seemed proof of the fact that a God-blessed, biracial era was dawning and that, with native preachers spreading the word to distant parts, all Americans might live in harmony.

That illusion was intensely alive south of Boston, where two of John Eliot's missionary colleagues had had even more success than he in establishing Christian communities among the native peoples. There, on Cape Cod and the offshore islands, the missionaries were dealing with adaptable people who lived far from the laws and persecutions of Massachusetts Bay and who were quite willing to fit Christianity into their belief systems without losing their integrity in the process. The first of these Eliot colleagues was Thomas Mayhew, Jr., a Congregationalist whose work among the Wampanoag of Martha's Vineyard began in 1643. Like John Eliot, he received some financial assistance from England, that is from London's so-called New England Company (evolved from the old Society for the Propagation of the Gospel). But, also like Eliot, Mayhew operated on the strength of his own interactions with the local scene as well as his own communications with God; he could never be regarded as a church functionary.

Mayhew saw as his first duty the turning away of the Wampanoag from their demeaning devil worship and "false gods." But he also respected with all possible care the overlordship of Massasoit, their sachem, as well as their other cultural traditions—even the role of their powwows. When a "universal sickness" gripped Martha's Vineyard in 1645, Mayhew and his disciple Hiacoomes had more success with cures than did the medicine men. Furthermore, Hiacoomes willingly tested his faith against all the "diabolical craft" that the powwows could heap upon him. The beneficial effect of this competition was that, after the powwows succumbed to the missionary's evangelization, they became a part of the Christianizing movement themselves.

The results in Martha's Vineyard amazed all New England: By the fall of 1652, the total number of Mayhew's converts had reached three hundred adults. A school for further education in Christianity was established and a new kind of community was envisioned that would imitate Eliot's praying villages (and would, again, resemble the mission stations that had been established by Père de Brébeuf just a few years earlier). After Mayhew's death by drowning, his work was carried on by his father and by his widow and their sons. The Mayhew family's dynamic mission—which took the form of two operative churches by 1675—continued to spread across the island by native preachers, who soon succeeded in establishing it on Nantucket as well.

The other missionary whose work may be compared with Eliot's was an English lawyer named Richard Bourne. Following community leader Edmund Freeman from Plymouth to Sandwich in 1640, Bourne, though a layman, saw it as his charge to aid the stricken, local "South Sea" Indians (meaning those of the Cape Cod's Nantucket Sound shoreline). Like Mayhew, he took the course of directly engaging the powwows in a contest for spiritual leadership, preaching through an interpreter. After a four-year struggle in the mid-1650s—a struggle for leadership that is still recalled in Mashpee folklore as a fight against a gigantic, boulder-carrying devil—he emerged as the stronger force. Thereafter he acquired a working knowledge of the native language, as well as a stipend of upward of £15 from the New England Company. In 1660 he created the praying town of Mashpee, located on Cape Cod's largest, and some say most beautiful, freshwater lake.

Around the shores of that lake today, according to ethnologist William S. Simmons, you can hear children sing the mocking song of a chickadee that watched as the Devil approached Mashpee one day before his defeat by the missionary. As he soared across the heavens, the Devil carried with him projectiles in the form of beach stones; soon he could be seen from Mashpee, appearing against the sky "like a great black eagle hurrying over the hills." Fearing neither stones nor the evil spirit himself, the legendary chickadee sang out to him in mocking tones:

> Howdy, Giant,
> Howdy, Devil.
> You're gonna wrestle
> With Richard Bourne.
> You're gonna git
> The worst of it.
> You're gonna git
> The worst of it!

The stones that the frustrated Devil threw at the free-flying chickadee can still be seen in "Bourneland," a rocky contrast to the rest of the Cape's flat sandscape.

Significantly, Bourne had purchased the land for this long-lasting mission site with his own money (£15), for this was not a church or governmental effort but a family commitment, supported by Bourne's grandson and great-grandson after his death in 1682. Commenting on his motivations, contemporary clergyman Gideon Hawley wrote: "He was a man of [such] discernment that he considered it as vain to propagate Christian knowledge among any people without a territory where they might remain in place from generation to generation." The discernment Hawley referred to could only have occurred because Bourne, like other frontiersmen, was gaining through personal contact with the Mashpee Wampanoag a sense of the profound significance of the American land to its Indian people. That undying religious tenet lay at the heart of the first successful nineteenth-century (1833) rebellion of red Americans against white authorities, described in this book's last chapter.

Impressed by Bourne's work and the number of his converts, John Eliot and John Cotton, Jr., participated in his ordination and his installation as the pastor of the Mashpee church in 1647. As Richard Cogley remarks, "Bourne was probably the first Englishman ordained for a native congregation in colonial America." By 1674 the native-run church had twenty-seven communicants and ninety more baptized members; even more important, the church's educational program had produced a number of trained and seasoned Mashpee preachers ready to take over the pulpit after Bourne's retirement.

This was a pulpit and a church where Christian teaching was carried out not in the spirit of conquest but in harmony with local spiritual creativity. Indeed, within the Mashpee Meeting

House honor has always been given to local traditions as well as to Old and New Testament heroes. Outside, on the clapboard front wall, one can see this sign:

MASHPEE OLD INDIAN MEETING HOUSE

EST. 1684

INDIAN PREACHERS:

SIMON POPOMONET, SOLOMON BRIANT,

WILLIAM APES, BLIND JOSEPH AMOS,

Descendants of Massasoit

The last line makes the point of cultural continuity, not invasive conquest, most convincingly.

The historical record of those halcyonic mid-1600s years also gives a picture of a pro-native alteration in New England's cultural patterns. Both the English colonists of Plymouth and those of Boston had originally established tightly circumscribed communities, hedged from the surrounding land and life by palisades and prohibitions. Faith was identified with the special and holy space within or immediately surrounding the church or meetinghouse; lack of faith existed outside the church community's "hedge." Now, however, the Pilgrim and Puritan chronicles reported more and more escapes into the wilderness, departures on new adventures, beginnings of seemingly unrelated, even unchurched communities.

Of particular dismay to the Pilgrims was the centrifugal behavior of one of their own, Deacon John Cooke. Son of Francis Cooke (a *Mayflower* passenger who had belonged to the original congregation in Scrooby, England), young Cooke had seemed secure enough in his faith to be appointed to the post of internal security agent (heretic hunter) within the Plymouth community. But then he took off for Dartmouth at the western limits of the colony, seduced by the new philosophies of the Baptists and other breakaway denominationalists. The excommunication from the church that followed his defection did not stop others from emulating him. And thus it happened that down the river ways of southern Massachusetts spread fishing and farming communities whose undisciplined shapes and independent churchmanship and tolerant racial attitudes marked them as peculiarly American places. Might this be the pattern for New England's and America's future?

The increasing prominence of educated Indian churchmen in this mixed American scene—successful farmers and boat-owning fishermen—remained a blossoming marvel to those who believed in the furtherance of John Eliot's work and, at the same time, an insult to orthodox leaders in both red and white societies. John Sassamon, a Neponset who had been trained at Harvard and who, in his youth, had served with the English during the Pequot War, was in some ways typical of this educated and respected group of literate and bilingual Indians. He helped Eliot the Apostle pull together the *Indian Primer and Catechism* and proofread it for accuracy. But in other ways he was typical of nothing other than man's congenital fallibility, being so often in the wrong place at the wrong time.

Though unordained, Sassamon, a second-generation Christian, was regarded as devout (if not exactly trustworthy). He preached regularly as a layman at the Natick church and seemed ready for the ultimate test that would cap his career. When Massasoit, the much respected grand sachem, died an undeviatingly pagan death in 1662, the Apostle saw an opportunity to start up a mission among the Wampanoag Pokanoket. Responding to

Massasoit's son's request for a teacher, Eliot selected Sassamon and sent him to Shawomet (Warwick, Rhode Island) and nearby Mount Hope. There the newly installed sachem, Massasoit's son, bore the name Metacom, but the English bestowed on him, after he had received his royal inheritance, the flattering title of King Philip—the name by which the terrible war of 1675-1678 would be known. In the commencement of that war, Sassamon, with his ripe but not necessarily wise view of the colonial and native authorities, would play a key role.

Having served Massasoit's son as secretary for a number of years—and having witnessed in that court both the fraudulent land deals that were imposed on Philip and the prince's own illicit sale of Wampanoag land to interested Rhode Island buyers—Sassamon returned under a cloud of suspicion to Natick. Rumor had it that Sassamon, while working at Mount Hope, had made a draft of the young sachem's will that benefited the drafter as much as the inheritor. Questions had also been raised about whether Sassamon's Christian commitment had lapsed when living among the Pokanoket—or had he merely been playing a part beforehand? To clear the matters up, he hastened to Plymouth, bearing many self-justifying tales of his own behavior. He also reported that Philip, in a hostile mood, was not only continuing to sell land that was supposedly covenanted by Plymouth, but was also surrounding himself with battle-ready warriors.

Sassamon subsequently took up permanent residence on the shore of Assawampsett Pond (near present-day Lakeville, Massachusetts) among his wife's people. There the aging courtier existed as a part-time preacher and continual intelligence agent between the land-hungry, trigger-happy Pilgrims and the callow, imperious prince to the southeast. One is tempted to compare him to Polonius, a learned, somewhat doddering figure from another generation, half-hidden behind a screen. He was to have his Hamlet.

NEW ENGLAND'S SHAMEFUL HOLY WAR

From King Philip's viewpoint, Sassamon, for all his decades of service and Christian respectability, looked like a traitor and a turncoat. Far more strongly than his father, Philip distrusted Christianity culturally and personally. In one famous episode, the young sachem, having received a visit from the Apostle John Eliot, reached across the space between them and took hold of a button on his guest's coat. "I care no more for your gospel," he said, "than that!" Christianity represented both a challenge to his political control—a number of villagers and subchiefs having already drifted away in the direction of the praying towns—and a threat to his freebooting way of life. When word came to him that Sassamon had whispered to the Pilgrims news of his preparations for a raid against the town of Swansea (although Sassamon had received Plymouth's promise that his role in imparting this report would never be revealed), Philip concluded that the troublesome old man needed to have an accident.

Most writers—including this author, in the 1990 book, *The Red King's Rebellion*—date the beginning of King Philip's War from the discovery of Sassamon's body beneath lake ice in February 1675. The bruised figure was found with his neck broken, quite obviously a murder victim. Plymouth seized on the incident to bring on a summary trial, with Wampanoag allowed to sit in the court as spectators but not as jurors. The trial's result was the hanging of three presumed murderers, one of whom had been a key councillor in Philip's court. What marked the incident as particularly significant was the religious language and imagery with which it was surrounded. Blood had spouted from Sassamon's body when one of the accused murderers walked by, it was said; comets were observed in the night sky. Plymouth considered that, given the arming of the natives and the murder of a native saint and the cosmic disturbances, some sort of supreme test now faced them.

In Boston, too, news having arrived of a possible fight between a disgruntled Pokanoket sachem and the stressed citizenry of Plymouth, signs indicated that something dreadful was happening in the heavens. Cotton Mather wrote that the beating of drums had been heard at night; ghostly armies were glimpsed marching through the woods. That very day word came that the Pilgrims had heard troops of invisible horses rushing back and forth. An event involving unknown forces of the spirit world seemed to be shaping up.

At Mount Hope, where Philip was considering how to preserve some part of his shrinking territory and diminishing authority, he received counsel not only from aroused youthful warriors but also from senior powwows who agreed that a time of finalities was upon them. Externally, there was the threatening expansion of neighboring farms owned by colonists whose fences failed to keep omnivorous hogs and wandering cattle in their appointed fields. Internally and personally, there were the humiliations of Philip's being called repeatedly to Plymouth to hear new regulations against his men bearing arms. John Eliot, in protesting that these prohibitions were insulting (as well as unrealistic), raised a lone voice.

Philip's powwows, also fearing the loss of their authority in the face of the encroaching white culture, advocated violent action. They promised on the basis of their communications with the spirits that Philip himself, as military leader, could never be hurt by a blow from the English enemy—a prediction that turned out to be correct. Reflecting on all that had happened to him and his people since the arrival of the colonists some fifty years earlier, Philip stated (in testimony given at a peace conference in Providence): "But a small part of the dominion of my ancestors remains. I am determined not to live until I have no country." By having no country, he would have no life, no soul.

And thus New England's second, vastly more destructive, religious war began. Philip himself had wanted to delay a few weeks or months until he had gathered additional allies (particularly from nations like the Narragansett and Mahican, sufficiently strong of sinew and of spirit to have resisted both disease and Christianity). But his enthusiastic young men dashed into the field with raids on Swansea, Taunton, Dartmouth, and other nearby towns. Plymouth, though urged to treat the raids as merely that and to think deeply about root reasons for the uprising, also seized on the occasion to saddle up and ride to war. Joined by 110 eager "volunteers" from Boston (many of whom were prisoners especially released for this purpose), a Plymouth-led strike force eventually succeeded in crossing over from the mainland to the peninsula where Philip's Mount Hope headquarters was located. Surprisingly, Philip and all his men had withdrawn from the scene but then returned, to the colonists' shock, in a punishing attack. The strike force retreated and English colonials reconsidered their situation. Unimpressed

by Plymouth's military capabilities, some Bay Colony magistrates advised that the whole interracial contest be brought to a
swift halt.

By then the Algonquian were rallying to Philip's cause.
Both in the areas surrounding Boston, where the Nipmuck arose
to storm the agricultural town of Brookfield, and in the Connecticut River valley, where the Pocumtuck and Norwottock
assaulted the frontier communities of Deerfield and Hatfield,
a widespread, apparently allied offensive of Native Americans
burst upon the English, an offensive that seemed to be powered
as much by clever generalship as by religious zeal. Those terrifying, flaming attacks of spring and early summer 1675 were
followed by what many viewed as a particularly convincing
demonstration of the powwows' might, an August hurricane
that uprooted the oaks and shook the timbers of Massachusetts
Bay. A Puritan commentator wrote that the powwows "farther
say, that as many Englishmen shall die as the Trees have by this
Wind been blown down in the Woods."

It was a terrifying prospect. To Cotton Mather it appeared
that the colony was totally surrounded, that America's all-
powerful Indians had "risen almost round the country." The
Puritans concluded that they must join Plymouth and strike
back against Philip with all the majesty of their true God. At
this point in the seventeenth century, the myth of the Puritans'
divine election was so firmly set in place that it could not brook
challenge. With the remembered triumph of 1637 and the uprising of a new and militant self-righteousness in place of the old,
strictly religious and communal objectives, the Puritans at this
time of crisis saw themselves in the role of biblical Hebrews.
They were charged with taking the land—the God-given and

blessedly profitable land—from pagan forces of evil. The Apostle's little towns were all very well, but God surely judged military conquest as an even more effective form of civilizing the pagans. Carrying on in the tradition of Cromwell, the Puritan forces would be led into battle by a "pillar of fire."

Defeating Philip's perceived legions from Hell and demonizing all Indians (even Christian ones) as servants of the Devil became twinned objectives for the Puritans. It was in this mood that the Massachusetts Bay Council ordered all Indian men, women, and children, even the praying Indians, to be rounded up, marched through the countryside, and interned on Deer Island in Boston Harbor. In the eyes of the oppressed Algonquian, the imminent possibility of their being shipped off to the West Indies as plantation slaves was an even worse fear than imprisonment on that bleak sandbar. Yet to many Puritans—despite the impassioned objections of John Eliot against this well-established practice—slavery appeared to be one of the livelier, more convincing rationales for assisting Plymouth in the war.

Among even the most faithful of the praying Indians, the vengeful and racist attitudes of the English colonists sundered their peaceful beliefs. In one praying community, Hassanamesit (today's Grafton), an attack band of Nipmuck allied with Philip slipped into town just before the arrival of government troops who had been detailed to march the village's inhabitants to Boston. The Nipmuck informed the town's minister, Tuckapewillin, that the inhabitants' choices were basically two. One was death at the hands of the native attackers or death (possibly slavery) on the Bay Colony's dreaded Deer Island. Another, safer way was to join the many Algonquian who were rallying to Philip's cause (including deserters from other praying towns). Reluctantly, Tuckapewillin and his people agreed and departed with the attackers—though the minister himself, plagued by inner doubts, subsequently fled back to the English side.

Many months later, on meeting with Eliot, his beloved Apostle, the captive Tuckapewillin expressed his undying loyalty even in the face of persecution. He said, "I thought within myself it is better to die than to fight the church of Christ." Perceiving that his family, his town, his land had been taken away from him in the passions of war, he told Eliot, "I have nowhere to look but up to God in Heaven to help me."

By that time—the winter of 1675-1676—the allied Indian forces that Philip was credited with commanding had accomplished more than had at first seemed possible. Even as the interned Christian Indians froze on Deer Island—bringing forth the sympathetic comment from Eliot that "the Island was bleak and cold, their wigwams poor and mean, their clothes few and thin"—terrified colonists streamed to the capital, grateful for any shelter they could find. These thousands of refugees, stripped of all possessions and with no homes to return to should peace ever come, could only be declared wards of the state.

Nearly half of New England's ninety-five settlements had been laid to waste or soon would be. Everything west of Concord (some twenty-five towns) was either reduced to ashes or suffered from repeated attacks. Historian Jill Lepore, author of *King Philip's War and the Origins of American Identity*, discovered a letter from Bostonian Nathaniel Saltonstall to a friend in London in which Saltonstall contemplated the desperate situation. He surmised woefully that, "Nothing could be expected but an utter desolation." The English were being pushed into the sea, apparently by brilliantly deployed warriors and (it seemed to some) by demonic forces too powerful to be resisted.

This being in some large part a spiritual contest, the Puritans looked in all corners of their souls to explain God's abandonment. From pulpits in still standing towns came the word that God had intentionally "chastened us with his rods." The most severe preachers blamed the losses on general immorality—particularly on excessive leniency toward the Quakers. The most liberal preachers (including John Eliot, who was held to be one of the war's causes and was reviled by laymen and clergy alike for his pro-Indian attitudes) pointed to Plymouth's expansionist policies as one undoubted cause. Plymouth's struggles against the Bay Colony for control of southern New England, fruitless and terminal in character at this time, had indeed threatened the status quo. But Eliot's charge against Plymouth, though accurate, was regarded as pertinent by few.

Another cause for the war and for English defeats, as seen by terrified contemporaries, was the devilish personality, the innate "naughtiness," of Metacom (i.e., Philip). He undoubtedly was a talented and clever leader, though perhaps not capable of such grandeur as his father achieved. Well acquainted with English ways, he is most accurately seen as a native leader with his back to the wall, employing whatever tactics might be available to retain his domain and, thus, to serve his people. Ethnohistorians of today, in their praiseworthy attempts to right the record by presenting events of the past from the Indian perspective, have made the additional point that, to Philip's eyes, the major issue was how to retain the loyalty of his Wampanoag (and, if possible, other tribes as well). Infuriated by the success of the praying villages, and fearful that all tribesmen might veer away into some kind of accommodation with the English, he commenced nativist oratory and actions in order to attract all Indians of the area—particularly the youths—to his cause. In this, one continues to see a strong religious theme, if only in reaction to the process of Christianization.

Yet the chief reason for the Bay Colony's military defeats was not the dazzling genius of Philip but the dreadful mistake made by Puritan leaders once the drums of war had struck up the beat and stirred the passion for victory. Casting caution aside, they rashly decided to attack New England's mightiest native nation, the Narragansett. Even Roger Williams, once the Narragansett's friend, agreed with the Bay Colony's decision to launch an unprovoked campaign in December 1675; he accepted the rationale that those self-sufficient Narragansett had aided and given refuge to too many of Philip's Wampanoag Pokanoket. So into the heart of Narragansett country stormed the mightiest force New England had ever assembled, some one thousand men including scores of Indian guides and ancillaries. Narragansett chief Canochet's headquarters proved a formidable target, both because of its hidden location (in a great swamp near present-day Kingston, Rhode Island) and because of its great strength. But when it fell before the remorseless English assault—an assault made feasible, it must be repeated, by the native scouts who helped the English find the fort—hundreds of no longer neutral, now infuriated Narragansett streamed north to join Philip's companies.

These were the soldiers who helped make the Algonquian alliance so mighty. Yet the alliance did not actually have great numbers on its side: Philip and his allies were never able to muster more than a few thousand men against the united colonies of New England's five thousand soldiers. Additionally, the English were aided both by more advanced technology and by dedicatedly loyal scouts. These hundreds of Algonquian ancillaries (including praying Indians) who served in the cause of New England were responsible, in the opinion of John Eliot and many others, for the turning of the tide in King Philip's War. It was one of them who aimed and fired the musket that put the ultimate lead ball through Philip's heart, thus fulfilling the powwow's promise that the sachem would not fall beneath the gun of any white man.

Philip and the other Indian leaders had fought with tremendous skill, both in the woodland engagements and when besieging bastioned emplacements. Yet in their bold attacks, as man after man fell to English bullets, they counted each loss dearly, each man as irreplaceable. Their spirit may be read in a sign they posted for English eyes after the successful attack on Medfield in May 1676:

KNOW BY THIS PAPER, THAT THE INDIANS THAT THOU
HAS PROVOKED TO WRATH AND ANGER, WILL WAR THIS
TWENTY-ONE YEARS IF YOU WILL; THERE ARE MANY INDIANS
YET, WE COME THREE HUNDRED AT THIS TIME. YOU MUST
CONSIDER THE INDIANS LOSE NOTHING BUT THEIR LIFE;
YOU MUST LOSE YOUR FAIR HOUSES AND CATTLE.

Their emphasis on numbers revealed their anxiety. They were even more anxious about the effectiveness and god-connectedness of their powwows. In that same bloody and rainy springtime of 1676, when Tispaquin—a sachem and shaman who was one of Philip's prime lieutenants—was commanding an assault on the Plymouth colony town of Bridgewater, a thunder and lightning storm suddenly burst upon the scene. Despite the fact that several buildings had already been put to the torch and it looked as if the Algonquian could easily wipe out the twenty-six defenders, Tispaquin ordered his three-hundred-man war party to halt in midassault. He wanted to consider the heavens and (according to an Indian account) went through the process of convening a powwows' council in order to give adequate attention to what the storm might portend.

In response to the shaman's ritualistic conjurings, a devil appeared. As the legend is written, "It had the Shape of a Bear wlkg on his 2 hind feet." If the vision had been a deer, the Indians believed, "they would have destroyed the whole Town & all the English." But because the appearance was that of a bear, they "followed him and all drew off." And so Tispaquin, despite the superiority of his numbers on that day, could not bring himself to press the attack.

Yet the English had enormous respect for this Tispaquin, who was a religious nobleman, a *pniese,* just as Hobomock had been. When he finally surrendered after the death of Philip, Plymouth's commander Benjamin Church (whose personal experience with the Algonquian had taught him much about fighting in the frontier mode) stated that he wanted to employ the captive Tispaquin as an officer in his Algonquian brigade. But other English shouted down the idea, pointing out that since *pnieses* thought themselves to be invulnerable to bullets, let the matter be put to the test then and there. As Church reported the trial by fire, "[Tispaquin] was found penetrable by the English guns, for he fell down upon the first shot, and thereby received the just reward for his former wickedness."

Before the turning of the tide of battle in the spring of 1676, Philip's greatest difficulty as commander and statesman lay in the fact that he had no additional allies (beyond the Narragansett) who might rally to the Algonquian cause. But always hoping that additional tribes might see the danger and the weakness of the English, he had set forth during the preceding winter on a recruiting trip to the northwest corner of New England. There he hoped to lure the Mahican of the Hoosick River valley into an alliance as well as other people resentful of Dutch and English traders. What he succeeded in doing, instead, was in alerting the Mohawk Iroquois to his presence—the very people of whom Père Druillettes had warned the English and their Algonquian friends a dozen years earlier. By now, however, the Iroquois negotiators had established a solid relationship with the crown's representative in Albany, Sir Edmond Andros. Hearing of Philip's incursion, Andros requested the Mohawk to take care of the problem. In response, Mohawk warriors punished Philip's small force so brutally that he never again gained full command of the remaining Algonquian alliance.

Finally, when it became clear after Philip's death that the remaining Algonquian forces could not carry on the war effectively in southern New England, the Puritan commanders decreed that most of the interned praying Indians could be released. As one Bostonian commented, "God was pleased to mollify the hearts and minds of men towards [these Indians], little and little." By then, however, more than half of the original group on Deer Island had died of illness or starvation. Although Joseph Tuckapewillin survived, he still faced the threat of being shipped off for sale as a slave (the fate that awaited Philip's wife). Natick was allowed to open its doors again and the Christian Indians of Mashpee and the islands survived intact. But the days of two-faith cooperation had passed in Massachusetts.

Mercy was definitely not a quality of the deity summoned by the Puritans to aid them in their time of trial. The pastor of the First Church of Boston proclaimed from his pulpit that, given the chance, he would "carry fire in one hand and fagots in the other to burn every Quaker in the world." The Indians deserved even worse. This was to be the enduring, cursed, militaristic legacy of the Puritans—a legacy reevaluated even today as Deer Island becomes a site for public commemoration of the Algonquian interned during King Philip's War.

If there was any winner in that war, it was probably the Mohawk. They not only punished the rebellious Pokanoket prince, but also gained recognition for carrying out English orders to run down those Algonquian who chose to carry the war to Maine. Finally, Governor Andros decreed an end to the whole thing with the Treaty of Casco, in 1678. The Puritan ministers and magistrates were revealed as not winners but losers. Not only had they demonstrated an incompetence to protect their own people in the face of a native uprising, but they had also required outside forces (including Andros, representing British imperial authority) to terminate the bloodshed. Dreams of a proud and independent and religiously dominant Massachusetts Bay were doomed forever. Certain New Englanders had, however, found a new identity in the war; they had discovered that the alleged wilderness was actually a place of fascination and richness where native people had managed to flourish mightily. Thereafter they streamed to the western frontiers, far from Boston, where they opened themselves to new spiritual experiences.

John Eliot spent his final days trying to get a revised edition of his Bible published (which he barely succeeded in doing in 1685, paying for the publication with his own funds) and in encouraging the native preachers to stand firm. To his deep regret, he learned that many of the praying Indians who had gone to war on the English side had become total soldiers, their faces painted, their crosses left behind. They had been transformed, once again, into individualistic fighting Americans. Yet when the Apostle died in 1690, aged eighty-six, he was able to concentrate on purely heavenly matters. His last words were, "Welcome, Joy!"

In London, only a decade before John Eliot's death, a young and highly educated Quaker named William Penn received, in payment for a debt owed his father, the royal charter for a colony in America. It was to be a "Holy Experiment," that is, a colony where religious and political freedom could flourish, for the benefit of men and women of all races and conditions. Soon after arriving in his new province of Pennsylvania in 1682 and after laying out the rectilinear City of Brotherly Love, he received a report from emissaries he had sent to the Bay Colony, now renamed (along with Connecticut and Rhode Island) the Royal Dominion of New England. They described it as an exhausted, burnt-over territory, deeply in debt, its religious passions spent, its native peoples fled or extinguished, and its land-hungry farmers looking for fields far from the established towns. Yet William Penn trusted that, given the failure of those early and severe religionists, some kind of more enlightened holy space might yet be created and flourish in this green land.

PART II

CHAPTER 5

The EARLY EIGHTEENTH CENTURY'S FLOWERING of HOPE: The GREAT AWAKENING

W HEN A HOST OF Delaware consented, in response to a call from recently landed William Penn, to confer with him and to put their marks on his so-called Great Treaty of Peace, no formal Christian prayer sanctified the pact. Nor did any field artist record the event. But young America's first painter of historical subjects, Benjamin West—born a poor Pennsylvania Quaker, ultimately a prosperous artist for King George III—chose in later days to portray the convention of 1682 as a portentous, mythic event. He imagined it as happening at Shackamaxon on the banks of the Delaware River (now the industrial neighborhood of Kensington), under an elm tree with an appropriately awesome spread of branches.

The contemporary philosopher François Voltaire, known for his remark that "if God did not exist, he would have to be invented," was convinced that Penn would stay true to his humanistic promises that "the Indians and English must live in Love, as long as the Sun gives Light." While respecting Penn's principles as sincere and "very wise," the skeptical Frenchman noted with customary wit that the pact at Shackamaxon was "the only treaty between these peoples and the Christians which was not *sworn* to . . . and which [therefore] has not been broken." Yet here at last, he concluded, was proof for all rational men to see that people of many beliefs and races could lead the good life side by side without need of autocratic restraints or ecclesiastical mumbo jumbo.

Romanticists as well as rationalists warmed to the theme, entranced by the prospect of perpetual peace among pacifistic settlers and cooperative Algonquian. Benjamin West's Shackamaxon elm tree accordingly appears and reappears as a hoary symbol in all those depictions of *The Peaceable Kingdom* produced by American primitivist Edward Hicks (1780–1849). Hicks's innocent-eyed animals and sympathetic, diminutive Quakers appealed enormously to sentimental, nineteenth-century viewers. The theme of manly brotherhood also appealed to later eras: in Philadelphia folklore, the Delaware chief at the Shackamaxon signing became known as Tammany; as mentioned in chapter 1, the Sons of Tammany went on to form a powerful political organization, replete with rites and costumes, to commemorate the chief's steadfast spirit. At the end of the eighteenth century, enthusiasts even elevated him to "Saint" Tammany. His name was adopted by an organization that initially provided support for the racially oppressed and economically underprivileged but that eventually deteriorated into New York's notorious Tammany Hall. In these and other ways did the signing at Shackamaxon twist its way into the spirit and the history of America.

But long before the sanctification of Tammany, both the authentic religiosity of the Delaware and the dynamism of Penn's holy experiment had lost their deep spiritual roots. The

Delaware—who worshiped Cautantowwit, the same great god from the southwest whom the Narragansett and other Algonquian revered—were once known as the Lenni Lenape, the "grandfathers" of all eastern Indians. But during the first decades of the eighteenth century, they saw themselves diminished, divided and betrayed by the combined efforts of Anglo-Americans and Iroquois. William Penn's colony unfortunately betrayed itself by its own tolerant and undiscriminating pluralism—a contrast to the homogeneous and discriminating Puritans, who failed to evolve into Americans because of their concentration on an exclusive elect. With Penn's death in 1718, the great planter's avaricious heirs and land-hungry newcomers waged a battle for the mastery of Pennsylvania and its borderlands that would confound the Quaker legislature and subvert the old treaty in the most shameful of ways. Although Quakers would continue to grace the American intellectual and cultural scene with the "inner light" of their beliefs, chances of their persuading American culture, native or white, to follow that light had been dimmed.

Yet Penn's experiment can be closely likened in another sense to Winthrop's "Citty upon a Hill," for both were seventeenth-century religious-social imports from Europe; both, while failing to fulfill their universal objectives, made major impacts on the emergent complexities of American culture. And both survived in the moral genes, as it were, of American society, refusing to die like a discarded literary style or an overhunted species, or even to be replaced by the religious sentiments that flowered in the eighteenth century. Indeed, to see Puritanism and Quaker-derived principles resurface from time to time in American history, like old roots bearing new fruit, is one of the living joys of the study of comparative religion. But what is even more wondrous is to see how, in a quite different way, the undying, evolving principles of the Native American people (including the Delaware) have also had an impact—a perhaps unintentional impact, as in Tammany Hall—that would help shape the totality of American culture. In the words of historian James Axtell: "While all people to some extent define themselves by contrast with other people, the English colonists forged their peculiar American identity more *on an Indian anvil* than upon any other factor [italics added]."

No better era may be selected to illustrate that intercultural truth than the mid-1700s, the time when Puritanism and Quakerism were no longer radical imports from Europe but quiescent American orthodoxies and when Iroquois and Algonquian beliefs were also aged themes awaiting renewal. This was also the time when the "natural" religions advocated by Voltaire and John Locke were penetrating the American colonies. In the very years when Boston and New Haven and Philadelphia were becoming comfortable cushions for matured religions, they were also experiencing a worrisome secularization and a reflected enlightenment that threatened to blank out the spiritual heritage of the preceding century and to replace it with Deism (not to mention the penny-wise secular morality of Franklin). The unorthodox belief that an individual might attain salvation not solely through the will of God but through the individual's good works—a deviant concept that, in John Eliot's day, was shudderingly called Arianism after the fourth-century theologian who had dared equate Christ with God and that continued to plague orthodox Calvinists—now advanced to the point where humans (including, ultimately, the modern American) were seen as free and omnipotent.

Into that time of crisis for Anglo-American and native religions erupted a spiritual force that has come to be called the Great Awakening. Historians give much credit to this psychic spasm of the early and mid-eighteenth century as the individualistic urge that inspired colonials to separate state from church and to take up arms against the Crown. But America's cultural historians have generally failed to recognize the Great Awakening either as an event that affected *both* red and white peoples or as a long-range movement that, refusing to die, created ultimately as much damage as benefit. It played the effective role of a dark angel both in the development of America's homegrown, nationalistic religion and in the change from the optimistic accommodation of the Delaware at Shackamaxon to the transcendent rage of those who followed Pontiac and Tecumseh.

JONATHAN EDWARDS'S "ENTHUSIASTICAL TOWN"

On the last day of February 1704, the prosperous and comfortable frontier village of Deerfield, Massachusetts, suffered a nighttime assault, a knife thrust into the body of Protestant New England. The thrust was delivered by a newly invigorated task force of French troops and Indian allies (mostly Roman Catholic Abnaki) that had been ordered to disrupt and possibly break the remarkably successful alliance between the English Crown and the Five Iroquois Nations. Forged in the years when the English were taking over Dutch assets and strengthened in the recently completed King William's War (1689–97) and known as the Covenant Chain, that grand and historic alliance resisted most of underpopulated New France's previous efforts to break or bypass it.

Deerfield, situated in the lush Connecticut River valley, shone forth as a perfect target for the French and Abnaki, not only because of its ripe wealth—its forty-one well-appointed houses and storage sheds were known to be cornucopias of grains and meats—but also because of its brilliant pastor, Harvard-educated John Williams. A commanding preacher and a gifted land speculator, he headed the family that presumed to lead Massachusetts in the development of multitudinous church-spired farming villages along the colony's western frontier. To strategists in Quebec, those presumptuous English efforts had to be brought to an end.

Under cover of darkness and aided by hard-packed snow in their approach to Deerfield's palisades, fifty Frenchmen and two hundred Abnaki (the largest war party yet sent forth by the new administration in Quebec) swept upon the sleeping town in a mood of merciless fury. Sharpening the attackers' zeal for scalps and for captives were memories of the slaughter of their kin at La Chîne, a few miles upriver from Montreal. There, fifteen years earlier Seneca-led Iroquois on English orders had wiped out the entire community and, in a drunken orgy of roasting bodies, had claimed revenge for previous French military insults. Now it was the Abnaki's turn. Among the first victims whose skulls they cracked open were two of Pastor Williams's children, axed before their parents' eyes.

Only one brick house was able to withstand the assault, as tomahawks broke down doors and knives separated scalps from skulls. Fifty-three settlers perished before the two-hour-long rampage ceased; 111 adults and children, in varying stages of undress, were marched off along the snowy trail northward, the Abnaki knowing that the French governor would pay in gold for English captives. Ransomed successfully two years later, John Williams wrote so vividly of his experiences among the heathen that few New Englanders could keep those horrors from their innermost minds. Heightening the grotesque appeal of his best-selling, biblically allegorical book, *The Redeemed Captive Returning to Zion,* was public knowledge that one of the author's own captured children, seven-year-old Eunice Williams, was never returned to safety.

Indeed, having been taken to the Indian village of Cauhnawaga on the St. Lawrence River where she was instructed in a mission school, Eunice forgot her Puritan catechism entirely and, as a young squaw, became the bride of the very brave who had carried her on his back away from the smoking ruins of Deerfield. In later years, she would return to New England for obligatory visits to relatives but, blanket-clad and accompanied by dark-eyed children, she found the scene there strange and uncomfortable. By that time, thanks to her father's stirring book and the ceaselessly beating drums of war, the very name Deerfield had become a legend and a rallying cry for the conquest of the Canadian French and their Algonquian allies, a troubling reminder that, devils on the march, the Kingdom of Heaven was not yet at hand.

As frightful as the Deerfield raid appeared in New England eyes, a subsequent event in New Haven vexed the Old Lights of orthodoxy even more. These were the strict upholders of Puritanism (versus Arianism) who, while letting certain aspects of the faith fade into routine adherence, defended the supremacy and unexpandability of the elect. What shocked them occurred immediately following the Yale College commencement of 1722. In his closing prayer, Rector Timothy Cutler startled listeners by his use of the Anglican phrase, "Let all people say, Amen!" The next day Cutler and two resident tutors further startled a board of inquiry by denying the validity of ordinations performed by the recently introduced Presbyterian church (whose John Knox–inspired system of organization had been seen by many as the best way to bring the varieties of Congregationalism into proper order). Instead, Cutler's group defiantly went further to the right, espousing the Episcopal rite and declaring in favor of the Church of England. Four ministers from neighboring towns, formerly quite orthodox, joined them in this great apostasy. Cutler and his fellows were immediately dismissed ("excused") by the college trustees, who, in order to prevent the repetition of any such scandal, required Yale's faculty henceforth to subscribe to the Presbyterians' Saybrook Confession of 1708.

But the harm was already done: All the world could see that, a century after its foundation on American shores, the church of the Puritans was deeply riven within and cruelly vulnerable from without. Since the drastic changes in the charters of the New England colonies (most tellingly, the seizure of political power by the Crown after King Philip's War), even the Old Saints of Massachusetts feared that they could not credibly present themselves as God's chosen people. With mercantile pragmatism calling the tune in the capitals and with naturalism and even Anglicanism capturing the intellects in the universities, from where might come a robust defense of Puritan Jehovah? The fact that a sufficient leader did come forth—Jonathan Edwards, America's most eminent (some say singly eminent)

philosopher of the colonial period—supports the cultural theory that religion as a creative and defensive strategy will usually
assert itself in times of stress. The ancient, prophetic strain will
speak out, working like an antibody to repel infection. The alternative is cultural collapse.

Jonathan Edwards, the notable theologian and prospective
healer of New England's threatened body, has admittedly received terrible notices in today's popular American culture.
Robert Lowell attempted to write a biography of him but found
the subject too formidable. Twentieth-century poet Phyllis
McGinley described preacher Edwards's God thusly:

> Abraham's God, the Wrathful One,
>   Intolerant of error—
> Not God the Father or the Son
>   But God the Holy Terror.

But no one can deny either the intellectual brilliance with
which Edwards attacked the challenges he saw in the world
around him or the authentic personal passion with which he
made his case. Also, what scholars are now discovering is
that Edwards's contact with Indian religious values during this
culturally intermixed time of the mutually disturbing Great
Awakening ultimately did much to revise his fiery exclusionist
theology.

Born three years earlier than Benjamin Franklin and educated at Yale within the humanism of John Locke and Bishop
Berkeley, Edwards believed in the methodology of science
as well as in the theology of Calvin (not to forget the divine
purpose of the Puritan fathers). To him the pairing of science
and faith represented no contradiction, for he saw the absolute

sovereignty of God in every corner, on every meadow of the universe. He saw the workings of the spiders (which he had studied as a precocious child in Windsor, Connecticut) and the sins of man as being equally the creations of God, as revealed in Hebrew and Greek scriptures. While he referred to his work as "experimental religion," it was undertaken, in all of its aspects, as confirmations of God's divine plan.

Having graduated from Yale in 1720 at age seventeen (a not unusual accomplishment in that era), and having experienced conversion at age nineteen (perhaps as a reaction to his "nigh to the grave" encounter with pleurisy), Edwards was still on the New Haven campus as a graduate student when Cutler staged his disrupting defection to Anglicanism. Soon after his ordination, the good-looking, six-foot-tall, very ambitious youth journeyed to Northampton, Massachusetts—the largest congregation beyond Boston—where he would serve as proper assistant to his famous grandfather, Solomon Stoddard. That patriarchal figure, often referred to as Pope of the Connecticut Valley region, had sought to save Puritanism for future generations in a unique manner: by relaxing the standards of church membership. By his liberalized rules, a young person could be admitted to the church without having endured a conversion experience.

Also, as one of the more imaginative leaders of the so-called New Lights (clergy who chose to break away from the elitist formalisms of the old structures and to serve broader congregations), Solomon Stoddard strove to open the church doors even wider by staging emotional revivals. Jonathan Edwards arrived in Northampton in time (1727) to witness the fourth of the hugely successful revival meetings—men and women on their knees, weeping in repentance before the altar. Although harvests from the earlier so-called awakenings had been impressive, this final one coincided with an earthquake and seemed therefore to be of a new and even greater import.

At his grandfather's side, the observant young man learned how vivid language and cosmic references could serve to keep God at the center of popular thought. Earthquakes, hurricanes, Indian raids—all such evidences of His displeasure should be seen as occasions to demand that congregation members cast off their old, sinful ways. They must demand of themselves not "what can I do to change this earthly scene?" but "What might I do to be saved?" All people should be welcomed to that contemplation, and the most interesting place to gather in town must be the church, not the tavern. Solomon Stoddard raised the pulpit to that focal position, but within two years of young Edwards's arrival, the grand old man was dead. His congregation mourned him and his attractive policies as well as his steady hand on the helm of power, and viewed the future with intense apprehension. Edwards carried on the revivalistic tradition with an impressive conversion-success ratio—but with a certain theoretical aloofness.

The young theologian's revivals of 1734 and 1735 confirmed one of his ideas about how to build on his grandfather's achievements. He directed his energies particularly toward young people, those confused postadolescents who were "addicted to night-walking, frequenting the tavern, and lewd practices." As his experiment succeeded and as the number of professed converts mounted into the hundreds, trendy Northampton (only a dozen miles downriver from Deerfield) became known as the "most enthusiastical town" in New England. Many parents followed their young converts to the rail, allowing Jonathan Edwards to conclude that his town was uniting behind him.

Yet this was an illusion. In fact, New Englanders, once long ago unified in theology (as well as in terror of the unknown wilderness and its presumably hostile savages), were now being divided as old fears eased. The region's Protestant clergy argued with each other from their fixed Old Light and New Light positions (as well as inveighing against the other, more rationalistic philosophies); the no longer homogeneous society split itself between contented haves and rebellious have-nots. This division widened as easy years of peace (1713-1745) and fortunate harvests banished old fears.

When the fully crowded balcony of the Northampton church collapsed without a single person being injured, many saw the event as a favorable omen. Surely God, in selecting Jonathan Edwards as pastor, had sent a prophet who would deliver New England from its divisive, backsliding ways and would restore the power and majesty of the old order. A few years previously, on a pulpit visit to Boston in 1731, Edwards had put the entire colony on notice that the current self-sufficiency and smugness observable in its capital were symptomatic of a perilous illness. His Boston sermon, published under the no-exceptions-possible title of *God Glorified in the Work of Redemption, by the Great Dependence upon Him, in the Whole of It,* warned that sinners must look to God and God alone for salvation. Further, only by the abasement of man could the church exalt God. "Justification by Faith alone" became his grand theme. Though men and women might glimpse God in all his sovereign glory through such events as the church balcony's harmless collapse, they could not comprehend His divine plan and certainly not alter His predetermined intentions for them.

Cruel and condemnatory to modern ears, Jonathan Edwards's dire warnings of doom were met in Northampton and elsewhere with outpourings of joy and tearful conversions. He took note of these "outcries, faintings, and fits" and described them in his *Faithful Narrative of the Surprising Work of God* (1737) as evidence that—good news!—God was at work here in America. Indeed, he proclaimed that the "glorious work of God so often foretold in Scripture...will begin in America," by which he naturally meant New England. Perhaps Edwards's most memorable sermon (in terms of numbers of people who suffered ecstasies of repentance and remorse on hearing it) was the famous *Sinners in the Hand of an Angry God*, delivered at Enfield, Connecticut, in 1741. In response to this terrifying description of the hellfires over which God holds the individual, scores more self-convinced sinners fell to their knees and cried out for salvation.

Edwards's own wife, Sarah, a beautiful and aristocratic (born a Pierrepont) but pious and practical helpmate, with whom he had eleven children, became "exhausted by joy." Some feared that what she had really suffered was a nervous breakdown, not surprising in the face of the tensions engendered in Northampton by the religious fevers. She and Jonathan analyzed her condition on their knees, hand-in-hand, assessing the nature of her experience as a real "affect" of God's mercy (he having written much about the false varieties of affects). Finally she regained sufficient balance to cope with daily affairs. Nonetheless, it seemed to her and others that the town hummed with an excess of excitement—and with disappointment, too, for life's problems continued to seem onerous even after conversion. Furthermore, a "spooky invasion of crows" kept Northampton neighbors on edge.

The religious revivals of the watershed decade of the 1740s coincided with the sense that something particularly American and probably divine was happening to the population, something especially pertinent to those individuals whose spiritual condition had never mattered before. Whereas New England had been suffering through what James Truslow Adams would later call a period of "glacialization"—in which the vivid imagination of original Puritans had been replaced by little more than chillingly correct observances or icy intellectualism—now anxious men cried aloud in public and attention-starved women suffered "fainting fits." In more southerly colonies, too, this widespread emotionalism made headlines as a profound social phenomenon, particularly after the arrival of the noted English evangelist, George Whitefield, in visits of 1739 and 1741 to Georgia and the mid-Atlantic colonies. His success even in rationalistic Boston (where he attracted the greatest crowd the city would see until the time of Daniel Webster) led Old Light ministers to fear that Christianity, by becoming more popular, was being perverted rather than revealed. Indeed, these religious archconservatives asked, What revelation could there be other than the Bible? And who gave these itinerant preachers on the frontier their authority?

Whitefield, though an ordained clergyman in the Anglican faith, and though a colleague of the English Methodists John and Charles Wesley, had broken away to pursue a far more evangelical variety of Protestantism. On his trips to America, he found not only a readier reception to his message on these shores (both in the awakened South and in religiously agitated New Jersey) but also a more profound response than in England. Although he was mocked in some areas for his beetle-browed appearance—being called, among other things, Dr. Squintum—his message was so arousing that the audience frequently stood as one, to follow him to the altar rail. One female writer reported that Whitefield's speech was so "magical" that, upon his pronunciation of the word *Mesopotamia,* one of her friends fainted with emotion. Ultimately, he informed the Wesleys that the revivalism that flourished in America in the 1740s was far different from that in England. It was, he said, a matter not of the church being revitalized as an arbiter of established truth but of the individual being self-realized as a liberated agent. He admired this American style of conversion. Although Harvard issued a "testimony" against him, Whitefield chose to end his years not in England but in Newberry, Massachusetts.

In reaction and confusion, many Old Light Congregational clergy tried to deny that anything was going on at all. Seventy-five percent of them claimed that no traces of revivalism existed in their towns; others said that the reported numbers of converts were greatly exaggerated. Zeroing in on those remarks, revisionists of recent times have attempted to discount eighteenth-century American religiosity. Such revisionists point out, quite accurately, that the very term *Great Awakening* was invented in a later age, in the myth-hungry nineteenth century. But the records of affected witnesses continue to speak louder than the doubts of the skeptics. Ninety ministers met in Boston in July 1743 to testify to "the great work of the revival." They presented the Reverend Charles Chauncy, most doubtful of the city's Old Lights, with a letter attesting to the genuineness of the multitudinous conversions they had witnessed. Contemporary accounts in New England—particularly in hardscrabble areas of the Berkshires, inland Connecticut, and Essex and Middlesex Counties—demonstrate how the evangelical message, with its strange mixture of blood-and-thunder Calvinism and individualistic spiritualism, provided new directions for pre-Revolutionary New Englanders.

Indeed, the revivals and the struggle between Old Lights and New Lights now appear to be parts—vital, spiritual aspects—of a larger, evolutionary whole. For, although the "wondrous facts" of hundreds converted do confirm the reality of Jonathan Edwards's and George Whitefield's Great Awakening, they say nothing about its psychic cause or historic effect. Anglo-American society, having shed its European skin, was then struggling to find its new, multicultural identity—a tremendously complex and differentiated process. For some men and women, the Great Awakening, in fact, did not happen at all; for others, it provided new life.

Even black slaves and native tribesmen were swept up in the revivals. Joseph Park, the minister at Westerly, Rhode Island, recorded that, while "there [had not been] above ten or twelve Indians that used to come to meeting at all, there are now near an Hundred that come very constantly." The stirring of the spirit that could be felt across the colonies—most strongly, perhaps, on the frontier—was not solely a Christian matter or a white matter. Princeton University's Frank Lambert's recently concluded study of the Great Awakening emphasizes that

> At the same time Anglo-Americans were discovering a "Great Awakening," many Indians were finding or inventing their own version. According to one historian,* a cluster of Native Americans in the Susquehanna and Ohio Valleys began in the late 1730s to follow "prophets" who proclaimed the necessity of a new spiritual encounter; but unlike that of the white revivalists, this one was rooted in nativist traditions.

Meanwhile, back in Northampton where Jonathan Edwards continued to contend with Arianism even while accidentally fostering individualism, he was regarded by the gentry as a dangerous anachronism, an unwelcome reminder of the time when Puritan magistrates ruled the roost. Edwards's aloof personality, his minatory intellectualism, even his number of swooning converts, rather than being testaments to his service and God's powers, became social embarrassments. This all-too-famous theologian, so often out of town on preaching errands, was no longer in touch with the leadership of his community—the landed gentlefolk who scorned the spiritually roused country people and their "clownish" enthusiasm. Edwards's vision of the soon-to-come Kingdom of God—wherein the lamb might lie down with the lion and where Jonathan Edwards himself might fulfill his desire to "lie low

---

*Gregory E. Dowd in *A Spirited Resistance: The North American Indian Struggle for Unity, 1745-1815*. Baltimore: Johns Hopkins University Press, 1992.

before God . . . that He might be ALL and that I might be as a little child"—could no longer control the powerful personages of Yankee society. Nor could his interpretation of Christian majesty be expected to calm or conquer the resentful Indians. On the contrary, the Algonquian, in their French-aided frontier actions, now seemed poised to strike once more at New England, in all its disorder.

Fearful of both their religion's lack of control and the Indians' building strengths, Massachusetts Bay authorities decided on the extraordinary move of inviting their exotic allies, the resolute Iroquois, into the capital to put on a show of strength. A Connecticut physician named Alexander Hamilton, having traveled to Boston, happened to witness this bizarre presentation in 1744. He reported how formidable and elegantly dressed the Mohawk sachems appeared as they paraded down the capital's streets. Who could doubt, native or white, that the authorities, able to put on such a show of might, were firmly in charge?

When war with France did break out again briefly in that same year (King George's War, 1745-1748), controversial religious figures like Jonathan Edwards seemed all the more irrelevant to the real issues of society. His kind of saintly leadership was needed no more. And when Fort Massachusetts—fifty miles to the west of Northampton in what would become Williamstown—failed to hold off an Indian force under French command (another Deerfield slaughter!), the wealthy families of the colony's interior valleys determined that they must bolster their defenses against all opposition. A mounting financial crisis that peaked in 1750 convinced them further that they must seize control of the reins of power for themselves.

The THEOLOGIAN in STRATEGIC EXILE

A smashing attack by the French on Charlestown, New Hampshire, farther up the Connecticut River from Deerfield, intensified frontier fears. Added to the spiritual hysteria, the increased tension in Northampton became too much for that community to bear. Uneasy citizens met to talk about ousting Jonathan Edwards from his pulpit. Matters came to a head when the preacher lambasted certain privileged youngsters who had been caught reading a midwives' manual—reading it for something other than its medical advice. Edwards's high-powered sermons against such sinfulness among the youth included barrages against their fathers' well-loved taverns in which he portrayed them as engaged in "tippling and chambering."

Women gossiped about the aristocratic Mrs. Edwards who had been seen wearing a gold chain and locket that her husband had given her even while he preached against show and riches. The final crisis came when Edwards demanded that the rather easygoing church-admission standards instituted by his grandfather be reversed. This was among the basic issues dividing the New Lights from the Old; that is, the more extreme new evangelicals from the exhausted upholders of orthodoxy. Henceforth, after Edwards's retrogressive restrictions were imposed, only the elect—that is, those who had endured a credible conversion experience—were admitted to communion. Thus he and his fellow New Lights revealed themselves as not "new" at all, in the sense of more tolerant, but as throwbacks to the early Puritan extremists.

As onetime friends took sides against new enemies, Northampton's two hundred families fell apart in discord. Rather than calming matters down, the Treaty of Aix-la-Chapelle, which signaled the end of King George's War and peace between England and France, played a further part in unnerving all New Englanders. The Crown, in its imperial wisdom, had decided to return the great Nova Scotia fortress of Louisburg, which had been captured by colonial fishermen and merchants, back into the hands of King Louis and his Algonquian allies. Upland Yankees joined coastal Puritans in seething fury. Scapegoats were needed; when the vote for Jonathan Edwards's removal was held in the spring of 1750, the count was two hundred yea, twenty-three nay. Even the first selectman, who happened to be Edwards's unstable cousin, Joseph Hawley, voted against him (though Hawley later recanted).

Thus at age forty-seven, Jonathan Edwards, the rejected upholder of the Word of God, with ten living children to support, was ushered out into the wilderness. He soon received several invitations from relatively prestigious churches, but none struck him as true challenges or calls from God. On the other hand, the region of westernmost Massachusetts, now known as Berkshire County, was in urgent need of a take-charge leader. There in the wilderness, among those closest to nature, he might be able to demonstrate the immanence of God's Kingdom. Hired to head a promising-sounding community of Algonquian and white settlers on the Housatonic River at Stockbridge, Jonathan Edwards was given a salary that stemmed equally from the Massachusetts legislature and from

London's Society for the Propagation of the Gospel in Foreign Parts.

Yet why would anyone, whether concerned about religious outreach or colonial strategies, view Jonathan Edwards as an auspicious candidate for such an assignment? The expectation remained firm in Christian hearts that, with God in His heaven, a saintly clergyman had the power to make such a community work, even in the face of the French and Indian thrust from the north and west. Indeed, Stockbridge stood at a key point on the New England frontier—where Massachusetts strove to assert its territorial claims against both land-hungry, Dutch-descended New Yorkers and a variety of Indians, including French-allied Algonquian and settler-hating Iroquois. The Iroquois's many years of war against the French had left most of the Five Nations nominally united with the English in the famous Covenant Chain (though they labored to remain as neutral as possible in Europe's recurrent imperialist wars). However, some western Iroquois had concluded by the mid-1700s that the acceptive French empire, with its aggressive program of new forts from Lake Erie south to the Ohio River, offered a better chance for survival than the haughty British.

Although France's seventeenth-century connections with the peoples of America's western lakes and rivers had been more culturally intense than imperially successful, her new king, Louis XV, committed himself to bringing those people and their territories into his Catholic embrace. He forged new alliances with the distant Ojibwa (the most populous of the woodland nations) and the Shawnee and Wyandot (who, like the Huron, had been cruelly punished by the Iroquois), along with the Ottawa and Potawatomi. He also sent one of his most daring officers, Captain Pierre-Joseph Céloron de Blainville, on an epochal voyage of exploration and diplomacy down the Ohio River (*La Belle Rivière*) in 1749. De Blainville traveled all the way to the Miami River and reported back to the king of France not only that the proposed anti-British, anti-Iroquois alliances were feasible but also that sending out Catholic missionaries and building up French forts would be quite acceptable to the western tribes. The beneficent memory of Père de Brébeuf aided the project.

At the very same time—in this moment of supposed peace between the European nations—the British king made a grant of half a million acres of Ohio valley land to a group of Virginia speculators. The acres lay, more precisely, between the Kanawha and Ohio Rivers in territory that the Iroquois claimed was theirs to give away by right of conquest. Functioning with great facility as international diplomats, the Iroquois had also, just a year previously, generously yielded lands not truly theirs when they signed unto Pennsylvania a royal grant for territory belonging to the Delaware. Their collusion with Pennsylvania speculators was a feature of the Treaty of Lancaster (1744), to which the king swiftly gave consent, thanks to the work of John Hanbury, the Quakers' clever agent in London. Having won a solid alliance and great rewards as a result of their illicit giveaway, the Iroquois sachems had paddled home from the Lancaster treaty session with some £1,100 worth of trade goods.

Yet some objected to this cozy, pragmatic alliance. Conrad Weiser, the German-born expert in native languages and trusted frontiersman who served as translator for the colony of Pennsylvania, pointed out candidly that the Delaware, not the Iroquois, were the rightful owners of the trans-Allegheny territories coveted by speculators. The Delaware would from now on justifiably regard themselves as swindled. Weiser could see, on the other hand, that the Iroquois—depleted in population (their number of warriors reduced to twelve hundred from twice that) and lacking in victories (the Ojibwa having hurled them out of Ontario)—were then in such decline (modern historians mark the Iroquois peak at about 1700) that they had to make major moves for their own survival. Authorities in Boston and Albany also protested against the basically illegal maneuvers of the competitive Virginians and Pennsylvanians into Ohio territories, maintaining that their previously existing agreement with the Iroquois, the Albany Treaty of 1722, had limited the western expansion of those colonies to the crest of the Appalachians. The fact that neither speculators nor colonial authorities nor the Crown heeded that restriction led directly to the war that capped all the preceding frontier struggle—the Seven Years War of 1754–60, also known as the French and Indian War (and to some global historians as the first World War).

Thus by the time of Jonathan Edwards's assignment there, Stockbridge, obscure Stockbridge, on the strategic western border of Massachusetts, had assumed a position of some importance for the engaged parties: the imperialistic French and the British, the trade-conscious Iroquois and the Algonquian, and the competitive New England and the mid-Atlantic colonies. Whoever held this frontier might dominate the entire theater of operations. When a band of dislocated Algonquian repeatedly requested a school for their children at Stockbridge back in the 1730s, the Bay Colony's governor and leading churchmen had responded positively. They saw the requests as an opportunity to secure both their secular and their religious domains. Jonathan

Edwards might be the Moses, the creative spirit needed for this occasion; perhaps his vibrant brand of theology, stimulating hearts in the raw Stockbridge community, would shape human-God relationships in the proper manner. As Massachusetts authorities viewed the scene, they may even have hoped that this community, located in a valley stretching north like an arrow toward New France, could provide a base for future military actions. Altogether, Stockbridge represented a bizarre congruence of Christian purpose and colonial policy.

Another question remains: Why did Stockbridge's Algonquian want to entrust their destiny to the heirs of Boston's ironclad Puritan leadership? Stockbridge's native people were actually Mahican, originally lords of the economically and strategically valuable lands in the valley of the Hudson River that stretched from Long Island Sound to Canada. After a century of success in accommodating themselves to changing economic circumstances, they had been both battered by the Mohawk and squeezed between unsympathetic Dutch New Yorkers and advancing New England settlers. Now many sought refuge among their neighbors to the east, the Algonquian Housatonic. Indeed, the westering Yankees tended to call all these Stockbridge people not Mahican but Housatonic.* For along the borderland river of that name, numbers of Mahican and other tribesmen had gathered, breaking old tribal patterns and forming new communities. Even some Iroquois Mohawk joined them, for polyglot settlements of this sort represented

---

*The hospitable Housatonic actually lived farther north (around present-day Pittsfield).

the international way of life forced on a diversity of people by the instability of the frontier.

The so-called Housatonic finally succeeded in getting a favorable proposal from the Massachusetts legislature and the colonial Mission Board in 1734. The official plan envisioned an English-structured Indian settlement with a school, a church, and outspreading farms along the river's meadowlands; it looked like a bold experiment in a strategic location. But unfortunately the plan had at its heart neither the inspired imagination of John Eliot nor the communal sensitivities of the Moravian missionaries who were then settling in Pennsylvania and in nearby New York. Although the Housatonic were granted most of the land in this model town—handsome and arable acres for them "to have and to hold"—a few English inhabitants were invited to join in and lend their talents in the governing process. Thus this was not to be an *Indian* community where pride in their accomplishments and in their (adopted) faith might be worked on and celebrated, but an oddly configured community, in which the Indian families, despite their initial majority, would contend with a minority of English families (whose families grew even faster than their ambitions).

One of those Anglo-American families, as fate would have it, was the Williamses, a colonial dynasty that in previous decades had risen in status among the elite river lords of the Connecticut valley. John Williams had been a lion of his day; now his cousin Ephraim Williams, Sr., commanded most of the attention. Within but a few years of his moving to Stockbridge in 1736, this Williams increased his holdings from the original 150 acres to 400 acres (ultimately acquiring more than 1,500 acres), despite the community's basic law that the white contingent should not gain lands from the Indians by dispossession. Having come to regard Berkshire County as his own fiefdom, Ephraim Williams was by no means pleased to hear of Jonathan Edwards's appointment in 1750.

It happened that Edwards's uncle, John Stoddard (a survivor of the Deerfield Massacre) had been the first to propose a Yankee settlement in strategic Berkshire County in 1722. The so-called engineer of western expansion, this Stoddard had optimistically commented on the "friendliness" of the Algonquian Mahican and had invited them to join in the Albany Conference of that year. But Ephraim Williams, Sr., had fought alongside and befriended certain Mohawk warriors in King George's War; he seemed to have a special place of friendship for the Iroquois. He also spoke out as an ardent New Light. So it was in this town of family antagonisms, racial tensions, and religious expectations that Jonathan Edwards was expected to bring the particular magic of what came to be called the Great Awakening.

When it had originally heard reports of the Stockbridge Indians' desire for a school, the Mission Board hoped to employ someone of undisputed religious authority who, among other functions, would be able to face down secular contenders for power. So it happened that the very first pastor whom the Mission Board had sent to Stockbridge (Jonathan Edwards being the second) was the talented John Sergeant, a Yale graduate and promising linguist. Additionally, Sergeant had been blessed with a pleasing personality and "a beautiful countenance" (which had immediately attracted the attention of Colonel Williams's lissome and strong-willed daughter, Abigail).

He was also, unfortunately, hampered by a maimed left hand and a weak constitution.

Sergeant had immediately asserted himself as the guiding force of the cultural experiment at Stockbridge. Within a few years he had not only set up the school for the Housatonic children (with upward of eighty in attendance) but had instituted farming instruction programs that helped the Stockbridge Indians produce marketable crops. The resident Algonquian had sung his praises; Chief Konkapot and his family were accepted for baptism at the church's font. Hearing this, a number of Mohawk were attracted to come in from the west (perhaps to prevent the Algonquian from controlling this well-funded post). Happy with the young cleric's success, Ephraim Williams, Sr., quickly accepted Sergeant as husband for his daughter. It seemed an excellent match, though it did draw Sergeant into the Williams coterie. Unfortunately, he died in 1749, aged thirty-seven, before his program for Stockbridge could prove itself. Then came Jonathan Edwards, who seemed well positioned to build on Sergeant's success.

The controversial theologian had demonstrated an interest in missions among the Indians many years before, both in his own theoretical work and in his backing of the widely renowned missionary, David Brainerd. The two men seemed inseparably connected. When Edwards had made his initial 1737 announcement that the "Great work of Redemption" was actually taking place in New England, he had included the Indians in his statement that the awakening was "reaching all sorts of people without distinction." And he had included Brainerd's many conversions among the Delaware as additional evidence of the Kingdom's approach.

Published in 1749, just before his expulsion from Northampton, Jonathan Edwards's biography of David Brainerd was
so laudatory of his harvest of native souls in Pennsylvania that,
if Puritans ever hailed saints, they would surely have nominated this young missionary to that heavenly rank. Indeed, to
understand Edwards's attitude toward the Indians—and to
gauge Stockbridge as but one aspect of the Great Awakening's
mixed contribution to the evolution of the American spirit—it
is necessary to step back and review David Brainerd's very rel-
evant accomplishments in New Jersey and Pennsylvania.

The MODEL MISSIONARY MEETS
the INDIAN REFORMER

Brainerd made his final, saintly statement by dying within the
embrace of the Edwards home in 1747. Aged twenty-nine, and
already famous as a kind of hinterland hero, he won yet more
hearts in the role of the pitifully deceased, deeply mourned fi-
ancé of Jerusha Edwards, daughter of Jonathan and Abigail.
Compounding the tragedy of his death, the young missionary's
tuberculosis had infected Jerusha while she nursed him; she
died soon thereafter. Then there was Brainerd's life.

In his short days on earth, Brainerd had been a strangely
appealing man, though characterized by the sort of self-
flagellating self-concern that modern tastes find morbid and
destructive. William James might have commented that the
"soul-sick" aspect of Brainerd's spirit showed him to be a typical, profoundly religious personality, yearning to be at one with
God, even for death, because that would surely lead to God.
Brainerd's story of death and life—advertised by Jonathan Edwards as the "example" of true religion—made such an impres-

sion on the popular mind that his soul-suffering, self-loathing form of spirituality unfortunately became the highest form of *imitatio Christi* for many American Protestants (devout and otherwise), even for those not on the evangelistic wing.

In his earliest days at Yale, Brainerd had developed hopes of following in the tradition of the great revivalists. Such hopes seemed blasted, however, when he was expelled from college because of a remark he had made likening a conservative instructor to a piece of furniture. The expulsion (seemingly the end of all his ministerial aspirations) "broke his heart," as contemporaries remarked. Ever thereafter afflicted with a martyr complex, he spent years of his brief life trying to right himself with the university's "grandees." Partially in reaction to that hasty explusion and to the straight-laced spirit that had caused it, Brainerd's New Light friends, Aaron Burr, Sr., and John Dickinson, founded in 1748 the New Jersey institution that became Princeton University.

Soon after leaving Yale, lay preacher Brainerd received funds and an assignment from a missionary group in Scotland. He took particular interest in "evangelizing the heathen" in Pennsylvania and other colonies where European immigrant groups like the Moravians and German pietists that had been welcomed by Penn were advancing what British Calvinists viewed as the wrong flavor of Christianity. The Scottish Society signed on the impassioned young evangelist with a hefty allowance.

Because of contentions then raging among Penn's heirs and other speculators for land in Pennsylvania, the Scottish society thought it best for Brainerd to delay his work briefly and to study Algonquian with John Sergeant at Stockbridge. That term completed, Brainerd's initial experience as a missionary-in-training occurred in 1742–43 in westernmost Connecticut among the Schagticoke, a mixed group of Algonquian refugees from the previous century's New England persecutions who had put themselves under Iroquois protection (and who would, in subsequent years, vent their anti-English bitterness in an attack on Stockbridge). Brainerd's first real post, however, was across the border in the royal colony of New York. There, at Kaunaurueek, slightly northwest from Stockbridge and eighteen miles south of Albany, he attempted to set up a refugee community and a school with the aid of a translator whose name is transcribed as John Wauwaumpequunnaunt. Preaching two English and two native-language sermons each Sunday, finding the weather ceaselessly grim, and experiencing continuous bouts of ill health, he made a weak impression on the suspicious natives.

Brainerd's unhappy years at Kaunaurueek had occurred in the years of dread when decades of peace on the frontier seemed to be ending in French-induced Indian attacks. With the actual commencement of King George's War (the war in which the Williams family's beloved Fort Massachusetts fell to the enemy)—and with the frightening news that many of the western Indian nations were siding with the French—Brainerd urged the people of his threatened mission to move to the safety of Stockbridge. There, these variegated Algonquian believed they might benefit from the experimental community's openness, if not its sanctity, and from the vocational training offered by the English school.

David Brainerd then went in pursuit of the Scottish Society's main objective: to work among the Delaware of Pennsylvania. As previously mentioned, these were people of an extraordinary heritage, for under their own name of Lenni Lenape ("The Genuine People"), they regarded themselves as the grandfathers of all other Algonquian. That claim rested on their tribal memory of an arduous trek across the entire continent thousands of years before, the narrative having been preserved in haunting memories of ranges surmounted and rivers crossed. It also rested on the antiquity and vitality of their religious rituals, particularly the busk ceremonies (i.e., dancing) around the central, symbolic pole of their longhouse. John Heckewelder, longtime missionary among the Delaware, reported, significantly, that they viewed nature as a great whole, "from which they have not yet ventured to separate themselves." Beyond the sun and moon, the spirits (manitous) that they worshiped were the household gods, Indian corn, and the four directions. From time to time, Cautantowwit (or Kiehtan as the Narragansett also called him) would emerge from their pantheon, standing supreme among others.

As described by the earliest white settlers, the Delaware territory originally stretched from the Hudson River to the Potomac. Once a populous nation of more than twelve thousand people, they had been forced to figure out, during their perennial contests with the Conestoga of the south (called Susquehannock by John Smith) and other Iroquois people to the north, certain defensive techniques for survival. They did not, however, have the power to prevent the Iroquois's duplicitous sale of their lands. Yet they did consider themselves skillful in working with or defending themselves against the peaceful Quaker immigrants; the Delaware had seen to it that the Shackamaxon Treaty of 1682 gave adequate honor to their national integrity. Gentlemanly Governor Penn had enjoyed conversing and walking out with the sagacious Delaware chiefs. He even staged leaping contests among the people, the Quakers taking off their broad-brimmed hats and heavy costumes for the event.

But by 1722 many of the Delaware had concluded that co-existence with the expansive and not consistently honorable European settlers was unfeasible. They began an evacuation of their territories and a westward drift toward the river valleys of Ohio that would continue for the rest of the century. Most heinous of the dispossessions endured by the Delaware was the so-called Walking Purchase of 1737. This extortion was the work of James Logan, the unscrupulous manager of the Penn family properties after the founder's death and the agent responsible for making pacts of mutual interest with the Iroquois. Under the cover of Iroquois protection, he negotiated with the Delaware for a modest piece of land west of the Delaware River, a portion whose western border might be paced off by a man in, say, a day and a half—presumably twenty or thirty miles. But by hiring a crew of three champion hikers to perform maximally for eighteen hours, Logan succeeded in stretching the border from Bristol, Pennsylvania, some fifty-five miles up through the Lehigh Gap, thereby grabbing a tract twelve hundred square miles in extent. From their strongholds in the north, the well-informed Iroquois discerned how the Delaware (whom they regarded as conquered vassals) were selling off chunks of their land and being cheated of much more. The Iroquois decided to make it even more clear that they were in charge of the region and the Delaware should get out of the way.

When the Delaware sought further protection against the English from their self-appointed Iroquois overlords, they were instead banished from their homeland. The cruel and contemptuous words of Iroquois chief Canasatego* to the Delaware chief Sassoon, delivered in July 1742, on the latter's being forced to sign the so-called Great Treaty with the Five Nations in Philadelphia, have come down to us in the orthography of the day:

> You ought to be taken by the Hair of the Head and shaken severely, till you recover your Senses and become sober. . . . How came you to take upon you to sell Land at all: We conquered you; we made Women of you; you know you are Women and can no more sell Land than Women; nor is it fit you should have the Power of selling Lands, since you would abuse it. The Land that you claim is gone through your Guts; you have been furnish'd with Cloaths, Meat and Drink, by the Goods paid you for it, and now you want it again, like Children as you are . . . And for all these Reasons we charge you to remove instantly; we don't give you the Liberty to think about it. You are Women. Take the Advice of a wise Man, and remove immediately.

The Iroquois gave the Delaware only two choices for their new location: one in Wyoming Valley on the northern branch of the Susquehanna River (site of present-day Wilkes-Barre, Pennsylvania), the other farther west at Shamokin, the forks of the Susquehanna (today's Sunbury, Pennsylvania). Before the Delaware's large-scale departure, David Brainerd set up a small mission station at their base on the river of their own name, seeking to serve among those few allowed to remain.

---

*This was the very same Canasatego who had so impressed Benjamin Franklin at the Treaty of Lancaster in 1744.

There, and at another station farther south on the New Jersey side of the Delaware River (Crossweeksung), he began to enjoy some success. Many of the demoralized but unfailingly cordial Delaware, whose own culture was now in tatters, turned to him for assistance—though some reactionary powwows threatened his life with displays of symbolic weapons.

Even as King George's War exploded on the more distant frontiers (1745), an increasing number of Delaware came to hear Brainerd preach. In this effort he needed a new translator, for the Algonquian he had learned among the Mahican was far different from this dialect. He hired a Christian member of the group named Moses Tattamy to be his guide, a man known as much for his fondness for liquor as for his skill at languages. Tattamy had learned English in the course of his employment by the Moravian leader Count Nikolaus Zinzendorf, who had successfully established settlements in eastern Pennsylvania (including Bethlehem) and in New York for his communally minded followers. The Delaware, whose social mode was also communal, found the pacifistic Moravians and their form of re-vivalism particularly congenial—here there were no demands to plow fields in straight lines as the Europeans did or to have your hair cut short as the English did. But now they all, the Christianized Delaware and the simple Moravians as well, were threatened by the blind punishments of war.

With Tattamy's help, Brainerd hosted increasingly large re-vivalistic meetings for his diverse flock. On one fortuitous occasion, his village of ragged refugees discovered three deer readily at hand, as if waiting to be sacrificed for a feast. Brain-erd, in the spirit of the Great Awakening, seized on this as a spe-cial sign of grace. Encouraged, the congregation swiftly grew from a few dozen to sixty or seventy participants. The Delaware's response to Brainerd's fervid message went from a general recognition of the mutual, human passion for repentance to tearful breakdowns and specific confessions. Equally important to Brainerd, there was a noticeable change in the native peoples' behavior patterns, as liquor was forsworn and devil worship abandoned. Even some of the stolid Quakers, who had come to observe the meetings, found themselves on their knees, seeking God's unknowable, unearnable mercy.

So it happened that the Great Awakening arrived on the New Jersey frontier and at the forks of the Delaware River. By the end of Brainerd's service there, he had swayed a bit from strict Calvinism, paying heed to his congregation's own traditions and adapting the Bible's message to their needs. "What amazing things God has wrought!" Brainerd exclaimed. By then, as he reported the glorious facts, forty-seven people had been baptized (twenty-three adults and four children, two of whom were Tattamy's); he even succeeded in converting a powwow. The total who regularly flocked to his outdoor meetings—both whites and natives—eventually exceeded one hundred. But, much like John Eliot in a different time and place, Brainerd was forced to recognize that many neighboring farm families were upset by the prospect of a biracial citizenry. It was necessary for this missionary to move on to another frontier community.

Ranging farther west, Brainerd was tortured by crippling sinus headaches, bloody coughing spells, and near starvation. Forced so often to sleep in the wilderness, with but little protection against the rains, he was frequently too weak or fevered to go on. But on he went. In an attempt to explain his determination to proceed with his mission, he once wrote, "[I] long and love to be a pilgrim, and want grace to imitate the life, labors, and sufferings of St. Paul among the heathen." Yet in other places he writes more with disgust than with sympathy for the pagans and their "dancing and hallooing," apparently tired of trying to wean them away from their own difficult-to-comprehend religion.

Brainerd admitted, however, that the morality witnessed on more than one occasion among the Algonquian seemed superior to that of the white settlers, particularly to that of the renegades then flocking from famine-stricken Europe to America in response to Pennsylvania's come-one-and-all policies. In his journals he reported a sachem's derogation of the white man's rectitude, word for word:

> The Christians [the sachem said] would lie, steal, and drink, worse than the Indians. It was they first taught the Indians to be drunk; and they stole from one another, to that degree, that their rulers were obliged to hang them for it, and that was not sufficient to deter others from the like practice. But the Indians, he added, were none of them ever hanged for stealing, and yet they did not [ever] steal half so much; and he supposed that if the Indians should have become Christians, they would then be as bad as these. And here upon he said, they would live as their forefathers lived, and go where their fathers were when they died.

Confronted by such not unreasonable attitudes, Brainerd realized that he faced an uphill battle as a Christian proselytizer and as an ambassador of Anglo-America. When the missionary took his first journey farther west to the forks of the Susquehanna, he heard without surprise or affront the tirade of the local chief, who said Brainerd really had no right to implant a post in that sensitive area. That chief spoke with authority and with broad knowledge of the intercultural and international situation of which David Brainerd's work was but one small and potentially dangerous part. This wise man, named Shikellamy, held a position nominally inferior to Sassoon's (the Delaware whose back had borne the insults hurled by Canasatego), but actually possessed more authority. Sassoon suffered from numerous illnesses, including alcoholism, whereas the younger and lower ranked Shikellamy had been selected by the Iroquois overlords to be their man at Shamokin, one of the most important trade and information centers in eastern North America. To this busy place at the river forks came preachers and agents of varying rank and credibility. Brainerd, who had finally been ordained in 1744 (Jonathan Edwards having joyfully granted his approval of the event), understood that he, though a humble missionary, might also be regarded as something of an official personage.

Although David Brainerd's personal call, as he perceived it, came from heavenly offices, his sustaining salary and his earthly orders came from British colonial interests. Nor was the Native American he now faced a mere village headman. Just a year after Brainerd's ordination, Shikellamy had been promoted to executive deputy of the Grand Council of the Iroquois Six Nations. Thought to have originally been an Oneida chieftain (or possibly a Frenchman captured and adopted by the Oneida in his youth), he had been baptized by a Jesuit priest in Canada. Count Zinzendorf is quoted as having said of Shikellamy: "He was truly an excellent and good man, possessed of many noble qualities of mind . . . laying claims to refinement and intelligence."

Significantly, since taking over at Shamokin in 1728, he had become a close friend and colleague of Pennsylvania's colonial
agent, Conrad Weiser, who had also been adopted into one of
the Iroquois nations. With Weiser he succeeded in working out
most of the treaties and the agreements that passed for law and
order on this section of the American frontier.

Given the kind of adept and flexible, if not exactly idealistic, control that he exercised over Shamokin's mixed-race,
mixed-religion populace, Shikellamy represented one species of
hope for peace and equity (Hiawatha's ancient concepts) in the
mid-eighteenth-century borderland. Learning of Brainerd's approach and purpose, he called for a gathering of the Delaware,
convened in his substantial house, to discuss the missionary's intentions. When Brainerd informed them that, operating under the
governor's orders, he planned to stay in Shamokin for two years
and to build a church there, Shikellamy concluded that the time
had come to correct the young man's impression of the situation.

In words that reminded hearers of the sanctified Two-row
Wampum Belt (mentioned in chapter 3) and later recorded by a
contemporary Moravian missionary, Shikellamy explained,

> We are Indians, and don't wish to be transformed into
> white men. The English are our Brethren, but we never
> promised to become what they are. As little as we desire
> the preacher to become an Indian, so little ought he to de-
> sire the Indians to become preachers. He should *not* build
> a house here.

For the sake of both people, it seemed clear to this boss of
the borderlands that religion was something too culturally particular and special to be spread lightly and loosely over the land,

Miles Standish and Hobomock The 1620 treaty between the Pilgrims and Chief Massasoit's Wampanoags worked well for both people, in part because of their religious steadfastness and in part because of their mutual, pragmatic dependency. In this painting by J. E. Baker, the Wampanoag leader Hobomock is seen guiding Miles Standish and an armed force of Pilgrim "Saints" to an attack on the rival colony of Wessagusset (now Weymouth, Mass.). *Library of Congress*

Discovery Dance The dancers in this George Catlin painting of the 1830s are members of the Sac and Fox nations on the Illinois frontier who are performing an ancient ritual common to many Native American tribes. Their "discovery dance," an expression of religious belief and communion with nature, mimics hunters spying game or enemies and reporting their finds to the village. *Smithsonian American Art Museum, Washington, D.C./Art Resource, N.Y.*

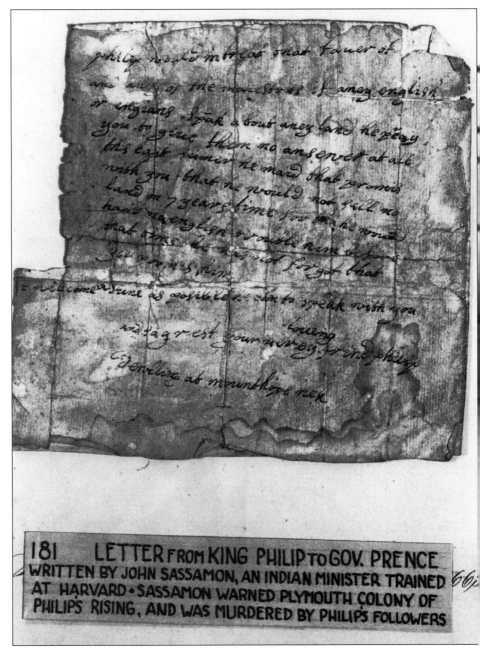

Sassamon's Letter Written a decade before King Philip's War (1675–78), this letter from Philip to Plymouth's assistant governor, William Prence, was crafted and penned by Christian convert John Sassamon, who entreats the English on Philip's behalf not to deal with any other parties in the critical issue of land sales. *The Pilgrim Society, Plymouth, Mass.*

Eliot Preaching This depiction of John Eliot preaching to Chief Waban and his Massachusett people is a typically romantic, nineteenth-century re-creation, showing a handsomely headdressed chief and attentive, robust villagers. Yet the depiction is accurate in one detail: it portrays the Apostle to the Indians wearing not the black robes or clerical collar of a preacher but the rough trousers and open shirt of a woodsman. *Natick Historical Society, Mass.*

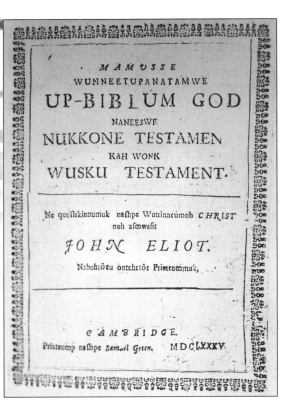

Eliot's Bible Not only the first Bible to be printed in a Native American language but also the first Bible in any language to be published in the New World, John Eliot's translation represented a truly prodigious effort both by Eliot and by several native colleagues. Completed in 1663, *Up-Biblum* was revised for two later printings; the title page of the 1685 edition is shown here. *The Pilgrim Society, Plymouth, Mass.*

Moravians Baptizing Delawares When memorializing the mid-eighteenth-century baptism of three Delaware and Mahican converts, an unknown French artist turned what was surely a dramatic meeting of different peoples into this static tableau. As shown here, the male members of the Moravian community stand on one side of those being baptized; the women (one carrying a child) on the other. At rear are graduates from the respective Indian nations. *Moravian Archives, Bethlehem, Pa.*

Jonathan and Sarah Edwards While serving as master of the Indian mission school in Stockbridge, Massachusetts, in the 1750s, Jonathan Edwards posed for the upcountry artist Joseph Badger, a sometime glazier and sign painter. The portrait (at left) shows undying fire in the famous theologian's eyes but gives no hint of his metaphysical sympathy for Native spiritual themes. An anonymous and even less tutored artist portrayed Edwards's much loved and reportedly beautiful wife, Sarah Pierrepont Edwards (at right), reflecting only her often-noted hauteur. *Yale University Art Gallery and Stockbridge Library Association*

Samson Occom America's greatest Native American preacher of the Christian (Calvinist) Gospel is shown here not in the pulpit but in a leafy bower, as painted by Nathaniel Smibert, America's most skillful early portraitist. The Mohegan preacher, trained by the ambitious Eleazer Wheelock for service on the racially fraught frontier, served there in the era of Pontiac's War. *Bowdoin College Museum of Art, Brunswick, Maine, bequest of the Honorable James Bowdoin III*

Joseph Brant The Mohawk warrior Joseph Brant, captured by the portraitist Gilbert Stuart in 1786—that is, after Brant had failed in his Revolutionary War attempts to consolidate the Iroquois under the British flag and the Anglican faith—continues to look undaunted and magnificent on canvas. He was at this time making his second appearance in England, where to his regret he could not secure a meaningful commitment from the Crown to the cause of Indian independence from the U.S. *New York State Historical Association, Cooperstown, N.Y.*

Sir William's Certificate Standing beneath an Iroquois religious icon, the Tree of Peace, a British official is seen at the top of this certificate presenting a weighty medal to a Native American ally. Designed by Sir William Johnson, Great Britain's Superintendent for Indian Affairs (and Joseph Brant's brother-in-law), the certificate and its inset illustration represent his hope for peaceful brotherhood and uninterrupted trade on the imperial frontier. *Collection of the New York Historical Society*

Treaty of Fort Stanwix The Treaty of Fort Stanwix (1784) marked the end of the Revolution and the war on the Six Nations (the Haudenosaunee). The treaty established peace, but New York state's constant abrogations of it led to the significant conference at Canandaigua ten years later. *Buffalo and Erie County Historical Society*

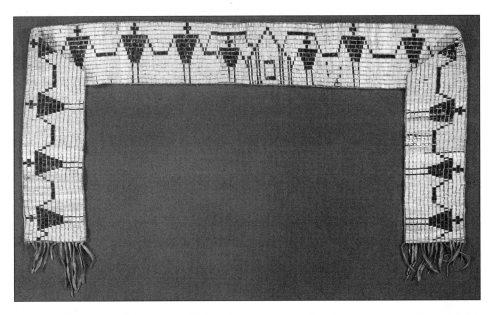

Washington's Covenant Belt This historic, six-foot-long wampum belt, called the George Washington Covenant Belt, was created to commemorate the signing of the treaty of Canandaigua (1794). It shows the Thirteen Fires, original states of the U.S., linked to two small figures standing on both sides of the Haudenosaunee council house. The figures represent either the keepers of the Haudenosaunee's eastern and western doors or George Washington and the council house's traditional speaker, Tadodaho. *Courtesy of Chief Irving Powless, Jr., Onondaga Nation, and New York State Museum, Albany, N.Y.*

Open Door Tecumseh's brother, The Prophet (also known as Tenskwatawa, "The Open Door"), sat for the westward roaming George Catlin in 1830. Half blind and never a match for his superbly physical brother, Tenskwatawa had wielded tremendous power as a spiritual force. But here, wreathed in sacred beads and clutching a holy "fire stick" against his people's enemies, he faces the end of his days in the reduced role of chief of a lesser Shawnee village. *Smithsonian American Art Museum, Washington, D.C./Art Resource, N.Y.*

Tecumseh's Death After his defeat of Tecumseh's and The Prophet's confederated forces at Tippecanoe, General William Henry Harrison faced the onslaught of British and Indian allies in the War of 1812. Upon the British victory at Detroit, Tecumseh rode into that city in triumph. But, following the Americans' successful defense of Fort Meigs (May 1813), Harrison pursued the enemy allies into Canada. On the Thames River in October 1813, General William Henry Harrison's curiously hatted Kentucky militia (at right) hunted down and killed Tecumseh, thus ending all hopes for the separate, religion-based Indian nation of which the chief had dreamed. *Ohio Historical Society*

Red Jacket's Medal When the great Seneca orator Red Jacket visited Washington, D.C., in 1792, President George Washington presented him with this silver medal. The scene etched into it is heavy with symbolism: an archetypal Indian, having discarded his war ax, extends the pipe of peace to a benign president; in the background a shining future opens up to the agriculturally productive natives. Red Jacket wore the medal on grand occasions for the rest of his life, trusting that (in an Iroquois metaphor) any imperfection in the relationship between the U.S. and Native American nations could be removed as easily as tarnish from the medal's surface. *Buffalo and Erie County Historical Society*

like pollen in the spring. Furthermore, to build such a mission house as the one Brainerd had in mind was the same as erecting a fort from whose tower waved a flag of conquest. The Iroquois would not tolerate it.

Understanding if not agreeing with the message, Brainerd withdrew. He traveled farther down the Susquehanna (which would become known as the River of Missionaries), hoping to find another downriver community where his mission might prosper. At length he came to the river's junction with the Juniata River, where a collection of wandering tribesmen (including Shawnee and additional, displaced Delaware) was attempting to survive amid frontier pressures. There, near the present city of Duncannon, he encountered yet another group of displaced Algonquian, these the Nanticoke, who had a distinctive reputation for witchcraft and for ceremonially tending to the remains and spiritual legacies of their ancestors. "They appeared friendly," Brainerd wrote later, "and gave me encouragement to come and see them again."

It was also there, at Juniata Junction in 1745, that Brainerd met a charismatic Indian figure known only as the Reformer. Remarkable in himself, the Reformer was a further demonstration of how, in the era of the Great Awakening, spirituality among historic Indians and white frontiersmen expressed itself through personalities preaching ancient religious themes. The appearance of this latter-day John the Baptist foreshadowed other nativistic visionaries. As author David Wynbeek points out in his biography, *Beloved Yankee,* "Brainerd's succinct account [of the meeting] is one of the earliest records of a [native] religious reformer—or, as Brainerd described him, 'a restorer of what he supposed was the ancient religion of the Indians.'"

On that day in a lodge at Juniata Junction when the excited fellow came dancing toward Brainerd, furiously rattling corn within a dry tortoise shell on a wooden handle, the missionary shrank back, though he knew that this was a test of some sort and that he had to find a way to counter the shaman. Brainerd wrote,

> His appearance and gestures were so prodigiously frightful that no one should have imagined that he could be human. Every part of his body, including his fingers, was covered by his "pontifical garb" [a great coat of undressed boar skins that reached his toes, buckskin stockings, and a half black, half tawny wooden face], with an extravagant mouth, cut very much awry.

No creature Brainerd had ever witnessed appeared as frightful, "or so near akin to what is usually imagined of *infernal powers.*"

Yet, when the dancing within the ceremonial lodge ceased— the earthen floor having been pounded "almost as hard as a rock" from the repeated stompings of previous dancers—the Reformer seemed willing to listen to Brainerd's gentle words. While tolerating some parts of Christianity as set forth by Brainerd, he violently rejected some other parts. "He told me," Brainerd recorded in his journal, "that God had taught him his religion and that he would never turn from it, but wanted to find some that would join heartily with him in it; for the Indians, he said, were grown very degenerate and corrupt."

Brainerd could not help being impressed by the zealous yet courteous Reformer. In his passion to oppose his fellow Indians' alcoholic binges and to help them differentiate between good and evil, the shaman seemed both naturally moral and truly inspired. "It was manifest," Brainerd observed, "that he had a set of religious notions that he had looked into *for himself*, and not taken for *granted* upon bare tradition." Many of the Reformer's tenets were set forth with an accompanying phrase, "So God has taught me." He believed, for example, that all departed souls went southward, the good souls being admitted there into a beautiful town that sounded quite heavenly in its high walls and exclusivity. "I must say," Brainerd concluded, "there was something in his temper and disposition that looked more like true religion than anything I ever observed amongst other heathens."

The unique frontier civilization that was aborning here, with its wise Shikellamy and its inspired, pantheistic Reformer—as well as with its native refugees and white settlers and its crooked traders and evangelistic missionaries—might seem to be America-in-the-making. Although Eliot's praying villages and native saints had not quite led to an accommodating, biracial civilization in southeastern Massachusetts, might it not happen that here, in these greening valleys of the mid-Atlantic region, a secure and religiously diverse society could be built? Unfortunately, despite the fact that such a society was approved by both the ruling Iroquois on the Susquehanna and the European powers reigning in Philadelphia and Quebec, that prospect was severely jeopardized in the years of Brainerd's visits.

All too soon, two swirling, interconnected wars would break out, on a wide front. In one, the westward-moving Delaware would be assaulted by the Iroquois-allied Shawnee; in the other, additional pressure from French in the west (reflecting King

Louis's renewed determination to hold transmontane North America) would provoke additional contests with the British. When Brainerd returned from Crossweeksung for a second visit among the religiously inclined Nanticoke, their Reformer had disappeared. The combined nativist and Christian Great Awakening, having flamed here briefly, was quenched by other forces.

But on a subsequent visit to Shamokin in August 1746, Brainerd found Shikellamy holding firm in his mind and his faith even as others deviated toward Christianity. With the northeast in tumult and with an increasing number of people succumbing to an illness known as "the flux," Brainerd urged the faithful Delaware to move not west but east, to find greater security among established communities of converts on their home river. He felt that the Scotch-Irish churches on the New Jersey frontier were fully charged with the same brand of fiery Calvinism that he admired, ready to hear the confessions of all comers to the tents of the Great Awakening. The original, Irish-born founder of New Jersey's Presbyterian churches— that historic figure, William Tennent—had done his part to rattle the structure of Old Light orthodoxy by setting up a "Log College" for the training of dynamic New Light preachers at Neshaminy on the banks of the Delaware River in 1726. His place was now being taken by his son, Gilbert (later known as Son of Thunder), who became a strong friend of George Whitefield and who joined with New England's preachers to develop the main thrust of America's distinctively Protestant culture.

After sickly David Brainerd's reluctant departure from New Jersey and withdrawal to the north, it happened that Shikellamy himself, desiring further conversations with his Moravian friends, moved to Bethlehem for additional instruction. There he died a Christian, the records show, on December 6, 1748 (Moravian calendar). By the time Brainerd reached Northampton for a reunion with his beloved Jerusha Edwards in the springtime of 1747, the missionary recognized that he was mortally ill. Tuberculosis rampaged through his chest; malnourished and exhausted from his wilderness travels, he counted on no miracle. Yet he and his host Jonathan Edwards felt strongly that God supported them: When Brainerd's brother John arrived with news from New Jersey that the communities of converts there were flourishing, the mood in Stockbridge was joyous. Additional evidence had been given that God's Kingdom was at hand! Within a few months, the young man expired, and within a few years Jonathan Edwards was expelled from Northampton to western Massachusetts.

By then, however, Edwards's book on Brainerd's career had become so popular that Americans came to believe that they, like the dauntless, backcountry missionary, could accomplish great works for God and themselves even in the tangled wilderness, and even among the Indians. In those sufferings they would triumph, not in claiming territory for any government but in demonstrating that the care of all human souls was the proper function of the pilgrim missionary. What further proof was necessary beyond Brainerd's life? Yet ironically, the struggling religious communities in which David Brainerd had worked so ardently in the cause of brotherhood were first steps not toward new Jerusalems, but toward mixed-purpose villages that would be destroyed with a fury resembling that unleashed against Père de Brébeuf's mission stations. Perhaps something was lacking, perhaps something was too short-lived in the up-beat emotionalism of the Great Awakening. Perhaps those ex-cited expressions of faith were too erratic to be a major factor either in implanting God's Kingdom or in building an inte-grated continental civilization.

The ULTIMATE VICTORY

In Stockbridge Jonathan Edwards, though frustrated by the powerful Williams clan, attempted to exert a powerful, binding, and healing influence—though he considered himself "fitted for no other business but study." Finding that the fifty-odd chil-dren in the intercultural school were all learning by rote (that being the educational style of the time), whether they spoke English or not, he insisted that schoolmaster Timothy Wood-bridge see to it that all of them be familiar with the meaning of the words. Furthermore, noting that the Indian girls were left out of the instruction process, he brought them into the school, thereby instituting a radical program of coordinated education of both sexes.

Because of his inspirational and integrationist work among Indian families (that is, because of his apparent success in turn-ing the Stockbridge experiment into a reality), he was sum-moned to Albany in 1751 for a rally that British colonial officials had called for regional support against the French. Edwards's low-level function was to aid discussions about how to swing both the Algonquian and Iroquois to the British cause. When in Albany, he talked with William Johnson, the physically impres-sive, Irish-born adventurer who had staked out a fur empire for himself along the Mohawk River, had married a Mohawk, and had won royal thanks for his marshaling of Mohawk forces at the time of King George's War. The two men spoke at length, most concentrated on how to keep the Indians from straying away from "British interests." Whatever imperialistic sentiments Edwards may have felt, he deeply dreaded the prospect of the French gaining the allegiance of the borderland Indians—for, as he saw relations between heaven and earth, such a turn would show God's disfavor toward the Anglo-American colonists.

Despite their enormous differences, William Johnson and Jonathan Edwards (the former an Anglican and perpetual royalist, the latter a Calvinist and neo-American) both saw the Indians, the well-schooled and properly non-Catholic Indians, as key in the early 1750s to successful defense against the popish French. The two men lent their mutual talents to the writing of a treaty (replaceable, of course) that would accomplish that purpose by giving gifts, guaranteeing lands, and promising everlasting support. The discussions were held a bare three years before the more famous Albany Conference of 1754, at which Benjamin Franklin did what he could to bring the individualistic English colonies into a united American front against the French and into harmony with the Indians, particularly the Iroquois.

Edwards even volunteered to learn Mohawk in order to aid British strategy as a diplomatic agent. (Some commentators see this as a move on his part to leave Stockbridge for greener pastures and to slip free of the Williams clan's reins.) Yet, despite his willingness to defend the frontier in the British king's name and even to serve in harness with heavy-handed William

Johnson in the then looming, cataclysmic war for the continent, he differed with British policies in one important area:
He felt that the Crown should *not* send professional armies to
the frontier. Instead, Britain should let the Americans take
care of the war with their own colonial militias and proven Indian allies, the king supplying arms and matériel from his
empire's vast wealth. Johnson, who knew to what extent the
French had committed themselves to the building of frontier
fortresses and to consolidating their American holdings, believed strongly to the contrary. In no way should the British
be Americanized—either in changing their fighting techniques
or in yielding command to the individualistic, independent-
minded, crazily religious colonials and their supposedly loyal
Indian allies.

Before the outbreak of the war (1754), Jonathan Edwards
had time enough to win another kind of battle, the power
struggle with the Williamses. Abigail Williams Sergeant, widow
of Stockbridge's competent first missionary, had married the
colony's Indian agent, Joseph Dwight. Eager to claim the monies
that were coming into the school for the education of Indian
boys, Dwight agreed with his wife's plan that she head up a
school for Indian girls that would be equal with the boys' day
and boarding schools. It mattered little that Abigail had no
competence for such an assignment. Becoming aware of her
mismanagement, Jonathan Edwards remarked, "It is enough to
make me sick." The theologian then swung, rather uncharac-
teristically, into action, writing a series of public pamphlets that
pointedly accused the Williamses of using the charity funds for
their own purposes.

Edwards knew that Stockbridge—with its day and boarding schools of fifty-five Indian children and its church congregation of forty-two Housatonic and several white families—
was a crucial lynchpin for any colonial society in which Indians
might have a distinctive part. In such a community as Stockbridge, they and their children could not only learn English and
acquire vocational skills that would aid their survival, but they
could also find a new religious base for their disrupted lives.
With Brainerd as his model, Edwards saw that the Indians truly
needed new inspiration and that their distinctive life ways deserved toleration. Furthermore, he recognized that the community's dislocated Indians were totally justified in complaining
that Abigail Williams Sergeant Dwight was excessively unkind,
untrained, and unfit; only three girls of the Stockbridge Indians
and one newly arrived Mohawk signed up for the grand lady's
offered instruction.

Even as Edwards studied the situation and wrote his persua-
sive pamphlets, he failed to appreciate that the additional Mohawk who had come to Stockbridge for schooling (totaling one
hundred, many of them children of veterans who had fought
beside Ephraim Williams, Sr.) represented a power play of another sort. They embodied a conscious, political effort by the
Iroquois to take power away from both the resident Algonquian
and the English colonists.

That aggressive move unfortunately contributed to the
trouble within the Stockbridge boys' boarding school. One of
two hostile factions was headed by Gideon Hawley, an enthusiastic and imaginative Yale graduate who had been sent out
from Boston to instruct the Iroquois (Mohawk and Oneida); the

other was led by an old and intemperate and nearly illiterate war veteran named Martin Kellog, a factotum of the Williams clan.* Seeing the collapse of the school and sensing this struggle (as well as Kellog's incompetence), many Housatonic withdrew their children from instruction. Leading Stockbridge Indians protested to the provincial government, some journeying to Boston to present their complaints about the inadequacies of the school. The whole divisive matter was finally resolved when the school's English backer, Isaac Hollis, decided to heed the Indian objections and channel his money only through the hands of Jonathan Edwards.

In the struggle for colonial and church funds, Edwards clashed not only with Joseph Dwight, who showed where he stood in the matter of interracial harmony by condoning Captain Williams's landgrabs. Not only did he frostily disapprove of Edwards's unwillingness to bow before the owners of property, he also supported the anti-Indian attitudes of a friend who had slapped a Mohawk child on the cheek. Additionally, Dwight condoned the arrogance of Captain Ephraim Williams, Jr., Abigail's widely traveled and continentally mannered brother, who publicly called the theologian a "very great bigot." When Edwards appeared to be winning the feud, young Williams dropped a provision from his will that would have given the In-

---

*This Indian-oriented interpretation, suggested by the work of Professor Kevin Sweeney of Amherst College, gives new depth and importance to what had been previously seen as merely a Hatfields-and-McCoys feud between two white, colonial factions. It demonstrates that the Iroquois and Algonquian still regarded themselves and their future life in communities along the rivers as what the frontier was all about, even as empires clashed.

dian school more funding. Irrelevant to this story (but otherwise interesting enough), those funds, after Williams's death in battle at Crown Point, were used for the endowment of Williams College.

Meanwhile Ephraim Williams, Sr., in a spasm of dementia, made a manic bid for total control by trying to buy up (or burn down) all the properties in the community. When that approach failed and rumors of arson spread, colonial authorities came down on the side of the respectable, resident pastor. By then it was all too clear, however, that the English leaders, clergy as well as lay, had made a total disaster of Stockbridge, though it had once been so promising a demonstration that Indians and white colonials could live and pray together.

During many of these turbulent midcentury years before the French and Indian War, peace had been tenuously preserved not only by well-intentioned religionists struggling to hold contending cultures together on the frontier but also by the collaboration of merchants in Montreal and Albany. Together they strove to keep the beaver pelts coming in from distant lakes and the processed furs shipping out to Europe on deep-burdened freighters. This sacrosanct business required both effective alliances with the native people (hunters and go-betweens alike) and harmonious relations between New France and the British colonies, particularly New York and Pennsylvania. Whatever it was that kings ordered as sporadic demonstrations of their sovereignty, generals and admirals had to obey. But between those spasms, merchants ruled, as did their desires to keep peace preserved and trade moving. They saw to it that the continentally important Albany Conference of 1754 was convened in the spirit of pragmatism. Quaker legislators from Pennsylvania,

Puritan descendants from Massachusetts, and Iroquois accompanied by shamans arrived in Albany full of the same mercantile ambition. Only the individualistic rovers from Virginia seemed bent on troublesome ventures, their eyes not on the business at hand but on prospects beyond the Appalachians.

Whether the trans-Allegheny West was ruled by kings or merchants or even parsons, the speculators of Pennsylvania had no intention of being excluded. They would exercise whatever wilderness wisdom they possessed to win their points. After the 1744 Treaty of Lancaster (which had confirmed their partnership with the Iroquois), a compliant, Christianized sachem named Tedyuskung had been among those few Delaware allowed to stay in his native territory by the Iroquois-Pennsylvania power brokers. He easily slipped into the role of a passe-partout between the eastern and western Delaware, something of a Sassamon-like figure—and thus made himself an ambiguous factor on the frontier as antagonisms between the French and English grew progressively more tense in the mid-1750s. Though definitely no missionary, he was the true product of the Great Awakening's raw frontier communities, working ardently for and benefiting much from peace and racial cooperation in the borderlands. So did the residual Quakers and variegated newcomers of Pennsylvania favor peace, preferring to turn blind eyes to French fort builders along the Ohio. It was not possible to hold that peaceable posture for long, however. All too soon the notoriously aggressive adventures of Virginia landowners like George Washington caused a fracas on the frontier that required a backup from royal forces.

Then came terrible news: A combined army of seven hundred Virginia militia, two hundred Iroquois guides, and fourteen hundred British regulars, headed by the so-called Bulldog, General Edward Braddock, had been crushed by the French at Fort Duquesne (Pittsburgh). Although Braddock's troops had greatly outnumbered those in the French garrison, and although the general seemed on the road to success when he hacked a European-style highway through the wilderness for his mighty transports, he foolishly heeded the suggestion of an aide-de-camp (the above-mentioned Washington) to force combat on the French with a small attack group.

Not usually reported in accounts of the ensuing disaster is clarification of how the French, despite the terrifying rumors of the size and might of Braddock's army, kept great numbers of Indians of a variety of nations fighting on their side. The explanation lies partly in the creativity of a spiritually attuned French officer, Daniel de Beaujeu. He rallied the natives on the eve of battle, leading them in rousing war songs, and reminding them of the mysterious unity of their wilderness brotherhood. To a man, they responded to his leadership, joining the French in an inventive defense against the on-marching British. Braddock's regulars, surprised by an eight-hundred-man French and Indian ambush, had no time to form and fight in the only style of battle they had been trained for. Routed, losing hundreds more in their flight, they surrendered their scalps to the knives of the French-commanded Algonquian and their displaced Delaware colleagues.

The carefully constructed Albany Conference—originally such a bold, all-American conception—fell apart in despair and terror when the news of Braddock's destruction spread among the delegates. The Delaware, remembering all the sins committed against them by Pennsylvania land-grabbers and encouraged

in their fury, loosed a terrible revenge through the western settlements. Yet the British saw that if the Delaware and other Algonquian could be turned around, these Indians might be the
key to an eventual defeat of the French. It was a time for Loyalists and Christians of all stripes to be enlisted, once again, in
the cause of empire. It was a time to remind the Delaware of
the cooperative policies of William Penn and of the caregiving
Moravians. Such converted and steadfast Native Americans as
Tedyuskung were needed. This was the urgent message that arrived on his doorstep early in 1758—which was, for the British,
three desperate and losing years into the French and Indian
War—delivered by Conrad Weiser, the adopted Iroquois and
friend of Shikellamy who had served for decades as the colony's
wiliest negotiator. Talking earnestly with Tedyuskung and
learning from him who were the most powerful and amenable
chiefs among the western Delaware, Weiser selected a Moravian missionary named Christian Post to head out for a conference with those named chiefs. This young man's first task
would be to promote the list of promises made by Pennsylvania's governor and by Tedyuskung (to the effect that all previous land thefts would be returned to the exiled Delaware if they
would assume a neutral posture). Then, after what was expected to be the grand British victory, the Delaware would be
able to return as welcomed citizens to their native valley. That
spiel memorized, Christian Post headed off on foot through the
hostile forests and over the snowy passes to make a plea that
was, in fact, one of the most vital petitions in the history of
North American conquest.

Mission accomplished, Post returned to the Indian council

at Easton, Pennsylvania, in October 1759. The next month Fort
Duquesne fell to a large English force headed by General John
Forbes—a direct result of the extraordinary lack of supporting
Indians (most notably, Delaware) on whom the French had
hoped to rely. This key event in the French and Indian War is
rarely credited, as it deserves to be, to Tedyuskung's Christian
loyalties and to his skillfulness in identifying the crucial religious and political figures among the western Delaware who
needed to be wooed by Post. It should also be marked as yet
another occasion in which desperate colonial Americans saved
their skins by depending on native cultural structures.

Jonathan Edwards, who spent the war peacefully in gar-
risoned Stockbridge (his position having become a sinecure),
benefited from native culture in those years in an entirely different way. He and his children learned another side of God's Kingdom in America, its natural beauty, which they explored on long
walks with Housatonic friends as well as by means of instruction
from schoolmaster Gideon Hawley. That extraordinarily gifted
linguist and naturalist (who left Stockbridge in 1753 to serve
elsewhere on the frontier before going on to the church at Mashpee) delighted in telling the Edwards family the names and qualities of the native plants, a numinous experience for all. Later, he
would take young Jonathan Edwards, Jr., under his wing and
give him the knowledge of Indian languages that allowed the
boy to grow into one of America's first philologists, as well as
founder of Union College in Schenectady.

As a result of this exposure (one would not dare to call it a
conversion), Jonathan Edwards's sermons to his still devoted
flock became increasingly nature-rich in their imagery and

forgiving in their theology. Scholars* now are finding in the writings of his later Stockbridge years not only the mellowing of a condemnatory mind but also the subtle influence of the Indians among whom he lived—people he regarded no longer as "beasts" but as younger siblings. He would teach the Stockbridge Indians the biblical story of the creation, using adapted images; he spoke, like David Brainerd among his Indians, not of the rage of God but the pity of Christ, how it blessed the hearts of innocent believers. In some paragraphs, he sounded as if humankind might even regenerate itself, meriting an easement of God's fury—a position approaching that of the once despised Arminians. Perhaps this was the ultimate victory: New England's greatest philosopher had found room in his spiritual kingdom for some truly American considerations, learned directly from the source.

Edwards did go on to remind the Indians that they should not indulge in the worship of "the sun, moon, or stars, nor of images of saints, nor the Virgin Mary, nor serpents or beasts." Yet he used his harshest language not on the "devilish" shamans of the forest but on the Deists and those liberal Protestants who spoke of human sufficiency. In the contemporary trends among his fellow Anglo-Americans (for example, those who opened a

---

*See, for example, Gerald R. McDermott's essay in *The New England Quarterly*, Vol. LXXII (Number 4), December, 1999, in which he (associate professor of religion at Roanoke College) refers to Edwards's "reconsideration of traditional understandings of the limits of grace." McDermott's final words on Edwards's change of heart: "In that journey, he allowed himself to be accompanied, even influenced, by the Indians he not only taught but chose to serve."

tavern in Great Barrington), he found continuing evidence of man's sinfulness, few signs of God's destructiveness. Still an heir of Puritan judgments, Jonathan Edwards* approved when the governor of Massachusetts issued a ban against Moravian preachers, saying that the colony should tolerate "no vagrant preacher Moravian nor disguised Papist!" He continued to liken the French Jesuits to Satan and explained that the Moravians were subversive, not only because of their intermarriages with Indians but because their brand of Great Awakening revivalism seemed "absurd." This all was declaimed, of course, in a time of war, when pacifism seemed treasonous and foreigners could be enemies. In that mood, the Edwards family had received the awful news of Braddock's defeat.

In their household, where ultimate victories and losses were never thought to be won by earthly generals, the routing of the British army was interpreted not as a military but a theological event. "Oh, our sins! *Our* sins!" Jerusha Edwards exclaimed. Neither the premature conclusion among many Native Americans (before Forbes's victory) that French arms would win the war for North America, nor even the portentous earthquakes of 1755 and 1756 affected Jonathan Edwards's theological conclusions about how the cosmos spun or in what direction the American people should march. The divine work of redemption should brook no interference—so proclaimed the greatest (and nearly the last) of the New England Puritans. And precisely because of the purity of his message, he was seen as the

---

*Though writing from frontier Stockbridge, his opinions and literary works—most notably the brilliant *Freedom of the Will* (1754)—continued to dominate American philosophical thought.

most acceptable choice for presidency of the College of New Jersey, now Princeton University, upon the death of its second president, Aaron Burr, Sr., in 1757.

Burr had been a Yale classmate of David Brainerd and, as previously mentioned, had helped to found the Princeton college in memory of that missionary's self-sacrificing Christian vocation. Jonathan Edwards, recognized as Brainerd's mentor as well as Burr's father-in-law (his daughter Esther having married Burr in 1754), felt flattered by the invitation but hesitated to accept. Why leave Stockbridge now that his personal enemies had been routed and his life's ambition—to write a magnum opus on God's redemptive plan for mankind—might finally be pursued? Yet duty called, as did the potentialities of a larger pulpit from which to declare God's purposes.

The tragic end to Jonathan Edwards's remarkable history came when, having moved to Princeton with his family, he was urged to receive an inoculation against smallpox. This was very much in the enlightened spirit of the day, and Edwards, himself an exponent of the scientific approach, agreed that inoculation seemed prudent. Given his position, a doctor with the highest credentials, Dr. William Shippen of the Pennsylvania Hospital, was called to Princeton for the procedure. He administered the fatal needle on March 22, 1758; Edwards died the next day.

CHAPTER 6

In the TWILIGHT of an EMPIRE, a
MISSION-MINDED SCHOOLMASTER
and a PROPHET for PONTIAC

THE GLORIOUS AND continental victory of the British in the
French and Indian War, sealed by the 1763 Treaty of Paris,
imposed dependency and starvation on the people of the Algonquian and Iroquois nations. With their battle-scarred forests
depleted of game, their traditional economy destroyed, and
their tribes dispossessed and dispersed, tribesmen cried out for
emergency assistance from the triumphant authorities in Quebec and Boston. At the same time they repaired to their own
inner resources for new strengths and otherworldly salvation.
The frontier's violent disruptions—which peaked in the famine-
and plague-ridden years between 1765 and 1767—brought forth,
on one side, Christian apostles who believed they could aid the
Indian nations through a program of native missions and, on
the other side, a native prophet who believed that the divine
cause of Native America could only be won by welding faith
with warfare.

Throughout these final decades of the eighteenth century,
when the British empire made its ultimate efforts to control
North America, reformers and humanists and even pragmatists

kept striving to build equitable biracial communities—Jonathan Edwards's Stockbridge, David Brainerd's Crossweeksung,
and the Nanticoke Reformer's Juniata Junction having been
three hopeful precedents. Exceptions to the general rule of conquest and annihilation, these historic communities seemed to
demonstrate that, under the right circumstances, enlightened Indians could help secure the frontier. After the French and Indian
War, those precedents, plus a twin desire to advance God's Kingdom and to develop the fur trade, prompted a new set of adventurers to head into the wilderness. There they would construct
new missions and trading posts, thus praising God and King,
while simultaneously securing their own worldly positions.

An important factor that helped these faithful adventurers
was the Native Americans' desire for learning—a factor that
coincided nicely with the evangelical Protestants' compulsion
to teach. The Great Awakening had stimulated an interest in
self-improvement and Bible study as well as in educational outreach that lasted long after Jonathan Edwards's death. Among
the surviving Indians, both nativist and Christianized, there was
an eagerness to learn the English language as a medium of
communication across boundaries.

The shining star of the outreach-minded Protestant missionaries was a Mohegan preacher named Samson Occom, hailed in
his own time (1723-1792) as "an ornament to the Christian religion and the glory of the Indian nation." His mother had been
converted to Christianity early in the century, along with many
others of her accommodating nation; she had seen to it that her
son was exposed to the brilliant preachers then blazing through
New England. And thus the young Occom was prepared to suffer a conversion experience when he came before the Reverend

James Davenport, one of the most extreme advocates of the
New Light position. Davenport had won a peculiar kind of
fame when he burned his vestments as a demonstration of his
stark, John the Baptist-style connection with God. He had also
joyously described the grim Seven Years' War as Armaged-
don—after which God's Kingdom would be revealed. Both
revered as a saint and condemned as a wild man, he succeeded
in rousing many New Englanders to repent themselves of their
ways; among these converts was the impressionable, seventeen-
year-old Samson Occom.

For this impoverished youth, the means were fortunately at
hand for him to pursue the study of Christianity and to become
an evangelist of Christ's word. That door was opened for him
through the kind offices of a nearby neighbor, the Reverend
Eleazer Wheelock, who spotted in Samson Occom something
that might one day be advantageous. In 1735 Wheelock had
been named pastor of the Congregational church in Lebanon,
Connecticut. Although that community was a mere crossroads
(now the town of Columbia), he nurtured hopes of opening a
profitable school. Despite his pose that he was a simple "country minister of Connecticut," the pastor (a 1733 graduate of
Yale) had a definite agenda and a certain charisma. Some thought
he looked like the French King Louis XVI and that he might actually be the mysteriously disappeared dauphin.

But Eleazer Wheelock was pure Yankee, a stern Calvinist;
he would use any tool at hand to advance his program. Seeing
this bright-eyed and pious Occom on his doorstep, he admitted
him as a kind of servant-student. A year or so later, noting that
the lad was making extraordinary strides in comprehending both
English and classical languages, Wheelock developed a more

definite idea of how he could employ the youthful Mohegan's talents for the advancement of what he called his "Grand and Christian Design." He would establish an expansive charity school that would train talented young Indians as teachers and missionaries in the "savage" areas recently liberated from the French; it would attract funds on the strength of its demonstrated successes and its holy (and imperial) intentions.

Thanks to funds from a philanthropic parishioner named Joshua Moore, Wheelock's dream, The Indian Charity (or Moore's) School, soon became a clapboarded reality in Lebanon. Occasionally the founder revealed his school's subjective purpose—referring indiscreetly to it as his "Indian business"—but in the eyes of most contemporary advocates of evangelism, the school looked like the very fulfillment of Jonathan Edwards's and David Brainerd's educational ideals. The thirty-odd Indian youngsters who eventually came to Connecticut from the frontier to be housed at the publicly supported school did indeed receive the promised instruction as well as good food (including Indian pudding) and adequate housing. But between and after lessons—which were most often conducted in the mode of a spelling bee, with students called up one after the other to recite—the students were pledged to work the chores of Wheelock's farm.

Far worse, they suffered under the lash of the headmaster's racist scorn. In a letter to George Whitefield, Wheelock once wrote of the "Difficulty of Educating the Indians," saying: "They would soon kill themselves with Eating and Sloth, if constant care were not exercised for them." He understood not at all that in insisting on the external "civilizing" of his charges, he was threatening their innermost beings. Yet somehow, Samson Occom, by his extraordinary strength of character, endured that stressful conflict, that alienation from his own culture, and emerged ultimately as a recognized apostle of his adopted religion both among Native Americans and internationally.

His eyes almost ruined by constant study, and his body clad in a few charitable castoffs, Occom graduated from the school after four years of study. Soon thereafter he was allowed to take a brief trip to Boston, more specifically to Natick. In that "famous town" (as he called it) he familiarized himself with John Eliot's heritage—the still vibrant New England tradition of native preachers in a productive, self-governing community of Christian Indians. For any who might ever doubt the reality or effectiveness of that native preaching tradition, Samson Occom would be the eternal proof of its validity.

On returning home from Boston to Connecticut in 1749, he was informed by Wheelock that the Missionary Society had named him to be teacher and counselor to a group of Montauk on the eastern end of Long Island. Although this was not a wholly Christian community, the residents had requested a schoolmaster and "judge" who could provide rules for equity, in much the same way that Eliot had once been asked to provide judicial aid for nonconverted villagers on the outskirts of Boston. Occom went happily and lived among the Montauk for nearly a decade, receiving only a tiny allowance from the Missionary Society. This occurred in the Great Awakening era of the 1740s and 1750s when New England, New Jersey, and New York experienced a surge of prosperity and individual accomplishment as well as of missionary achievement. For the Montauk (who yearned for better tools, clothing, and even English-style houses), their teacher opened a way to those gleaming possibilities, though he dwelled in a wigwam like everybody else and offered no easy answers to life's problems.

For enthusiasts of New Light Protestantism, Occom's successful mission offered proof and promise. Here was a sign of divine blessings—and therefore an indication that funds could be raised among the pious and the evangelically inclined. Aaron Burr, Jonathan Edwards's son-in-law, came forward with a supporting allowance from the College of New Jersey for the work of the now famous missionary of Mohegan ancestry. The Missionary Society, impressed by the return on its investment, pushed for Occom's ordination, a widely reported event that took place on Cape Cod in August 1759 (a month before the fall of Quebec). And Eleazer Wheelock, whose innovative idea for a mission school had been based on Occom's potential, now felt confident about making even larger plans. Perhaps his school could be the official training base for properly oriented Indians who would secure North America for the Crown by bringing the more distant "savages" under imperial control.

Wheelock wrote to David Brainerd's brother, John, in New Jersey to suggest that some of the Delaware lads from the Christian communities there might become useful parts of such a grand continental program. And, with some trepidation, he considered making an approach to Sir William Johnson, who had received a baronetcy from the king as a result of his actions in the war and who now ruled the valleys of central New York as the Royal Superintendent of Iroquois Affairs. Sir William had succeeded, almost single-handedly, in marshaling Iroquois braves (mostly Mohawk) to serve in the French and Indian War, just as he had recruited them for King George's War. In the postwar era, he intended to rally the Mohawk in another cause, using educated youths as emissaries ranging westward among the untutored, vexatious Seneca. Surely Sir William would be interested, Wheelock reasoned, in sending some candidates to the Charity School (along with appropriate fees).

Now that there was a new world to be won in the west, Eleazer Wheelock trusted that his school's native graduates would be much desired personnel. Certainly the tamed Delaware as well as civilized Mohawk could render a variety of public services out there "near the Bowells of the Pagan Settlements" (as he indelicately put it). Gaining assurances in 1761 that missionary boards in America and Britain (particularly the Scottish Society for Propagating Christian Knowledge) would support his endeavors, he was finally emboldened to send his carefully worded invitation to Sir William in 1761.

That was the same year (not a mere coincidence) when Samson Occom, living proof of the effectiveness of the Lebanon school, was dispatched on a preliminary visit to the Oneida—the Iroquois nation slightly to the south and west of the Mohawk. Though newly married and regretful at leaving his own people in the east, Occom had the ebullient feeling that the "People of Connecticut" were sending him west for profoundly Christian purposes and that out there, he could help his fellow Indians in their transition to a godly, English-dominated society. Prior to his departure, he received a letter from an Anglican clergyman among the Mohawk, saying that the Iroquois peoples were eager for learning and ardently requested a minister. The clergyman added, "They appear to have considerable notions of a Supreme Being, and of Revealed Religion." Was this not a further hint that, although the Great Awakening had faded (and had, in some senses, failed), there were still grand opportunities for evangelical Protestantism among the western tribes?

Pondering such expectations, Occom and his assistant chose a route out that curved south and west along Long Island Sound to New York City. There, on the Sabbath, the Mohegan clergyman, to his dismay, saw citizens of various origins carrying on their business without pause and reveling without shame. These people, he concluded, were more heathen than the "wild Indians" whose lands he would soon enter.

The SCHOOLMASTER'S DESIGNATED APOSTLE

When Samson Occom made his adventurous departure from Lebanon, a student named Samuel Kirkland peered out of Eleazer Wheelock's barnyard door to watch him ride off. As he gazed at the diminishing figures, Kirkland may well have been wondering when he, too, would ride out to the western Indians. Son of a quarrelsome and frequently unemployed New Light preacher, this young man had always had to scratch for a living. In 1759, at eighteen, he had managed to get a place in the Indian Charity School by arguing that he was both rugged and smart enough to accompany the Indian missionary agents on their ways. He could help them through the varied confusions of interracial diplomacy—and so he did. Yet his success in accomplishing that goal was only the beginning of his exemplary career, a career in which he not only went on to serve the church as the most effective of all white missionaries on the frontier but also served his nation, first as heroic frontier agent during the American Revolution and later as founder of Hamilton College in Clinton, New York.

Before young Samuel Kirkland himself could ride out, however, he still had to complete two more years of the Charity School, learning the complexities of Greek and Latin and the ways of the Hebrew prophets in company with the Indian youngsters who had been drawn to the school in response to Eleazer Wheelock's invitations. The Mohawk delegation of would-be scholars (escorted back to Lebanon by David Fowler, the so-called Mercury of Indian Missionaries who had carried Wheelock's carefully worded invitation out to Sir William Johnson's domain) included three lads, two of whom were of special concern to Sir William. The first of these was his own bastard son, William Primus. The second and more promising was his brother-in-law and brilliant protégé, Thayendanegea, better known as Joseph Brant, who would later, in the decade of the American Revolution, bind the Mohawk inseparably to the British cause.

Samuel Kirkland and Joseph Brant became close friends. Although they would be rivals and would one day march to war under opposed flags, they never lost respect and admiration for each other; indeed, in the sure way of fellow students under a severe master, they each *knew* the other's mettle, tested and proved. Although Samuel was a year older, Joseph had had the more notable life in years before coming east to school. Like Samson Occom, he had been born to an intensely religious, Christian mother—in his case, however, the mother's denomination was not Congregational or Presbyterian but Anglican (an important difference, as future years would show). Joseph's mother's second husband was a man named Brant, and in their little community of Canajoharie on the Mohawk River, her son's name then became Brant's Joseph, later Joseph Brant. Even more significantly, her daughter, Joseph's sister Molly, became Sir William Johnson's wife. The broad-shouldered Irish baronet, perhaps because his antecedents had not been English, accepted Mohawk ways with all the ease of a Frenchman—in fact, with much admiration. He believed that the Iroquois adjustments to European ways should "flow" from themselves and from their traditions. He regarded bright-eyed Joseph fondly, as one of his true relatives and trustworthy heirs.

Back in 1755, when Sir William had persuaded a number of Mohawk warriors to join the successful attack on the French fortress on Lake George, Joseph had been too young to participate. But three years later, when fifteen years old, Joseph was allowed to march along with the other Mohawk in General James Abercrombie's army when it unsuccessfully attacked Fort Ticonderoga, and so he shared in the trauma of that defeat. Though he had behaved well, he recalled in later years how, on first hearing and sensing the battle all around him, he had had to grab a sapling to keep from collapsing. Later that year, he took a more vigorous part in Bradstreet's attack on Fort Frontenac and in Prideaux's campaign against Fort Niagara. When the latter general was killed in battle and when Sir William took his place, Joseph found himself fighting shoulder-to-shoulder along with British troopers against the French. His good conduct was rewarded by a gleaming piece of silver, with THAYENDANEGEA engraved on the medal's back.

So it was no mere child who was sent by Sir William to study in Connecticut. And, having shown himself to be an adequate student (though somewhat too proud for Eleazer Wheelock's taste), Joseph Brant immediately became a candidate for the schoolmaster's ambitious program to advance natives through higher education into the ranks of the ministry, following the pattern of Samson Occom. At this same time, encouraging messages had been coming from the Oneida capital (Old Castle) about Occom's cordial reception among those people: He had rapidly acquired a knowledge of their difficult speech (which was closely related to the Mohawk dialect of the Iroquois language) and had collected a circle of students.

It looked as if more clergy would indeed serve the cause of unity and, therefore, that preparation of Indian youths for higher education might be the missing key to empire. Eleazer Wheelock accordingly saw Princeton as Joseph Brant's proper objective along with his friend Samuel Kirkland. Having successfully graduated from college, the two young men could be ordained and could carry the word of Calvin's God out to the heathen world, whether that be in the contested regions of Pennsylvania or amid the hilltop castles of the Seneca. Little could Wheelock suspect how very wrong his preview of Brant's and Kirkland's careers would be—or, indeed, how paternalistic and one-dimensional was his view of intercultural spiritual exchange.

As a first step before Princeton, the schoolmaster concluded after further correspondence with Sir William that Brant and Kirkland should spend some important time in the Mohawk homeland. There Kirkland could study, in the person of Sir William, a real-life example of how British civilization might include the Indians while also respecting Iroquois traditions. Brant, though of low rank, could show himself as a potential leader among his own people there, while also listening to Sir William's strategies for manipulating the more distant Iroquois nations for the purposes of his fur empire. But Brant soon saw that the situation was far from solid: Sir William was receiving rumors of disaffection among the Six Nations. The most real of their resentments was that they had not been rewarded in the expected ways for their assistance to the British in the capture of Fort Niagara during the war.

Sir William was also disturbed by news that the Pennsylvanians and Virginians were crossing the Appalachians in increasing numbers—the former accompanied by Moravian missionaries, the latter impelled by the same lust for land that had triggered the just concluded war. There also were reports of new anti-British resentments in the breasts of the Shawnee and the western Delaware and Ottawa. If those troublesome nations succeeded in luring the Seneca into an alliance, Sir William's hopes for building a smoothly coordinated fur trade monopoly would be blasted.

Temporarily settled at Fort Johnson on the Mohawk, Samuel Kirkland enjoyed Sir William's hospitality but was shocked by deviations from the New England way of life. The Anglican mode of worship preferred by the Irish baronet and the chapels he had set up in some of the Mohawk villages seemed outlandish, if not papist. They offered baptism and communion and the Lord's grace to residents with no confession or conversion—perilously close to the theology of the Jesuits who had striven so mightily to install themselves here in the previous century. That irregularity, plus the rather free morals of the Mohawk, appalled young Kirkland, but he confided his thoughts only to his journals, and went about learning phrases of the Mohawk language. He also observed how great a love the people felt for their land, their clans, and their rites. The autumn visit all too soon concluded; he returned home proud to bring with him three promising recruits for the Charity School.

In Lebanon he found Wheelock discouraged by official disinterest in missionary work. The new postwar British policy toward the Indians was far more militaristic, epitomized by Lord Jeffrey Amherst. This general, the proud captor of Louisbourg and victor of other key campaigns, now sat enthroned at Quebec in sole command of British imperial affairs in North America. In his bellicose eyes, Native Americans were nothing but a bother—he would certainly not give them their traditional gifts nor let them hang dependently about the forts. To him, the wilderness-conditioned traders and borderland merchants (who obeyed neither King nor Cross) seemed equally troublesome. Historian Francis Parkman speaks of Amherst's "thick-headed, blustering arrogance," portraying him as a "worthy successor of Braddock."

The general is also known to world history for his infamous order, given at one point in the frontier wars, to supply the western Indians with plague-infested blankets. "Could it not be contrived," he asked, "to send the *Small Pox* among the disaffected tribes?" An even more striking manifestation of his frontier policy, as glimpsed by the very tribes whose affection he was supposed to court, was the construction of British forts—a chain of them running southwestward from Lake Erie to the Ohio River—forts that proclaimed British *ownership* of the land. The Iroquois Grand Council at Onondaga tried to make this construction policy seem unnecessary by assuring Albany and Philadelphia that they, in keeping with the Covenant Chain, had repaired all of their alliances and now effectively kept the western and southern nations under tight control. This they had promised to do in a carefully constructed agreement (the Treaty of Easton, Pennsylvania, 1757). Their promise having been kept, the king surely had no need to concern himself about either forts or furs.

Yet Amherst and other officers of the Crown suspected that the Seneca, at least the westernmost of them, were conspiring with the independent nations around the Great Lakes. These were the previously French-allied people of the northwestern woodlands who were determined to recapture lands now claimed by the British but once theirs. At the root of discontent among those confederated nations was the well-remembered Iroquois Grand Council's 1742 gift of Ohio River valley territories to the British. In fact, these were the historic homelands of the Shawnee, the Illinois, the Miami, and (more recently) the emigrated Delaware, over whom the Iroquois lordship was imaginary.

Now, to the dismay of the Ohio nations and the western Seneca, the British were implanting military outposts even more formidable than those of the French. Whereas the French had merely desired to set up a defensive line supplied by a few trading posts ("brandy for furs" being the controlling motto), all the while respecting the Indians' sovereignty, the British intended to impose *overlordship*. Their shifting laws and supposedly benign regulations seemed always to have loopholes allowing squatters to seize Indian land. The British also welcomed missionaries, both the Moravians and the New Englanders, whose historic, deadening effect on the independent Indian spirit could be seen all too clearly among the doomed eastern Algonquian. That perception was echoed later in Samuel Kirkland's career when the lordly Seneca warned his Oneida Indians that they should reject the missionary and his Bible, lest they become a "miserable, abject people," like their weakened neighbors beyond the Hudson.

Even the Oneida, among whom Samson Occom served so effectively, expressed alarm at the ever forward march of the British military installations as well as at the provocations of the traders and settlers. Addressing Sir William in what Parkman calls "the simplicity of their hearts," the Oneida pointed out that, with the war against the French won,

> we are now left in Peace, and have nothing to do but to plant our Corn, Hunt the wild Beasts, smoke our Pipes, and mind Religion. But as these Forts, which are built among us, disturb our Peace, & are a great hurt to Religion, because some of our Warriors are foolish, & some of our Brother Soldiers don't fear God, we therefore desire that these Forts may be pull'd down, & kick'd out of the way.

One can imagine how this sentiment was received at Amherst's headquarters (if Sir William even passed it forward to him). What did continue to reach the general's ears, however, were rumbles of war drums in the west. One of his officers at Fort Miami in Ohio country described a "general irritation" among the surrounding native peoples, particularly the Shawnee and Delaware. While that early report was dismissed as mere nervousness, typical of wary troops on the frontier, no one at headquarters doubted that French residents of the west—the *habitants* and *coureurs de bois* who had dwelled in or roamed the land for so many years—were doing everything possible to keep the natives uneasy and disinclined to deal with

British fur traders. Much of the commotion in the west seemed
to be focused on a certain Ottawa chief named Pontiac whose
service to the French in the recent war had been fiercely loyal
and memorably effective.

But what none of the apprehensive British high command
suspected was that the hostile Delaware among whom Pontiac
moved had been visited by a prophet preaching a universalist
message. In the heightened words of Parkman, "a prophet arose
among them." This force, embracing far more than any one
tribe's spiritual beliefs, would make of Pontiac's campaign something of greater consequence than a local, political uprising.

A prime location to which the Delaware had migrated and
which had long been considered key to British control of (and
thus to missionary work on) the frontier was the boisterous
town of Oquaga, spread along the north branch of the Susquehanna River, in New York near the Pennsylvania border. The
Iroquois chiefs, in their presumed authority, policed it, for
rough it was, and defended it against possible attacks both from
other tribes and white settlers. They allowed certain missionaries to come in as part of the mix, part of the medley of peoples
from all across the northern woodland. Jonathan Edwards's
friend Gideon Hawley, one of the initial missionaries at Oquaga
(1752), had reported that the Indians there seemed to have absorbed much white blood into their racial makeup. The town's
very name means "the corn soup place," for here all could dip
from the same pot.

As Colin G. Calloway points out in his book on Indian societies before and after the Revolution, Oquaga in all its diversity revealed that the outreach philosophy of Hiawatha's Pine
Tree was still in effect. Here the generous "shelter of the Great

Tree of Peace helped to offset the trauma and social disintegra-
tion that accompanied displacement of [native] people from
their original homelands, *besides placing barriers to white settlement on the southern edges of Iroquoia* [italics added]." Oquaga,
then, was a quite appropriate assignment for Joseph Brant,
one of Eleazer Wheelock's more promising missionaries-in-
training and his traveling companion, the Reverend Charles
Jeffry Smith, when it came time for their postings in the early
spring of 1763.

The two very green missionaries-in-training were told to
follow the usual route from Connecticut to Iroquois territory:
up the Hudson River and then west along the Mohawk before
going south from Joseph's home at Canajoharie to Cherry Valley and down the Susquehanna. Much of this was now friendly
Tuscarora country, for those people had emigrated north, under
the protection of the Oneida, several decades earlier. But rov-
ing groups of Delaware and Shawnee might be encountered at
any point; the trip, under the best of circumstances, was perilous. Yet Joseph must have been excited by the prospect of
voyaging to the west and into his new professional role. Now
no longer a callow warrior, he was an agent of Christian civilization, out to reconcile his people, not exactly in the way of
Hiawatha's Great Law of Peace but more imperially and in the
name of Christ.

Joseph liked Jeffry Smith, his black-clad, Bible-carrying
companion, well enough, for the young Mohawk had learned to
believe in the missionaries and their peaceable, reforming functions, even in such rough-and-tumble places as Oquaga. But,
personally, Joseph might have preferred his friend Samuel Kirkland as a partner. These thoughts must have been in his head as

he and his assigned clergyman sailed up the Hudson. But suddenly, when their boat paused along the shore, news came that completely scuttled their mission. The west was in flames, ignited by the Ottawa chief Pontiac; Oquaga and all other outposts were at risk as the apparently well-planned campaign of the combined western nations swept eastward from the Great Lakes. Joseph Brant and Jeffry Smith had no choice but to return to Connecticut. There, in Lebanon, Joseph found a message from his sister Molly waiting for him. He was to come home at once. This was the time for the whole family to gather its strength in the safety of its Mohawk valley, praying for protection.

The DELAWARE PROPHET'S MASTER of LIFE

The often told story of Pontiac and his western "conspiracy" deserves to be told again, but differently—this time as an example of the peculiar workings of spiritual energy in the wake of the Great Awakening. Pontiac should stand forth on the pages of American history not just as an astonishingly innovative military commander, not just as a national liberator, but also as an inspired convert to a dynamic native religion.

Pontiac's name first appeared in British military records as a force to be reckoned with when he commanded the Ottawa contingent with notable boldness against General Braddock at Fort Duquesne in 1755. His name next appeared in reports in 1760 when his men had the effrontery to halt a westward-bound battalion commanded by Major Robert Rogers. Famed as Rogers' Rangers since their daring and successful attack on the St. Francis Indians in the climax years of the French and Indian War, Rogers and his buckskin cadre were at this point headed toward the surrendered French forts of Detroit and Michilimackinac, under the special orders of Lord Jeffrey Amherst. At those outposts they were to raise King George III's flag over his new empire of the west. Never before had British arms penetrated so far into the wilderness. But now, without warning, representatives from Pontiac strode into the Rangers' camp, demanding that the Anglo-American troops go no farther until the chief had arrived and could rule on the admissibility of their march.

The next morning, Pontiac made his expected entrance and, having heard the British recital of the war's surrender terms, accepted Captain Rogers's plan to occupy the abandoned forts. The major was surely well informed of Pontiac's importance— how highly his military skills had been valued by Montcalm. But Rogers had no conception of the depth of Pontiac's devotion to the French cause (the chief had remarked more than once, "I *am* a Frenchman and will *die* a Frenchman"). On the other hand, he overestimated Pontiac's position among the neighboring sachems, believing that the Ottawa chief was "king and lord of all this country." In fact, Pontiac, who was then in the prime of his life (aged about fifty), had had to struggle for all the years of his youth and middle age to maintain leadership of his confederation of Ottawa, Ojibwa (longtime enemies of the Sioux), Potawatomi, Wyandot (including remnants of the Huron), and other shifting, contentious people of the northern lakes.

In recent years Pontiac had been seeking an even broader alliance with the Shawnee and Delaware, as well as with the disaffected and intermixed Seneca commonly known as Mingo. For some of these rank-conscious Native Americans of increasingly sophisticated eighteenth-century societies, Pontiac seemed a bit crude in his habits, recalling rumors of the Ottawa's canni-balistic habits. Though perhaps aware of his lack of polish, he "stood tall" (as Parkman expresses it) for his courage, resolu-tion, and eloquence. Every inch a chief, he immediately im-pressed Rogers with his physical bearing and implicit power.

Pontiac's people of the northwest, shocked at the shattering of France's long-established brotherhood with them and in-sulted by British military moves into their territories, were at the point of concluding that the time had come for a last-ditch, all-tribes war for survival. Pushing them in that direction was a spiritual genius generally known as the Delaware Prophet. His true name was Neolin, the Enlightened One; his advent on the banks of the Ohio and the Muskingum Rivers in 1762 has been well documented. A noted Moravian missionary, John Gottlieb Heckewelder, who spent some fifty years among the Delaware, was personally acquainted with this very real, very believable figure, and described how, in his revivalistic ecstasies, he was "constantly crying." Heckewelder also recorded, admiringly (but probably inaccurately), the singularity of the Delaware Prophet's devotion to the Great Spirit.

The haunting story of Neolin's first meeting with his divine "Master" was reconstructed in the nineteenth century by an-thropologist Henry Schoolcraft. He begins by telling the tradi-tional story of how the young man, equipped only with gun, ammunition, and kettle, had wandered into the wilderness in search of a vision. Having arrived at a dazzlingly bright moun-tain after many trials, he was commanded by an angel to ascend the slippery-as-glass height after stripping himself naked and purifying himself. Finally reaching a village of elegant houses, he was commanded to sit down, which he did by perching upon a hat bordered with gold. Then the story veers from the traditional path and takes on a unique character. Before the eyes of the startled youth, a celestial figure appeared, setting forth a series of commandments. "The Land on which you are, I made for you and not for others," the Master of Life declaimed. Further, the figure instructed, "Drive forth from your lands those dogs in red clothing [the British]"; also, "Do not sell to your brothers that which I have placed on earth as food." Finally, he gave the prophet a prayer, "carved in Indian hieroglyphics upon a wooden stick," which he was told to deliver to his tribal chief.

Despite the genuineness of this inspiration, skeptical commentators stress Neolin's mimicry of that era's Great Awakening themes and find strong Christian influence both in the monotheistic character of his Master of Life and in his social commandments (which included monogamy). Yet, to both his contemporaries and to modern religious historians, Neolin, an archetypical reformer, expressed the divine concepts that had existed among Native Americans from earliest known times. Indeed, he urged his people to return to the noble life of their ancestors, to lay aside the clothing and goods they had received from the white men, and to strengthen and purify their own persons (by the use of native herbs and emetics). By so doing, and by strictly observing all his precepts, as he received them from the Master of Life, they and their nations would be restored to ancient greatness. The warriors would be invulnerable, enabled to drive out the white men who infested their territory.

Neolin's fame first spread to the communities of the Ohio valley, including the strategically important, interracial settlement of Logstown, or Chiningué, downriver from Fort Pitt.

Then it radiated out among all the woodland tribes surrounding the Great Lakes. Wherever he preached, he found believers— at the same time that Samson Occom and Samuel Kirkland were finding believers only a few hundred miles to the east. Often, however, the Delaware Prophet's warriors would neglect his seemingly less practical tenets. They would not discard their muskets or trust solely in the painted sticks that he supplied for weapons in the forthcoming holy war.

In the autumn of 1762 Pontiac, one of Neolin's new converts, decided to act out the Prophet's militant message and to set the war machinery in motion. Westering Seneca, just a year previously, had urged him to take up the battle hatchet and to lead them in a coordinated strike against poorly defended Detroit from a nearby Wyandot village, but he had declined. The time was not ripe. As it happened the commander of the fort learned of the plot through an informer and nipped it in the bud, after informing Lord Jeffrey Amherst of the impending peril.

Since the departure of the French and the initial arrival of Anglo-American forces in his forests, Pontiac had tried from time to time to extend the hand of friendship to the British and had been patient with their brusque aggressions. But their inhuman attitudes toward the Indians proved to be intolerable. The Ottawa chief described their obtuseness in this telling anecdote: "When I go to see the British commander and say to him that some of our comrades are dead, instead of bewailing their death as our French brothers did, he laughs at me and at you." Furthermore, when Pontiac saw that the British had no intention of assisting the impoverished Indians, he knew that he must act before the balance of power tipped too heavily against him. So now, with the Master of Life aiding him, Pontiac was ready to fight for his kingdom of heaven and for his part of America.

He cried out to all who would hear him, "We must destroy [the British] without delay. Are we not men? There is no longer any time to lose!" Already he had sent out ambassadors bearing that message to the different nations. As described by Parkman, "Bearing with them the war-belts of wampum, broad and long, and the tomahawk stained red, in token of war, [the ambassadors] went from camp to camp, and village to village." Their recital of Pontiac's proposal for a grand alliance in the spring of 1763 was heard with widespread approval. His plan of action seemed feasible. The united blow was to be struck in May; first each tribe would destroy the British garrisons in its territory, then, "with a general rush," they were to destroy all settlements of the frontier.

The preparations were to be concealed with the greatest secrecy. The Seneca were warned specifically to see that no news of the plan reach Sir William Johnson (whose strenuous, single-handed efforts to keep business humming and the Covenant Chain intact were now seriously threatened). Despite the secrecy, it became obvious to British agents that as spring advanced and the Indians came into the settlements from their wintering grounds, the tribesmen were rallying in increasing numbers around specific forts. There they camped, as if waiting, committing themselves to dancing and to prayer sessions.

At the final war council, a few nights before the planned assault on Detroit, Pontiac took the stage and recited Neolin's description of his dreamed meeting with the Master of Life. In the telling, he emphasized that the people must now "lift their hatchets" against the British. "Hoarse ejaculations of applause echoed his speech" (oh, the vivid Parkman!); further legend has it that the next day clouds thickened the skies in such palpable blackness that people used the fallen rain as ink to write with. Creatures of both the earth and the heavens seemed to agree that something awful was afoot.

The formal siege of Fort Detroit commenced with a thunderous, full-scale attack on May 9, 1763. This was the first of the planned assaults on twelve British positions all across the five hundred miles of western wilderness, from the Straits of Mackinac on the Michigan peninsula to Fort Pitt on the Pennsylvania border. The six-month siege of Detroit—the longest siege of an American fort ever carried out by an enemy force—was marked both by mass attacks on the walls and by horrific ultimata that the English must withdraw downriver in their ships, or else there would be no restraining the scalping knives. Gradually Pontiac tightened his encircling noose, capturing the schooners that sailed in from Lake Erie with provisions and additional men and executing the few *habitants* who sought to provide the British with food. The Indians' attacks and sorties intensified as spring lengthened into summer and as heat beat down on the fort. Yet, as summer lengthened, some of the tribes considered withdrawing, for the immediate success that they had been promised seemed not so easily granted. Neolin struggled to keep their resolve firm, while hoping against hope that somehow the king of France would learn of the battle and would sail in with his armies of assistance.

In fact, Pontiac and his chiefs, for all their assembled might and spiritual strength, had but a dim idea of how to conduct siege warfare in the European style. Their own mode of fighting still consisted mostly of traditional hit-and-run attacks, with the sensible objective of minimizing loss of life, always avoiding conflicts in which the fight went on until the last man had fallen. In the recent wars, however, there had been numerous frays in which Indians successfully fought French or English forces in modern-style, long-lasting engagements. Indeed, when a large British relief force arrived from Niagara under Captain James Dalzell bearing supplies and provisions, Pontiac fought it head-on but was unable to prevent Dalzell's reaching the fort. Subsequently, when the reinforced British then made a concerted attack on Pontiac's camp at the end of July, he (apprised of their approach) won the day and inflicted heavy losses.

Beyond Detroit, Pontiac's broad strategy of frontier aggression was more successful. Of the twelve fortified posts attacked, all but four were captured with ensuing massacres of the inhabitants. As the British rushed relief expeditions to the front, these were met and repulsed with marked efficiency. Frontier settlements fell one after another, the farms plundered and burned, the women and children carried off into captivity after the slaughter of the men. Battered Fort Pitt, which had received a warning just in time from Major Gladwyn, and two smaller posts held out along with starving Detroit. But it gradually became evident to British officials in Quebec (as well as to missionary headquarters in New England and Philadelphia) that a new kind of native genius was at work here. Pontiac's field management of the war certainly deserves such a description, for he not only remained in effective communication with his multinational bands of warriors but also created a regular commissary department that allowed the base to keep supplying food and matériel to the field.

In this Indian thrust for a new, battle-won identity, Neolin functioned as the driving imagination, the seer of otherworldly victory. But it was Pontiac with his quiverful of talents who transformed the variegated Indians into one nation on the march. He not only created a treasury department that issued promissory notes but also inaugurated a state department that dispatched authoritative reports by means of messages written in hieroglyphics on birch bark (which Pontiac sealed with his tribe's totem, the otter). He employed two secretaries for this unique correspondence, each of whom he managed to keep in ignorance of the other. And thus, in a way that recalled King Philip but that was wholly original and grander, he became the image of an authentic and inspired Indian commander in chief of all nations. America would witness the reappearance of this brilliant, Charlemagne-like image again in the life of Tecumseh and again in the character of military leaders farther west during the Wars of the Plains.

The possibility of such a coordinated native operation had never been imagined, even by seasoned observers like Sir William Johnson, certainly not by newcomers like Lord Jeffrey Amherst. The concept of a pan-Indian movement (a virtual national uprising) also remained difficult for later Americans to bring into focus, for it defied all commonly accepted knowledge about the scattered, undisciplined Indian nations. Yet what Pontiac had brought about might be called the first large-scale revolution of the New World, for it was forged by peoples who, in their desire to liberate themselves from European rule, struggled to form a spiritually united American nation.

By the fall of the year, however, as the British held firm at Detroit and as wishful *habitants* lost belief in the return of

French armies and turned their backs on the Indians, many tribesmen heeded calls to return to their homes for prewinter hunting. Not even the fiery sermonizing of Neolin could keep them constant, excited about the chance of liberation, and willing to see more young men die in battle. At last, on October 30, Pontiac retired with his ever faithful Ottawa warriors to the Maumee River and abandoned the siege. Yet he was determined to find new allies to replace those who had withdrawn in the face of key British victories. Two months previously, Pontiac's eastern cohorts had been severely bloodied by a large-scale force under Colonel Henry Bouquet (second in command to General Forbes during the 1758 capture of Fort Duquesne). Near that same site, in what was perhaps the crucial military engagement of Pontiac's revolution, Bouquet outlasted the fort's besiegers in the Battle of Bushy Run (even though he lost 150 men, far more than the Indians). Bouquet then continued west across the Allegheny River to recover white captives from the Indians encamped on the upper Muskingum.

Bouquet had demonstrated that, despite the numbers of natives in arms and despite the new spirit that moved them, British troops were, at that time, the world's best. This lesson was repeated early the next year, when Bouquet and Colonel John Bradstreet (under instructions from Jeffrey Amherst's replacement, General Thomas Gage) swept irresistibly farther west and north to disperse most of Pontiac's allies and to relieve Detroit and other Great Lakes forts from the Indian threat. In Pennsylvania, Bouquet succeeded in so thoroughly routing the Shawnee and Delaware that they laid down their arms and sued for peace. Having failed to find allies farther west or in the south,

Pontiac, though unconquered and still a threat, had no option but to raise the white flag and join the peace talks.

EARTHLY and UNEARTHLY FORCES STRIVE to BRING an EMPIRE BACK TOGETHER AGAIN

The shock of Pontiac's War changed the attitudes of Anglo-Americans so massively that it might be said the destructive war had at least one constructive result—to wake up the world to the Indians' plight. Official British policies swung from Amherst's militaristic indifference toward the Indians to a sudden and overwhelming concern; missionary agencies on the frontier changed their approach from haphazard community building to government-supported campaigns. Many of the Indian nations, both those that had been Christianized and those that had been inspired by native prophecies, desperately tried to find creative ways of living with their contradictory white neighbors. But one terrible aftershock from the war overshadowed all the small victories and presaged a new black mood on the American frontier.

This fateful episode occurred during the winter of 1763–64, when the terrors of war were still sweeping all reason aside. Frightened by the successes of Pontiac's allies and angered by the disinclination of Pennsylvania's Quaker-dominated assembly to supply aid for frontier communities, the ragtag citizenry of Paxton (on the Susquehanna, slightly downstream from Shamokin) concluded they must take matters into their own hands. In their war-frazzled minds, it now seemed that all cross-cultural experiments were subversive, resulting only in white heads being cracked open by red hatchets; certainly no Indians, however converted or educated, could be trusted.

The Paxton Boys, as this band of immigrant squatters came to be called, first took cowardly revenge on all Indians wherever or whoever they might be by massacring peaceful survivors of the Conestoga tribe in Lancaster County, Pennsylvania. Then, their numbers swollen beyond five hundred, the boys moved against another band of refugee Indians, the people gathered by missionary David Zeisberger into the first Moravian community named Gnadenhuetten, near Bethlehem. Terrified by the mob, the Gnadenhuetten pacifists fled to Philadelphia, desperately hoping to find safety, if not brotherly love, in the capital. As the bloodthirsty frontiersmen approached, Philadelphia teetered on the brink of mass panic. Government officials protected the refugees by housing them in barracks surrounded by a battalion of British regulars. Storming into the city, the boys "uttered hideous cries in imitation of the war whoop," vowing to knock aside the king's men and kill the cowering Indians. Benjamin Franklin, called upon to save the day, finally talked the ruffians into going home. This he did by promising more funds for frontier guards to guarantee their security, and by setting a pay scale of legislative bounties for Indian scalps.

Such was the mood of frontier America after more than a century of religious and commercial attempts to find means of settling the two peoples beneficially side by side—attempts that had deteriorated into setting scalp bounties. Farther north, where Sir William Johnson still tried to work with the Six Nations to restore peace to the frontier and where British authorities strategized about how to put the empire back together, Pontiac's War and its aftermath forced a realization that radically altered policies must be tried. The first of these policies was the so-called Proclamation Act of 1763, which, even before

Pontiac's withdrawal, sought to appease Indian fears of settlers' encroachment by establishing a barrier line that ran from Fort Stanwix (modern-day Rome, New York) down along the mountain ridges to the Carolinas. On the western side of this, the domains of the Indians' reign would be respected eternally; east of the line the British would rule royally (that is, without consultation with the colonies).

When the defeated Shawnee and Delaware were summoned to a conference at Fort Pitt early in 1765, Neolin the Delaware Prophet was among those who appeared, somewhat reluctantly, out from the surrounding forests. He made a short but helpful speech, saying that the Great Spirit had commanded the Indians to lay down the hatchet and smoke the pipe of peace. This speech was received as an indication not of total surrender but of reconciliation for now. Following his ameliorating words, the Shawnee released their captives and announced themselves prepared to receive appropriate gifts.

Not long after, Pontiac declared himself ready to make peace and to cooperate in the reestablishment of the fur trade. Leaving his encampment on the Maumee, he undertook the lengthy water voyage to Oswego on Lake Ontario. At that traditional meeting place of European and Native American powers, which had been burned by the French in their final raid of 1756, Sir William Johnson awaited Pontiac, eager to start doing business again and to implement the peaceful dictates of both the Great Spirit and the king of England. There followed the expected round of lengthy speeches (Sir William wrapping himself in his red blanket with gold fringe in order to assume the stance of an Iroquois orator) with full pardon being awarded by the British to the Ottawa chief.

For his part, Pontiac promised to cancel the war eternally by recalling the wampum belts from nations recently allied in war; henceforth, he would "think nothing but good." He pointed out, along the way, that some of the belts had originated not with him but with the Seneca, an internal factor with which the Iroquois themselves would have to deal. Pontiac's flotilla of canoes was then loaded with presents, and he set off again, fully honored by the British, returning to his home valleys. One imagines him in somewhat the frame of mind of a disappointed convert from the era of the Great Awakening, the gods having failed him once again.

The story should end there, but Pontiac's inner struggle was by no means over. Neolin and his visions of a reformed and victorious nation having disappeared once again, like the smoke of yesterday's campfire, the aging chief could only hark back to the days when he held high command under French authority. He was occasionally glimpsed wearing the gold-trimmed officer's uniform that Montcalm had given him, traveling and plotting among the Illinois villagers who lived near the remains of ancient civilizations along the Mississippi. A fearful citizen of St. Louis retained a local tribesman (a Peoria) to cut the old warrior down. The fee was a barrel of liquor, the place Fort Chartres, the date April 1769. Those facts are known—as is the resulting vengeful campaign that the Ottawa then carried out against the Illinois nation, resulting in its near extermination. But those terminal facts do not diminish the more enduring truth. Although no tablet was put in place to mark the burial place of the defeated Pontiac, his heroic name and the sacred battle that he and Neolin once waged could never be forgotten.

While others struggled to recover from the wreckage of war, the once mighty Six Nations (including those Seneca who had broken from the league and fought alongside Pontiac) strove to find a means of reuniting themselves. This was accomplished through a massive conference in October 1768 at Fort Stanwix, up the Mohawk River from Sir William Johnson's headquarters. Some three thousand assorted Indians attended, including not only the Delaware, Shawnee, and Mingo from the western regions but also the Stockbridge Indians and others from the east. The Crown had determined that this treaty signing was to be an unforgettable occasion, a defining moment in the history of North America. The treaty would not only reseal the Six Nations' relationships with their troublesome neighbors, but it would also settle land divisions among all contending interests. The Proclamation Line, now moved west to the Ohio River, would be subjected to careful adjustments: While the Indian nations would rule supreme west of the line and would retain some holdings east of it, various special interests (including the ever pressing Pennsylvanians) would finally gain control over most of the long-coveted territories in the east. Through mandated adjustments, the Indians involuntarily gave up small parts of Pennsylvania and New York as well as major parts of what would become Tennessee, Kentucky, and West Virginia (from which eastern landowners would continue to move into their illegal claims across the Ohio River).

To Sir William's chagrin, missionaries from the moralistic New England denominations spoke out against this lordly compromise, claiming that the legitimate interests of their people— particularly the Oneida and Tuscarora, some of whose warriors had actually fought for the Crown against Pontiac—were not adequately protected. At particular risk was the profitable portage at Wood Creek (near Rome, New York, handy for boats bound up the Mohawk to Lake Oneida and beyond). British officials swiftly hushed such protests, hurrying to distribute food and gifts in massive amounts to cheer the hearts and gullets of the participants. Valued at approximately $50,000 in present-day money, these presents for Iroquois and other chiefs required some sixty freight canoes for upriver transport.

Joseph Brant observed the procedures with interest as his superiors, the Mohawk sachems, divided the gifts among their villagers. He had sat out Pontiac's War in nearby Canajoharie, having been conscripted for only a few strikes against the threatening Delaware. Then he had married in 1765 (the wedding being a bang-up affair, with Samson Occom in attendance and two guests stabbed amid the general revelry). Now he was interested in raising a family and achieving position in the community by resuming a career as missionary and educator. Brant recalled how his mission to Oquaga had been stalled by the war and wondered if the Mission Board would send him there again (they did so briefly in 1769, at which time he found the people in the community miserably poor and in great need). But he recognized that, among his own people—where the dominance of Sir William was so strong, and the affection for the Anglican church so powerful—missionaries trained by Eleazer Wheelock were by no means as popular as they once had been. His destiny seemed to lie in other directions.

Wheelock, though clearly lacking in greatness, might be called a grand opportunist; he understood this time of peace as a chance to extend his missionaries' outreach and thus to improve his own status and cash flow. He therefore dispatched

Samuel Kirkland to the distant Seneca immediately when the war drums ceased their beating in 1764. That region was still unsettled and tense with hostilities, perhaps too much of an undertaking for a novice missionary. For that reason Wheelock had initially thought that Samson Occom (who had been forced out of Oneida country by the dangers of the war) would be the best candidate for the trip. He presumed that Occom, himself a Native American and a proven man in the field, would be an acceptable ambassador anywhere throughout the woodlands. By this time, however, the no-longer-young missionary had acquired a wife and numerous offspring; to hire him and support that family was considered beyond the board's resources. Therefore the challenging assignment of going forth among the Seneca as an educational missionary fell to young Kirkland, even though he had to be pulled out of Princeton to undertake it.

What he accomplished in this eighteen-month journey into hostile territory, quite apart from his success as an advertisement for Wheelock's brand of missionary work, was to give Anglo-Americans, upon the publication of his journals, an astonished and new sense of themselves as Americans—the sense that with God's help they could successfully bear any hardship their wilderness (yes, *their* wilderness) had to impose. This thoroughly American evangelist made few converts, had no momentous spiritual encounters, and provoked no great thirst for further education among the Seneca. But he did pick up their language to some extent, did learn how to conduct himself in their councils, and did present himself—and established the reputation for other educators who would come after him—as a courageous and reliable (more reliable, that is, than traders or soldiers) human being with spiritual credibility. Additionally, having been instructed at Johnson Hall before he left Mohawk country about the type of information that Sir William was eager to acquire from the Seneca (this being the year when that ever eager merchant was about to relaunch his fur trade business out to the Great Lakes), he became a first-class intelligence agent.

Perhaps he succeeded so well, and proved to be so tough in the face of the elements, because of his own humble, farm-boy beginnings—that, plus his fearless New Light faith. Having arrived at his target, the eastern Seneca village of Kanadesaga (near Geneva, New York) by means of snowshoes in January 1765, he stayed long enough to become formally adopted into a Seneca family and to learn the basics of their language. Then he set up his little school (against some local opposition) and commenced a series of voyages into the surrounding countryside. These let him see the general erosion of the Seneca culture then occurring: Alcohol was taking its toll, interaction with French traders had done away with many supportive traditions, and agriculture as they practiced it was too inefficient for them to escape periods of starvation. Although the incitements of Pontiac had passed, desperation might make them follow other militaristic saviors in the future.

Now a seasoned man of the wilderness, Samuel Kirkland returned to Lebanon with his new Seneca "brother," Tekenadie, in May 1766. Already Eleazer Wheelock was trumpeting the news of Kirkland's success on the frontier, claiming that the Charity School's program was so productive of dauntless agents that it now deserved full support from churches at home and abroad. Although that posture irritated Kirkland slightly, he was pleased to learn that the schoolmaster had succeeded in persuading Princeton to grant him a degree on the strength of his missionary work. To his profound joy, he was ordained before the end of that year. Now, with God's further help (and increased funding from the Mission Board), his work of assistance and education among the Iroquois could continue—his next assignment being among Samson Occom's Oneida. He arrived there barely in time to witness, and to raise objections at, the Fort Stanwix conference.

Occom, that rousing teacher and trusted missionary, had also returned to the missionary field, but now he accepted a pulpit among his own Connecticut Mohegan. There, despite a personal drinking problem with which he contended all his life, he became so popular and transcendent in his leadership that he was recognized as that longed-for phenomenon, a native apostle of Christ. The congregation swayed to his music as he sang the psalms; he wrote new hymns for them (some of which are still sung today). He dared make the point to all who would listen that, although he remained grateful to Eleazer Wheelock for his education, he believed that some of the Lebanon school's purposes were suspect. More specifically, he made the time-tested point that missionary work by itself—resulting in repentance and possible conversion—was not sufficient to sustain the Indian. Equally necessary was a supportive community and access to some meaningful stretches of mother earth. As Occom farmed his small patch of land and cared for his children, he illustrated this lesson with his hands as well as with his words.

To his white neighbors, however, Occom loomed as more of a local danger than a local saint. His independent opinions and popular following—as well as his occasional difficulties caused by drink—made him an unwelcome personage. A clergyman, if you please! Put on trial for a misdemeanor, he was eventually cleared, though his reputation remained blackened. When he raised his voice in defense of Indian land claims in that area of Connecticut, the murmurs against him grew even more murderous.

This was the time, moreover, when Eleazer Wheelock's need for funds had become extreme. With Sir William Johnson's growing disapproval of the New England clergy's anti-Proclamation Line, anti-Crown attitudes, and with the consequent withdrawal of Iroquois children from the Charity School, support funds diminished alarmingly. Yet then another bright notion came to the inventive Yankee clergyman. Send Samson Occom to Great Britain, where he would surely appeal irresistibly to sympathetic philanthropists: Here was your truly noble, really Christian savage. On the strength of such sentiment, Occom might even appear before the king himself! The fund-raising idea had the support of George Whitefield, who continued to be influential among the New England New Lights (and who had been both favorably impressed and spiritually influenced by Occom). The leaders agreed the trip should take place immediately; Occom sailed for England late in 1767.

He made a triumphant tour of Great Britain, triumphant both in respect to his own credibility—as an intelligent Native American and as a rightfully ordained clergyman—and also in financial terms. Introduced to the proper circles by Whitefield's friends, he collected £9,497 before moving on to Scotland to garner an additional £1,500. Everywhere he went he found interested Christians, though some of the more financially minded among them criticized Wheelock's accounting practices at the school. Returning home in 1768 (the year of the Treaty of Fort

Stanwix), Occom and his treasure chest were welcomed warmly by the schoolmaster. It seemed to Occom, however, that Eleazer Wheelock was becoming less enthusiastic about the education of young, native missionaries for service in the troubled west. Richer fields were even then on the schoolmaster's mind— specifically in New Hampshire, where the population was growing and where schools were needed and fundable.

Occom perceived, in further conversations and correspondence, that Wheelock's new concept of a school in New Hampshire was a reflection of the schoolmaster's personal discouragement with educating what he called the "tawnies." Instead, the new school (which would become Dartmouth College) would be primarily designed for the education of Anglo-American clergy. What filled Occom with understandable rage was that the monies he had so arduously raised in England for missionary purposes would now be used for this "English" institution. Separating himself entirely from the former mentor who had so unforgivably betrayed him, Occom vowed to carry on his own missionary program with the assistance of truer friends.

Truest of them all was Samuel Kirkland, who had his own reasons for choosing to break away from Eleazer Wheelock. Unhappy with his former teacher's opportunistic tendency to take all credit for any missionary success and distressed by his irregular and inadequate support of the Oneida mission, Kirkland had developed a concept for a Christian community on the frontier that went far beyond the one-shot approach favored by Wheelock. It was as clear to Kirkland in the 1760s as it had been to John Eliot in the 1660s that the education or Christianizing of the Indians could only be effective if the community in which they lived was self-supporting and self-governing.

Yet how could such an economically self-sufficient community materialize if Wheelock continued to withhold farm implements and tools, as he now was doing? How could Kirkland help direct the community toward independence if Wheelock, busy with other matters, always turned down his requests (even his reminders that salary payments were overdue)? Wheelock seemed able to focus only on such petty details as Kirkland's habit of wearing a deerhide jerkin—which the bossy schoolmaster viewed as quite improper for a New England clergyman. The arguments between the two men seemed all the more hurtful because Kirkland had married Wheelock's niece in the fall of 1768 and had done everything possible to show Wheelock due respect. The mounting quarrel was breaking the family apart. It also fractionalized the thrust of the Protestant church's missionary effort once again—this at precisely the time when Christians needed to move with unity and compassion.

Kirkland believed that Wheelock's so-called Grand Design for educational work on the frontier just made for greater weakness and dependency; it needed fundamental restructuring. It needed a more broadly conceived divine vision. Kirkland's opinion that truly strong frontier communities must be established among the Iroquois now became a personal cause. In those agricultural communities the citizens would be able to live and work with pride and responsibility, thus enabled to weather storms of drought and starvation (such as the famines experienced in the plague-ridden years of 1765 and 1767). In that sort of productive Iroquois location—and only there (certainly not in the native-decimated east, whether Connecticut or New Hampshire)—a missionary school might have a chance to exist as a working part of the culture. A plan of these dimensions was growing within Samuel Kirkland's mind when he went on home leave in 1769; significantly, he went not to up-country Lebanon but to the capital, Boston.

There he found himself welcomed, if not exactly lionized. His reputation as a colonial American who could actually move through and live in the wilderness (all the while bringing back impeccable intelligence) appealed to the Boston Board of Missions. The board members and their British backers offered to pay Kirkland a direct salary, £80 yearly, and to find necessary funds for his Oneida community. Some of the funds would come from Harvard University (which had long sought to take over the missionary work on the frontier from such New Light dissenters as Wheelock); some would also be taken, despite Wheelock's objections, from the £11,000 that Occom had raised in Great Britain.

Henceforth, to his considerable relief, Kirkland reported to a treasurer in Boston, not to Lebanon. Among the Indians, Kirkland and his ilk would be known from then on as the Boston Men, this phrase referring less to their religious preferences than to their financial sources and their political (anti-Crown) persuasions. There was, indeed, a definite political edge to the preaching of the Protestant gospel—particularly from New England pulpits—as the 1760s came to an end and as men of power throughout the colonies recognized that attempts to put Great Britain's North American empire back together again were not succeeding.

In the eyes of the king's men, too, religious issues seemed linked to political ones. In 1766, Sir William Johnson declared his political-religious position by joining London's Society for the Propagation of the Gospel in Foreign Parts, the Anglican missionary board. He went on to seek additional Anglican missionaries for the Mohawk villages, having perceived how much more enthusiasm there was for that church's grace-granting theology among the Iroquois than for the Calvinists' stricter views of who qualified for baptism and communion. He called the Presbyterians "too precise and severe" in their Christian beliefs. The Iroquois, in his judgment, should stay as close as possible to their cultural roots, while also heeding the Anglican priests and reverencing their cross; that religious discipline should aid their devotion to the essential business of supplying furs to his team of British traders. The single reason why Sir William had agreed, in times past, to support New England–trained missionaries among the Iroquois was because so few Anglican missionaries were inclined to leave their comfortable home parishes.

It was therefore into a less friendly Mohawk Valley that Samuel Kirkland returned in 1770; unfriendliness turned to outright hostility when news came of the Boston Massacre. With an Anglo-American war a distinct possibility and Sir William resolutely dedicated to the Anglican church as well as to the king, Kirkland saw that he must move swiftly to establish his innovative plan—his American plan. Finally free of the uncomfortable, destructive entanglements with Eleazer Wheelock and clearly understanding the contradictions between his church and Sir William's old order, his job was to

persuade the Iroquois to trust in a new kind of heavenly and
earthly kingdom.

From MISSIONARY to PATRIOT

Kanowarohare, the Oneida community that Samuel Kirkland
built adjacent to Oneida Castle, may have a baleful name—
it means "head on a pole"—but it stands forth from its time
as one of the most successful missionary communities ever
founded in North America. Among its many historical plusses,
Kanowarohare helped Americans win the Revolution of 1775.
Because the Oneida and their Tuscarora cousins gathered there
agreed intellectually with the political concept of liberty and
freedom (a political commitment that broke the Six Nations
apart), these two exceptional Iroquois nations went decisively
forth equipped to fight key wilderness battles, including decisive Saratoga. Yet a terrible irony lies in the success of Kanowarohare as a war base, for it was originally designed to be a
place of peace and prosperity, a place where a very special
brand of Christianity would tame the wild spirit and refine the
mind. Also, its life was critically short—its structures as well as
its moral, interracial meaning were swept away within a few
decades of its founding. Few Oneida today choose to recall the
foundation work there of Samson Occom or the era of growth
with Samuel Kirkland; despite the fact that Occom was a Native
American, they regard his missionary efforts as equally extra-
neous as Kirkland's.

By 1772, Kanowarohare's first buildings had been completed: seventeen log huts for the resident Oneida. A smithy
and two mills were later additions, great boosts to the agricul-

tural productivity. But the most important engineering accomplishment was the new twelve-mile road to Fort Stanwix, for it
was over this road that needed supplies would come and agricultural products would be exchanged. At the heart of the community of some 720 people, Kirkland and his enthusiasts set
about building their church, a large and handsome structure
that had been specifically opposed by Sir William Johnson. It
measured thirty-six by twenty-eight feet on the ground; its
crossless spire soared sixty feet into the air for all to see. From
its belfry tolled a grand bell captured from the French at Niagara in 1759.

Within this large, rough building, Samuel Kirkland carried
out the usual, exhausting program of preaching and hymn
singing that characterized New England Protestant churches
in the eighteenth century. Preaching in the emotional style of
Jonathan Edwards, Kirkland called for repentance and public
confession of sins. Recalling how well the service had gone on a
particular Sunday, with his Iroquois gathered as usual for prayer,
Kirkland wrote: "A more solemn Assembly I never saw, not one
appeared trifling or unconcerned, and many flowed in tears....
My exercise was 2 Hours and a half long." Archaeologists believe there may also have been a separate council house of traditional Iroquois construction. A contemporary visitor spoke of
the "Sachems then sitting in Council in a Miserable old long
Hutt situated in the Center of their Town." He also reported that
nearby was a common, "one very large cleared Field, in which
all their Horses and Cattle graze promiscuously."

In his addresses to his flock, Samuel Kirkland did not re-
frain from pressing upon them a patriotic interpretation of the

then breaking events in Massachusetts and the other colonies. He wanted the Oneida to understand not only why the Anglo-American settlers felt that it was God's will for men to be free of tyrants, citing biblical precedents for the philosophy of freedom, but also why the Iroquois, too, might rightly be called upon to take action on the side of the rebels. This was, of course, precisely the opposite of what the Mohawk were hearing sixty-odd miles away in such towns as Canajoharie and Fort Hunter. There the Indians, gathered in Anglican chapels and in the conferences called by Sir William Johnson, were asked to pray for the king and heard tales about the reckless disobedience of the colonists. How deserved it was that because of the Bostonians' irrational refusal to pay their just taxes, taxes necessary to pay for the wars that had but so recently prevented their destruction, the wrathful king had decided to close their harbor! Yet, because of this limitation of trade along the coast, the Mohawk, too, were now suffering from a lack of goods. In response to their needs, Sir William struggled to arrange an official variance in the admiralty regulations, for the sake of his "children."

Among those who heard and ardently believed this presentation of affairs was Sir William's protégé, the bright, educated, and ambitious Joseph Brant. His natural attributes could never make up for his lack of close connection with the network of matriarchal Mohawk aristocracy, but despite that, he succeeded in building on the power derived from his sister's noble husband (Sir William), the superintendent of Indian Affairs. Now a fully grown man and rather formidable looking, Brant earned a respectable income from both translation work and, when necessary, hauling boats up and around the river's falls. Yet he yearned for a larger role in his people's affairs.

He was the proud father of two black-eyed children. When his beloved wife, Peggy, died of consumption in 1771, his grief was eased through the aid of an Anglican missionary named John Stuart. This was the priest who succeeded in bringing him closer to God, he felt, than any of the New England clergy with whom he had been so closely associated. Indeed, it was through the returned assistance that Brant gave to Father Stuart—helping in his translations of the *Book of Common Prayer* and the *Gospel of St. Mark*—that the Mohawk warrior would later gain a not quite deserved reputation as a scholar of the scriptures. In fact, Brant's command of English at this point was rough; he had a long way to go before becoming the polished courtier of later years. Nonetheless, he could handle intercultural communications handily, speaking bluntly but effectively in defense of Indians whose lands were sought by whites.

Although Brant considered himself a loyal citizen, loyal to both King and Cross, he regarded friendships made at Eleazer Wheelock's school as friendships to be preserved. Later in the decade, when he saw an angry Mohawk raise his hatchet to attack Samuel Kirkland (perhaps in response to orders from General Gage in Quebec), Brant intervened to save his classmate's life. In 1774 shocking news came to the valley of a campaign against Ohio Shawnee led by Virginia's splenetic Governor Dunmore, an aristocrat who had dissolved his colony's assembly after it had voted to support Bostonians blockaded by the British fleet. Laying claim to territory in Indian country way beyond the line set at the Fort Stanwix treaty, the governor and his fifteen hundred militiamen defeated Chief Cornstalk near the point where the Kanawha meets the Ohio, then pressed on to the Scioto.

As Brant and other Iroquois heard reports of Cornstalk's defeat with dismay and sympathy, Sir William used all his authority as superintendent of Indian Affairs to keep the Six Nations out of the fray (known in history books as Governor Dunmore's War). Yet the Mohawk and other Iroquois must have had doubts about that authority—that is, Johnson's ability to do right by the people who had loved and adopted him—when he allowed additional white settlers to move up the Mohawk River and settle on tribal lands after the threat of Pontiac's armies had passed. Then came word of the Quebec Act of 1774, which extended the southern boundary of that province all the way to the Ohio River and put territories along that frontier under the administration of Crown officers in Quebec. This act, perceived as favoring Roman Catholics, not only distressed the Iroquois but also inflamed Anglo-American and other Protestant colonists of different national origins. They translated their combined fury into a bellicose measure against the act when the Continental Congress convened at Philadelphia later that year.

At length the Iroquois's and the settlers' demands for clarification of the Crown's intentions became too much for Sir William to deny. Despite failing health and the rigors of a blindingly hot July day, the grand patron summoned three hundred Iroquois representatives to Johnson Hall and attempted to soothe them with his usual paternalistic assurances and references to the Great Spirit. Joseph Brant was there, too, among the sachems, listening, relishing the drama of the day, and assessing the forces at play. The meeting lasted until six in the evening—the sun then still being high in the sky but Sir William too exhausted to continue. It was expected that on the next day, after the chiefs of the Six Nations had counseled together, they would deliver to him an equally eloquent and lengthy reply. But two hours later, as the blazing sun sank below the horizon and night finally brought its ease, Sir William was pronounced dead. With that almost Wagnerian death, his lordly scheme for binding the northern woodlands together in the Covenant Chain and in the king's and archbishop's bonds of empire sank like the setting sun behind the treetops.

In Kanowarohare, Samuel Kirkland attempted to explain this turning of the times, this passing of Cross and King, to his Oneida congregation. His words struck his audience as confirming. They already knew that, while the king lived far away across the ocean, the "Boston Men" and the swarming Connecticut Yankees lived close at hand, with their sharp plows, numerous children, and available rum. The Oneida, as guardians of the "southern gate" to Iroquoia, also could see the expansive behavior of the Pennsylvanians who continued to settle along the rivers with their mighty oxen and strange mix of heritages. Trading and contending with this variety of Anglo-American frontiersman had become standard operating procedure. The Oneida were now far more comfortable with these neighbors than with the arrogant heirs of Sir William Johnson up in the Mohawk Valley—a way of life that no longer seemed as constructive as it had a generation ago.

Kirkland put all of his faith and personal credibility behind explanations of the patriots' intentions to liberate all people from the rule of foreign, feudalistic rulers; he illustrated his message with ready similes from the Bible. Religion aside, his political message fell upon ready ears. The Oneida had seen, in the Crown's drafting of the Proclamation Line (which had deprived them of key territories), just how little their previous loyalty was valued by the king. Furthermore, they no longer relished the traditional idea of continuously submitting themselves to their big brothers, the Mohawk. The time had come for new relationships.

Samuel Kirkland, considering what this change of orientation meant for his mission, saw that he must find a place for himself and for his congregation (potential citizens!) within the American nation then forming. Strapping travel gear on the back of his saddle and concluding hasty prayers for all left behind, he headed down the Unadilla River toward Philadelphia and the First Continental Congress.

PART III

CHAPTER 7

PROPHETS of TWO
SEPARATE REVOLUTIONS

SEEKING TO DISMISS and disaffirm the American Revolution,
Great Britain's King George III remarked that it was, at
heart, "nothing more than a Presbyterian rebellion." New Jersey's first governor, William Livingstone—a stalwart warrior
in the Revolution and member of the First and Second Continental Congresses—recalled that his state's largely Presbyterian clergy had been "almost all universally good Whigs,"
thereby seeming to agree with the king that John Calvin's and
Gilbert Tennent's strain of Protestantism had been at the root
of the American struggle for independence. Yet the kind of independence that Americans, both red and white, fought for in
their respective and simultaneous revolutions on the frontier
had only distantly to do with the credo of any European theologian or political theorist. They fought, both red and white,
for concepts shaped by North American encounters, concepts
perhaps derived from antecedent, cultural sources but more
surely related to the psychic stresses experienced in the forests
and fastness of this continent. It was because of those cultural
encounters that people of the borderlands responded so robustly

to the calls of their respective, revolutionary prophets in the spiritually complex eighteenth century.

To the Algonquian and Iroquois—competitive peoples who had so recently witnessed the British Crown's victory over French imperial forces—the American War of Independence looked like a fratricidal civil war among English-speaking power cliques. It gave further dreadful evidence that Anglo-Americans were not bound together in any meaningful religious commitment. A pious Mohawk convert and classmate of Joseph Brant, on hearing of the war's outbreak, exclaimed in distress, "Oh, Britain! Oh, no! Can the heathens now say: Behold and see how those Christians love one another?"

What that pious Mohawk lad may not have perceived, as he pondered the import of the British-American war, was that the Indians, too, were engaged in a life-or-death struggle among themselves. Beset by wrenching conflicts between traditionalists and radicals, the Iroquois and Algonquian peoples of the northern woodland were deeply divided by both political and spiritual issues. From 1775 until long after Yorktown, native brothers fought against native brothers up and down the Mohawk River valley; Algonquian villages went to war against neighboring Algonquian villages in the Ohio heartland—all for reasons customarily described as external (i.e., imposed by the white man's disruptive presence) but more truly seen as internal as well.

Within the continuum of Indian culture, a new generation of reformers and activists gave voice to emergent issues. Their audiences responded passionately, if not always affirmatively. Whereas a stirring of religious consciousness within Indian nations of northeastern America had occurred in the mid-1700s at the time of the Great Awakening, another expression of Native Americans' messianic and prophetic themes burst forth at the end of that century and the beginning of the next. At this historic, spiritual turning point, two significant leaders—Handsome Lake from the Iroquois Seneca and Tenskwatawa from the Algonquian Shawnee—would assert themselves in revolutionary roles, standing forth against the conventional wisdom and the archaic leadership of their own peoples.

The reformist and revitalizing voices of prophesy arising from the Indian nations were affected both by certain beneficial concepts within the philosophy of the American Revolution (including political liberty and egalitarian nationalism) and by disturbing events concomitant with that war. Among the latter must be included not only war's material events (revised borders, unforgettable butcheries, all-too-swift victories, etc.) but also the seldom examined, soul-searing significance of those events. In the words of Farmer's Brother—a Seneca chief who witnessed the birth of Handsome Lake's religion—the American Revolution was "a great tumult and commotion, like a raging whirlwind which tears up the trees, and tosses to and fro the leaves, so that no one knows from whence they came and where they will fall." Indeed, as anthropologists instruct us, people live and work out their lives not so much in a world of physical events as in a world of consequent meanings or interpretations.

The War of Independence certainly had a shocking and profound impact on native civilizations. Conversely, the Indians' inner contest and revitalized leadership had an effect on the character and purpose of white Americans' Revolution. For the

Americans' encounters with the Indians changed the thrust of the Revolution, most notably on the frontier. Consider these two points:

1. The military objectives of the war in America's interior territories shifted dramatically from an attempt to achieve freedom from Britain to an attempt to destroy the power of emergent, militant Indians (war commanders such as Joseph Brant and the Seneca leader Cornplanter, and ultimately Tenskwatawa's brother, Tecumseh).

2. The political and cultural attempt to end the war and thus define the United States as a nation was ultimately worked out not in the Treaty of Paris but in a series of treaties with the western Indians, treaties made and broken and remade under the watchful eyes of British commanders in the not yet surrendered forts on the Great Lakes.

Let it be remembered that Washington's army of Continentals launched its largest assault during the Revolution not against the British in 1777 or 1778 but against the corn-rich, spirited, unreconcilable Iroquois in 1779. When the war against the British appeared to be won at Yorktown in 1781, the war against their Indian allies continued until 1794. Only then did Great Britain—in declining to aid Indians fighting against victorious General "Mad Anthony" Wayne—signal her surrender by total withdrawal from American territory.

The dynamic spiritual forces behind the American Revolution—not limited to the Presbyterians singled out by King George III—succeeded in influencing Indian culture in ways far more telling than mere military conquest. The native holy men who gave heart to freedom fighters against the American generals proclaimed ancient principles and practiced age-old rituals; at the same time, they also rediscovered and absorbed certain aspects of the mixed-culture experience. These included, even beyond being a diverse nation, united in war, the experience of joining a syncretistic religion, formed from old and new. Thus, for many Indians, the American Revolution was a deeply challenging spiritual test. And for the Christian Indians who chose to fight in support of the American cause (and who were later robbed of their share in the victory), the Revolution provided an opportunity, though a tragic one, to experience another aspect of their sacrificial religion.

Between 1775 and 1794 (and continuing on through the War of 1812 until the time of the Indian Removal Act in 1830), the winds of revolution and war would sweep through both red and white civilizations. People would find in their religions both justification for slaughtering their neighbors and inspiration for revitalizing society. Although it might appear that the respective divinities then worked in ways more contradictory than creative, this was evidently a spring seedtime, a germinative era when the destiny of all Americans, red and white, was not in their own hands.

As one looks more closely at the War of Independence, it becomes a disconnected story not only of opposed philosophies but also of divinely inspired men of different religions, establishing quite different but equally enduring myths and behaviors—Indian nationalism and American evangelical imperialism (also known as Manifest Destiny). The lives of two one-time colleagues, Samuel Kirkland and Joseph Brant, reveal

how their divergent faiths and revolutionary actions helped
shape those long-lasting cultural patterns.

REVOLUTIONARY FAITHS of FORMER ACOLYTES

Before and after Samuel Kirkland's swift march to the Continental Congress in Philadelphia in 1774, he lectured "his
people" at Kanowarohare on the significance of the Revolution's ideals, ideals that he considered applicable to all humankind. Surely the Oneida desired to liberate themselves from
the tyranny of such overlords as Sir William Johnson and to become free! Surely, too, they yearned to separate themselves
from the ancient, suffocating arrogance of the Mohawk!

Kirkland's impassioned sermons to that effect became more
authoritative after he received official requests from the New
York Provincial Congress, urging him to do whatever possible
to keep the Oneida and Tuscarora, and even accessible Mohawk, in proper political alignment, for their own good. Their
health and survival were undeniably Kirkland's prime purpose,
and for this Christian attitude he was beloved (even though the
Oneida continued to rue the New England missionary's refusal
to baptize their uninstructed children). Neighborly relations between Kirkland and the British power center at Johnson Hall in
the Mohawk Valley had grown increasingly strained as 1774
ripened into 1775. The missionary had even been forcibly de-
tained by the Johnsons, but finally freed after Joseph Brant
saved his schoolmate's life in the famous episode of the knife-
wielding Mohawk.

Revolutionary officials at Albany anxiously requested Kirkland to bring wavering Iroquois chiefs to the provincial capital
for conferences and lectures and, of course, gifts. In those par-

leys the missionary served not only as translator but also as a kind of sympathetic social worker. Never losing sight of the condition and the needs of the people, he demanded that two blacksmiths be sent to live as instructors among the Oneida (an argument he had made often with Sir William but never won). He also demanded, with less success, that American officials, instead of haranguing the chiefs with their demeaning, propagandistic phrases, employ the kind of religious imagery in their rhetoric that the Iroquois regarded as essential to civilized, diplomatic contracts.

In recognition of Kirkland's emerging position, the colony's revolutionary council gave him a stipend that made up for his loss of financial backing from the Missionary Board in those disruptive times. Indeed, Kirkland's role became increasingly that of an official agent, a paid hand for the revolutionary government. This function—half spy and half ambassador on the uneasy frontier—might seem a strange role for one of God's ordained ministers. But, as biographers now present the man and his times, Kirkland himself was experiencing a remarkable transformation, transformed by the pressures of the Revolution into another kind of missionary, the herald of American evangelical nationalism.

Speaking to this point himself, Kirkland remarked a year later (when he had become a military chaplain), "I find it more agreeable here [at Fort Stanwix] than I had expected." And later he wrote:

I don't feel so anxious about events [in this role] as I have been for time past. I feel more disposed to attend to present duty and to confide in Infinite wisdom for the management

of all that concerns His cause & the cause of my country.
I find it more comfortable to rest the future Events entirely
with God.

In a way strikingly different from Père de Brébeuf, the
Presbyterian missionary had put divine contemplations on hold,
concentrating on becoming an effective part of his fighting
nation.

Earlier, even in the first year of the war and in support
of his new revolutionary faith, Kirkland assembled a number
of Oneida and Tuscarora chiefs to accompany him on a tour of
New England and New Jersey in order that they might observe
the democratic government and the Continental army in action.
Although the chiefs were somewhat skeptical of the U.S. pre-
tentions to victory, they behaved with admirable decorum as
the Revolution rumbled around them. Ultimately they were
won over by word of the American triumphs at Trenton and
Princeton.

Indeed, Oneida leaders of today make the point that their
historic allegiance to America-in-revolution was a choice of
their own making—not a decision they were pushed into by
beloved missionaries (if beloved they were) or clever diplomats. They pledged themselves to the cause, a cause whose
virtues they could understand, yet whose consequences they
could hardly guess. For those native leaders and their communities, the American Revolution would prove to be a trial by
fire, a test in which the patriotic mettle of many would be arduously proved. Unfortunately, for most of them the victory of a
battle-scarred United States would be a death-dealing fate.

Soon after Samuel Kirkland's first visit to Philadelphia
(from which he had returned to Kanowarohare equipped with
wampum beads—the still vital coin of both trade and diplomacy), Samson Occom had a memorable talk with George
Washington in the revolutionary capital. Occom, that paradigm
of native Christian saints, would have reason to recall this talk
after the war when his special talents were required once again
by the insecure nation. But now, in this first year of the war,
both he and Kirkland had to concentrate on winning government guarantees of security and reward for the friendship of
those Iroquois not automatically inclined toward Great Britain
by reason of trade.

With convincing arguments, the missionaries supported the
strategy of preserving the neutrality of the Six Nations—a
position favored by Washington and other officials wary of en-
tangling alliances. Washington, in seeming deference to Indian
independence, went so far as to decline an offer from one Mohawk chief in the St. Lawrence River valley to supply hundreds
of warriors for the pending attack on Quebec. Although reasons
for this neutralist policy were numerous—including the unde-
sirability of bringing the always volatile Indians into a white
men's war and the disadvantage of forcing the hand of the
British on the frontier—there were also arguments for taking a
more aggressive approach to the issue of Native Americans.

Neither Washington's cabinet nor the Continental Congress
wanted to be faced with the consequences of having treated the
Indians as equals during or after the War of Independence.
John Adams spoke darkly of the Indians as "very expensive and
troublesome confederates in war," and went on to mention the

"inhumanity of employing such savages, with their cruel, bloody dispositions, against any enemy whatever." Some years later, Major General Philip Schuyler, head of the Revolutionary command's Northern Department, found exculpatory words to express the general feeling that the Indians must, sooner or later, disappear. He wrote that the Iroquois "will be of no obstacle to our future ... for, as our settlements approach their country, they must from [the resultant] scarcity of game ... retire further back and dispose of their lands."

Even as they strove to stabilize the frontier and to negate the British-Iroquois threat, leaders of the Continental Congress could not resist involving the tribesmen in their own purposes, if only as passive protectors of the nation's vulnerable western flank. A trustworthy candidate (or likely tool) for that function presented himself in the person of a Delaware sachem named White Eyes. He appeared, in full dignity, before the Continental Congress in the winter of 1775 and spring of 1776. This was a man who had learned from his grandfather, a Lenni Lenape chief who had dealt with William Penn, that peace and harmony between red and white might be achieved. So personable and available was White Eyes that he gave even Samuel Adams reason to think this Indian might be a civilized American. "The Chief was dressed in a good suit of Blue Cloth with a Laced Hat," a congressman recorded. And, further, "White Eyes shook all the Members heartily by the Hand, beginning with the President."

White Eyes had become familiar with the principles of the American Revolution through discussions with his friend, the unusually honest trader George Morgan (slated to become the official agent for Indian Affairs in the mid-Atlantic zone). The

Delaware sachem recognized the ideals set forth by Morgan as implicitly sacred, quite in keeping with his culture's ancient religious tenets. In volunteering to represent the revolutionary cause among his kinsmen on the Ohio frontier, White Eyes asked only for a few things from Congress: a schoolteacher, a blacksmith, and a minister. Benjamin Franklin, one of the assembled representatives, then made a famous remark to the effect that, for Indians who looked forward to citizenship and a constructive life under America's new flag, a blacksmith would be far more helpful than a minister.

Lobbying patiently for a bill to fund his program on behalf of the Delaware, White Eyes finally won the vote of Congress. And, by gaining the requested assistance, he scored a major triumph—diplomatic recognition for the Delaware nation. The coup encouraged him to hope that his fellow nationals, along with other Indians who might join them in a long-sought confederation, might be recognized on some victorious day as the Republic's fourteenth state. Yet there were, as time would tell, many flaws and loopholes in the agreement written between the Continental Congress and the Delaware. One of the most glaring of them was that the minister requested and supplied was an Anglican. Although the nomination of such a clergyman was made in perfect innocence (for, after all, Anglicanism continued to be the faith of most people in the southern colonies), and although John Hancock himself approved sending an Anglican missionary, that choice of denomination would prove to be a continuing problem for White Eyes. His Americanism, in the opinion of many English-hating colonists (particularly by those under the Moravians' influence), would forever be suspect.

While attempting to defend their flank, the revolutionary nation's congressmen and military leaders were engaging in the first battles of the war; simultaneously, the heirs of Sir William Johnson were seeking to secure their own properties in the Mohawk Valley by keeping the Iroquois faithful to the Crown. Threatened by the ever expanding settlers of German descent twenty miles away in the Palatine Bridge area as well as by immigrants from New England, the Johnsons knew that their time as lords of the borderlands was limited. They and Joseph Brant, having learned to their dismay that Samuel Kirkland and Samson Occom had succeeded in subverting the Oneida and Tuscarora to the Americans, saw that the two-hundred-year-old Iroquois Confederation, that noble league of Hiawatha, was being wrecked beyond repair. In the language of the Haudenosaunee, "the central fire was covered." Yet, trusting that something remained of the old tribal and confederation loyalty, the Johnsons sought protection for their properties from loyal Native Americans in all parts of their former empire. But the Yankees were on the march!

Although first rumors of an "army" of patriots marching up the valley proved false, Guy Johnson (Sir William's son-in-law) was soon seized by local patriots and briefly held in house arrest in Johnson Hall. In May of 1775, when peremptory orders reached him from the revolutionary government in Boston that he must bring a delegation of Mohawk east to confer with them, Johnson saw that he and his family could not afford to linger. Joseph Brant also understood the need to flee, even as he imagined how the invading Yankees and German settlers might ruin his tidy home, his spreading farms, his beautiful chapel. Most of his fears were justified. Within a few months his home had been wrecked and his chapel turned into a tavern, the lectern serving as support for the rum keg. Collecting family members and scores of like-minded Mohawk, Brant and the Johnsons loaded possessions into sturdy wagons and rolled slowly north to Canada. Before he left Johnson Hall, Joseph took his tomahawk and slashed at the banister rail in frustration. The farewell scar can still be seen.

In Canada, the British military command debated a policy of Indian neutrality against the advantages of adding native ancillaries to their armies' strengths. In a move to counter the patriots' diplomatic conferences at Albany in 1775, they organized a massive assembly of tribesmen at Fort Ontario. Attended by nearly fifteen hundred Indians, this great British propaganda effort drew in participants from far beyond the boundaries of the Six Nations. Great speeches were heard about the sacred qualities of the Covenant Chain. At a subsequent meeting in Montreal, Joseph Brant (acting as translator) assured the gathered Mohawk that, after the inevitable British victory, the ever generous Crown would surely return to them whatever land they had left behind.

Yet Brant had the intelligence to ask himself what, in the long run, might be gained from King George III, and what price might the Six Nations have to pay for their alliance with that often weak-kneed monarch. Surely, he reasoned, before the Indians signed up to fight on Great Britain's side, they must receive guarantees of the king's total commitment to the war and the British must understand the everlasting nature of their obligations. To make those points, he sailed to England with Guy Johnson on November 11, 1775.

It happened that Ethan Allen, leader of the Green Mountain

Boys and hometown hero—conqueror of Fort Ticonderoga, was in the brig of Brant's ship, a manacled prisoner. Yet chains could not quell his mind. This burly and voluble Vermonter, captured during the recent attack on Quebec, was a phenomenon of nature. Here, even in European eyes, was not that regrettable thing—the English colonial who had turned traitor; no, here was an authentic product of the swamps and hillsides, an indigenous American mountain man.

Proud of his book-learned Deism and of his bare-fisted victory at Ticonderoga, Ethan Allen told and retold to all who would listen the story of that daring night attack. When asked that night by the fort's commander in whose authority he had acted, Allen boomed forth the reply: "In the name of the Great Jehovah and the Continental Congress!" Later in the final years of the war, when returned home in exchange for British prisoners, he flirted with Toryism and became his own press agent, publishing news of his wild adventures and even wilder beliefs. In his own spirited way, he remained an independent Yankee to the very end.

Although Joseph Brant avoided any onboard discourse with the American captive, he felt he should make his own demonstration of independence on arriving at the king's court. His official function there was merely to serve as a yes-man for Guy Johnson, who was seeking to be named superintendent of Indian Affairs. But the young Mohawk, at the time when all eyes were on him, shocked the court by declining to kiss the king's hand. This he did not by way of disrespect but as an indication that he was an emissary to the court from the Six Nations, not a subject of the Crown.

That point having been made, Joseph Brant went on to become a lion of British society, delighting in the costumes one had to wear and succeeding in impressing even James Boswell with his education (which was, in fact, not that impressive). On the diplomatic front, he succeeded in winning a windy statement of support for his cause from the king's ministers—a somewhat vacuous and very tortured pledge of assistance for the Six Nations. Brant loyally chose to believe it, went faithfully to church, and eventually returned to his native valley in the summer of 1776 very much the king's man. Now he was all the more eager to lead his Mohawk and all similarly minded members of the Six Nations into combat against the rebels.

One might ask, What had Joseph Brant really become? Partially, an ever ready and unquestioning soldier. Accordingly, having learned of the Americans' defeat at Quebec and of the ongoing campaign by Lord Howe to capture New York, Brant flung himself into the fray. But he was more than a red-uniformed red warrior; he now (aged thirty-five) perceived himself as a working part of the Mohawk leadership. In turn, he was regarded by his people as a kind of headquarters functionary, if only because of his education and association with highly placed British officers. Yet his biographer Isabel Kelsay stresses that his command of English was still imperfect and his rapport with British officialdom not close.

Nonetheless, he thought of himself as thoroughly British. Among the Mohawk, there was a tradition of each young man having a most beloved companion; the friend closest to Brant's heart was young Lord Percy, whom he first met in England, now an officer in Montreal. Here was Brant's ideal, his most admired

example of a moral and Christian courtier. Though the An-
glophile Mohawk could never become a British nobleman like
his elegant and devout friend, he *could* become an officer and
gentleman. And so he did, even amid the brutalities of the
double American Revolution, and even as his frontier foes,
bloodied in his raids, referred to him as "that beast Brant."

The spiritual struggles accompanying the War of Independence were, indeed, effecting strange conversions among people
up and down the line. The war's pressures changed Samuel
Kirkland from an otherworldly clergyman into an evangelist of
nationalism; they turned Joseph Brant, once a child of the forest, into a loyalist of Anglican faith and gentlemanly morals. An
overheard remark by Brant revealed how far behind him lay the
years of instruction by Eleazer Wheelock and Connecticut's
Calvinist clergy. Accidentally biting into an unpalatable apple,
he spat it out and exclaimed, "It's bitter as a Presbyterian!"

By the LOSS of a MEDICINE KIT, a SIEGE DEFEATED

Although General Philip Schuyler had his own jingoistic opinion of the inevitability of the Indians' disappearance before the
march of American civilization, he was sufficiently aware of the
power situation in the New York area to recognize that the Iroquois needed to be very delicately handled. Meeting with a selected number of Iroquois chiefs early in 1776, Schuyler asked,
through the verbiage of the time-tested protocols, if it might be
acceptable for the United States to occupy and repair old Fort
Stanwix at the head of the Mohawk River. As recorded in the
papers of DeWitt Clinton, the chiefs said that they would not
take umbrage at such a move, but that any passage of armies
through their territory, whether American or British, would be

regarded as a hostile and defining act of war against them. Schuyler replied that it was precisely to prevent such an invasion that the fort (whose name was soon changed to honor him) needed to be manned and improved. George Washington, well aware that the fort was key to defense of the western frontier— the only other frontier fort then in American hands being Fort Pitt—agreed to send troops (the Third New Jersey Regiment) to rebuild the fort in the summer of 1776. But by the time the Third New York Regiment joined the New Jersey contingent at Fort Schuyler in May 1777, reconstruction of the log fort was still not complete.

The establishment of an American presence at Fort Schuyler, including the emplacement of Kirkland as its chaplain, was of profound importance to the Mohawk on the one hand and to the Oneida on the other. From their respective sides of the American Revolution, they viewed the strengthened fort quite differently. To the Oneida, it seemed a convincing demonstration that the Americans had the spiritual and military power to take charge of the region; to the Mohawk it seemed a confrontational maneuver that interrupted their communications with the west (that is, with their pledged brethren throughout Iroquoia) and threatened to impose a new kind of domination. Who might help them win their own kind of freedom?

Joseph Brant, only recently returned from England, hastened along well-remembered trails to visit his scattered family at Oquaga on the Susquehanna in the spring of 1777. There he raised the British ensign and, in effect, opened a recruiting office for all who would join him in attacks on the presumptuous Yankees. He saw the American flag at Fort Schuyler as an affront both to his own Mohawk inheritance and to the religion and sovereign he had adopted as his own. That rebellious flag intruded upon his vision of a vibrant Iroquois state guaranteed by the eternities of the British empire.

In fact, Fort Schuyler's red-white-and-blue banner, offensive as it may have been to Joseph Brant, stands in history as the first American flag unfurled under combat circumstances. It was raised by the fort's courageous twenty-eight-year-old commanding officer, Peter Gansevoort, whose father had sent him forth into the Revolution with the Roman-style admonition, "Conquer or die!" Much like his opponent Joseph Brant, Colonel Gansevoort viewed Fort Schuyler as the place where loyalty to land and religion and nationhood would be put to the test.

Through his contacts, Brant soon learned of the grand British plan to quash the Revolution by a three-pronged attack—down Lake Champlain, up the Hudson River, and across Lake Ontario. It was the latter thrust, under the command of the volatile, bibulous Barry St. Leger (who had served well with Wolfe at Quebec), that particularly interested Brant. It would bring British and allied troops charging down his Mohawk Valley and would wipe out precisely those intrusive Americans whom he despised. Hastening to put himself and his band of volunteer followers on the line for that campaign, Brant was conspicuously in attendance at the July conference called by St. Leger at Fort Oswego on Lake Ontario. The young Mohawk leader did all he could to urge the other war chiefs of the Six Nations to do likewise—to assemble themselves and their warriors at the junction of the three rivers near Oswego where they might feast, receive due honors, and commit themselves to the British command.

Brant was well aware of the reluctance of many hereditary sachems to abandon their carefully considered positions of neutrality. But he counted on the British to provide enough gifts and enough promises of war pelf and increased trade to persuade the less militaristically inclined. Surely General Schuyler, leader of the stingy Yankees, would offer no such rewards, Brant pointed out. Come join the battle! Did the Iroquois wish to see the Americans hold this fort, located in their very midst, just as they had seized Fort Ticonderoga farther east? The chiefs responded warily, the Seneca agreeing to take part in St. Leger's expedition only as fellow travelers, remaining on the periphery of the battle—though willing to share in the fruits of victory.

For the Americans, there was a corresponding, initial resistance to join the militia corps commanded by a local farmer known to history as General Nicholas Herkimer. In his heavily accented English, betraying origins in the German-speaking settlements along the Mohawk River, the farmer turned general urged his fellow patriots to hurry up, gather their arms, and march with him upriver while there was still a chance to defend Fort Schuyler against St. Leger.

But descriptions of the size of the combined British and Iroquois army that was about to sweep down the valley continued to discourage volunteers. Then came word of the first successes of the enemy army commanded by Johnnie Burgoyne that was majestically moving down from Canada, as well as wild reports of his Algonquian allies' rapacious behavior. So bloodthirsty were those Indians that, as the story was told, they even scalped and violated the daughter of one of Burgoyne's officers—Jane McCrae, blessed be her name—and the godless

British chose to condone the ghastly act! At once, the farmers realized it was their land they must protect, their women they must save. As they signed up, General Herkimer assured them that, yes, indeed, God was on their side. They would also be protected on the march by sixty totally committed, wilderness-wise Oneida braves, good Christians all.

American history, the victor's history, has generally not told the story of the resulting battle (the Battle of Oriskany and the defense of Fort Schuyler) from the Indians' perspective. Viewing it that way, the point stands out that, with Oneida warriors committed to combat against their Iroquois cousins, this frontier battle was essentially a civil war among the League of Six Nations. Obversely, American history has most often viewed the story as an Anglo-American event, focused on the sweating farmers who followed General Herkimer on that blazingly hot day of August 6 and fell into a Mohawk-led ambush at Oriskany Creek, some six miles from Fort Schuyler. The ambush, led by the ubiquitous Joseph Brant (who had been warned of the oncoming Americans by his sister at Johnson Hall), succeeded in stopping and battering Herkimer. But the mortally wounded general refused to surrender the field, standing with a shattered leg supported by a tree stump and continuing to issue commands. This final, bloody phase of the combat also served to terrorize the Seneca, many of whom fell beneath the still firing muskets of the Oneida and the bayonets of the militiamen. This was no common wilderness engagement; this was a fight of cousins, to the death.

The conventional white man's history of the Revolution also tells of how, during the next month, a slightly larger and better trained force of Continentals under Benedict Arnold campaigned up the same trail in order to revenge Oriskany and break the siege of Fort Schuyler (which had been initiated by St. Leger on August 7). Arnold seized the day and relieved the fort without firing a shot—a rather surprising victory. Those conventional histories are vague about the details: How did it happen that the Iroquois allies on whom St. Leger had depended for support dwindled away so rapidly, forcing the befuddled general to slink back to Oswego? Thus the Crown's strategic plan to strike from the west came miraculously to naught, thanks to Gansevoort's superhuman courage and to Arnold's extraordinary good luck (plus a bit of earlier help from Herkimer and the Oneida).

For a deeper understanding of the situation, it is helpful to look more closely at the Indian-versus-Indian encounter at Fort Schuyler—a part of the Indians' own simultaneous revolution. The key episode in the struggle at Fort Schuyler (as emphasized by National Park scholars who have studied the documents and sorted through the local stories) occurred just when Benedict Arnold's battalion was approaching, preceded by much thumping of drums and by carefully promoted rumors that his men were as many as "leaves on the trees." One of the broadcasters of this misinformation was an apparently dim-witted and physically deformed Tory named Hans Jost Schuyler. Captured and released by the Americans, he finally reached the safety of the British lines; there he tripped over his words and foamed at the mouth in terror as he described the size of Arnold's army.

Because they were fascinated by unusual persons with twisted features and misshapen bodies, suspecting them of being otherworldly, the Iroquois gave special attention to Hans Jost and his rantings. That much of the story has occasionally been told and evaluated: The Indians began to fear that something was cosmically amiss. But the ultimate threat that darkened the spirits of the besieging Iroquois occurred when the Seneca returned from the bloody combat at Oriskany and found that their camp had been raided by Gansevoort's second in command, Marinus Willet. From the Seneca's camp Willet had not only taken away wagon loads of supplies desperately needed by his besieged Americans, but he had also in the process seized those holiest of objects, the medicine kits of the warriors. Bereft of these links with their divinities, upset by the portents and rumors, and unimpressed by St. Leger, the Iroquois chose to leave the British to themselves. Perhaps they would join them for a fight another day. Thus did native spirits, as perceived by their devotees, give the battle to Benedict Arnold and his Oneida rebels.

Along with other Christianized and revolutionized Indians—particularly the Stockbridge Indians—the Oneida fought as an essential part of America's armed force at another key battle, Saratoga. Winning this battle helped Benjamin Franklin persuade the French that this War of Independence might well result in a Franco-American victory and a stunning British defeat. Ironically, the Indians on America's side at Saratoga faced as their fiercest enemies not the British—mighty as Burgoyne's army appeared to be in the fall of 1777—but French-trained Algonquian warriors under the leadership of the notorious Louis St. Luc de la Corne. For these Algonquian, the American Revolution was not at all about political liberty or national emergence; they fought merely to keep their old mixed-race world as it long had been, securely under the triumphant British flag.

It was St. Luc de la Corne whose barely controlled warriors had taken the scalp of Jane McCrae. It was also this seasoned frontier fighter who is remembered for a notably sadistic remark to his assembled warriors, *"Il faut brutaliser les affaires"* (It's necessary to brutalize matters). And it was this commander's defeated Indians who, having been bested by the Oneida and Stockbridgers in both scouting and fighting at Saratoga, fled north with the most astonishing swiftness, only a month after St. Leger's defeat in the west.

In telling the story of their intertribal revolution and their breakaway from British and Mohawk masters, the Oneida take deserved pride in the role they played at Fort Stanwix and Saratoga. Even more important to them, however, is the treasured narrative of Polly's shawl. Hearing of the freezing and starving condition of the American troops wintering at Valley Forge in 1777–78, a number of Oneida women, carrying heavy loads of corn, trudged down to that distant camp to feed and care for their fellow Americans in their hour of near defeat. Motivated equally by patriotism and by human concern, the women labored in the huts of Valley Forge throughout that hard winter, preparing their "flint corn" (which requires special treatment before it can be cooked) and nursing the sick and dying. Their leader was a woman whom the soldiers called Polly Cooper. When spring brought easement to the soldiers' suffering and the army stirred itself again, Martha Washington gave Polly a richly embroidered shawl by way of thanks for her aid. To this day, the Oneida bring out that revered piece of cloth—virtually a religious token—to confirm their life-saving contribution to the war in which some Americans won their freedom.

The AMERICAN REVOLUTION through INDIAN EYES

These episodes of intense interaction and interdependency between red and white peoples during the Revolution might seem to recapitulate other such hopeful episodes dating back to the time of the Pilgrims. They might also seem to confirm that the two peoples, sometimes fighting together, were in the cultural process of becoming Americans together. But, no. The peoples were in the process of becoming Americans separately, and the Revolution was the time when that cultural decision was made in action and in blood and, most important, in spirit. In the words of historian Colin Calloway, in the case of both Indians and white Americans, "the story of who they are dates back to the Revolution." And nowhere was that more true than on the frontier where not formal armies and protocols, but raw emotions and free license called the awful tune.

Professor Calloway also recalls the charge given to American revolutionaries by Thomas Jefferson in the Declaration of Independence. Jefferson, that grand libertarian, painted a defensive picture of how it was that the people of these colonies had risen up against their king, for that tyrant had unleashed on the "inhabitants of our frontiers the merciless Indian savages, whose known rule of warfare is an undistinguished destruction of all ages, sexes, and conditions." Congress thoroughly agreed with this prejudicial racial description, one of its committees reporting that the Indians were "aggressors in the war, even without a pretense of provocation." Thus the War of Independence became, in the west, another crusade against the barbarians. When General John Sullivan led his troops into battle against the Iroquois in 1779, his officers greeted July Fourth with the words, "Civilization or death to all American savages!" Even worse, as the victors' history of the American Revolution is too often narrated, neither Indian efforts to remain neutral nor Indian support of the patriots would count for much. Those exceptional contributions were surely not important enough to affect the myth that the Revolution had been a glorious war fought exclusively by a white and righteous people.

Also dismissed too easily is the story of the Indians' internal revolution. White Eyes, the Delaware chief who had pledged to bring his people onto the side of the United States in return for tokens of recognition, found himself contravened at every turn by more conservative Lenni Lenape. They believed that the British, with their respect for traditions and their lack of interest in native lands, offered a far more trustworthy, if more paternalistic alliance. And they resented the fact that White Eyes, by choosing the American side, was suggesting a breakaway from the time-honored subservience to the Six Nations; such radicalism struck them as insulting to the established, religion-endorsed rulership.

In his eloquent and even tearful speeches in council meetings, as he attempted to explain the American way of life, liberty, and the pursuit of happiness, White Eyes reached out beyond current orthodoxy to the underlying sentiments, the fundamental theology of his people. He also evoked the spirit of an independence-minded grand sachem who had recently died, saying: "You know what our aged chief believed...that the Word of God is true. I take my young people and children by the hand and kneel before that Being. I pray that he may have mercy on us all."

Yet, even with such eloquence, advocacy of the upstart Yankees' cause continued to be difficult—particularly when George Morgan himself (the government's agent for this region) realized that the official stance favoring the Indians was a sham, not backed by popular opinion. Many of Washington's generals yearned to "chastise the savages," whether or not that punishment would harm the British. And the people of the frontier, with the winds of freedom in the air and authority absent, found in the Revolution opportunity to brand all Indians devils and to strike back against such fearful demons as Brant and the infamous slaughterers of Jane McCrae.

There were, in the popular mind, a few noble savages—the more dead, the more noble. The Shawnee chief Cornstalk, despite the perceived wildness of his western nation and despite his personal reputation as a warrior in Governor Dunmore's War, had won wide regard for having joined with the pacifistic Delaware in efforts to calm interracial fires on the borderlands. Yet even he felt the hatred of the frontiersmen. Hearing that Indian war parties were marching south armed with British muskets, he had bravely swum across the Ohio River to warn the American commandant of a nearby fort in Kentucky of the impending attack. Notwithstanding the patriotism of his deed, a number of the surrounding settlers, seeking vengeance for the recent scalping of an American soldier, broke into the jail where Cornstalk was secured. As local legend tells the story, Cornstalk and his son (who had come to assist his father) faced their assassins with calm, religious fatalism before they were seized, dragged out, and hacked to pieces.

Yet it was White Eyes, the idealistic proponent of the American Revolution, who paid the most painful penalty for his loyalty to the United States—betrayal. By 1778 he had earned a colonel's commission and a handsome blue uniform for his service to the new nation and for his willingness to lead combined forces against the British at Detroit. But high-command distrust and native jealousy worked against this newly fledged officer in their usual way: The promised battalion of regulars never came forth. In fact, the promises of higher command for him and possible statehood for the Delaware all turned out to be deceptions. Finally, having been summoned to Philadelphia to answer false charges of treason, then released, White Eyes found himself in the hands of the notorious Indian hater, General Lachlan McIntosh. The general's soldiers cut him down in an orgy of rage at what they viewed as his history of presumptuousness.

McIntosh's effort to attribute White Eyes's death to smallpox failed. But even after an official investigation had labeled the assassination for what it was, saying that the Lenape chief had been "treacherously put to death," cynics predicted that the vaunted treaty with the Delaware (the first Indian treaty in U.S. history) would be destroyed with as much zeal as its author had been butchered. From the Indian perspective, it appeared increasingly clear that loyalty to the British—as preached so fervently by Joseph Brant—was the preferable path to survival in the face of American race rage.

The Revolution that the Americans had brought upon the Native Americans, the Revolution that had produced more hatred than fraternity, was also profoundly damaging to the Indians' traditional lines of authority and their traditional ways of worship. Among the Delaware the perception was that the

Americans had not only murdered White Eyes but that they compounded that crime by interfering with the sacrosanct process of choosing his successor. This feeling of having been culturally subverted was shared by other Indian people. The Six Nations blamed the Americans for extinguishing their sacred fire, as well as for provoking their young warriors to dash off to war, on whichever side, quite heedless of the chiefs' counsels. The Revolution had shaken their fundamental religious order. *A Spirited Resistance,* Gregory Dowd's authoritative book on the Indians' age-old push for independence, quotes the Cayuga chief Kingageghta as lamenting in 1789 that a "Great Part of our ancient Customs & Ceremonies have, thro' the Loss of Many of our principal men during the War, been neglected & forgotten, so that we cannot go through the whole year with our ancient Propriety." Little wonder that the majority of the Six Nations' leadership resisted appeals from Yankee Presbyterian Samuel Kirkland to join the revolutionary cause.

Of Yankee settlements hated by British-inclined Iroquois and scorned by distraught Delaware, the prosperous town of Westmoreland on the glimmering north branch of the Susquehanna River was perhaps the most abominated. This rich watershed, blessed with abundant ore as well as copious agriculture, stretched beyond the town up the Lackawanna River and bore the attractive name of Wyoming Valley. For obscure, early colonial reasons, it was claimed by both Connecticut and Pennsylvania. Fiercely independent New Lights from Connecticut had migrated there in 1769 (over protests both from the Old Lights in their own legislature at Hartford and from the neighboring Pennsylvanians). They based their claims to the land on an agreement with the Indians reached at the Albany Congress of 1754. Now these settlers chose as their spokesman a Revolution-minded Connecticut man named Zebulon Butler. To him, Westmoreland in the Wyoming Valley represented evangelism and nationalism on the march together, the very spirit of the new nation. To the nearby Indians, particularly the Seneca to the west, Westmoreland represented change and dispossession of the most insulting kind.

The radicalized Seneca found it unreasonable to decline Joseph Brant's drum-beating invitation to come along and march with his Mohawk and Tories in a campaign of resistance. Another recruiter to that Tory cause was a revenge-minded Connecticut Loyalist officer named John Butler (relationship to Zebulon unknown). Despising his Yankee relatives for having joined the ragtag rebellion against royal authority, his resentment deepened during the defeat of his admired General St. Leger at the hands of Benedict Arnold's rough army of revolutionaries. Volunteering to lead a corps known as Butler's Rangers, and winning logistical support from the British, he toured the native villages for additional recruits. When he found that many of the Seneca nursed anti-American angers fueled by conservative shamans, he said that he would help them find release for their passions. For that bloody purpose, much abominated Westmoreland looked like the ideal target.

Hitting that town hard and fast in an early morning raid on July 3, 1778, John Butler burned it to the ground. He then directed his spirited warriors toward the neighboring, well-defended Forty Fort. By the slimmest margin, the American patriot Zebulon Butler succeeded in evading the attackers and escaping from the stronghold. But most defenders were slaughtered without mercy. The unsatiated Seneca were then ordered to ravage the entire valley. That rampage completed, they returned to their native villages with a lengthy string of prisoners and some 227 scalps on their belts.

This grim event—known to history as the Wyoming Massacre and vividly chronicled in Thomas Campbell's 1809 poem *Gertrude of Wyoming*—set ablaze white Americans' worst fears about the devilish savages and their fiendish leaders. Indeed, certain notable Indians had taken part in the attack, including the future prophet Handsome Lake and the Seneca chiefs Black Snake and Farmer's Brother. But, ironically, Joseph Brant, who received much of the blame for the bloody event, had been nowhere near the scene.

He was, in fact, at Oquaga where his family continued to live, recruiting warriors for his own volunteer strike force. His fearsome reputation among the white settlers, gained from far smaller sorties against such targets as Cobleskill, New York (where he also beat back a force of patriots that had come rushing up from Schoharie), had turned him into the "chief genius" behind the frontier war. In fact, Brant had few more than two hundred men at his command and throughout the war felt insufficiently supported both by Loyalist rangers like John Butler's son Walter and by the British high command. True to his own gentlemanly character, Brant had sought more than once to prevent the useless slaughter of women and children by any of his men, native or white. But those merciful deeds were not long remembered by the stressed patriots of the American frontier.

Brant's dual purpose in his increasingly intense raids was not only to drive the Americans out of Iroquoia but also to deprive Washington's invading armies of much needed food from interior farm communities. This intent—plus revenge for the swift destruction of Oquaga at a time when he was absent—was the motivation behind Brant's most important strike, the November 11, 1778, attack on Cherry Valley, New York. This extraordinarily beautiful community, established in 1740 by settlers from Londonderry, New Hampshire, could be reached from Brant's home village of Canajoharie by an easy march of little more than fifteen miles. The town's transplanted New Hampshire settlers, who considered themselves both intellectually and spiritually enlightened, had issued their own fixed resolution in support of the Revolution—they vowed to "Live Free or Die."

Combining forces with Walter Butler on that November day of early snow, Brant led a band of Loyalists and Indians that proved far too strong and too smart for the town's emplaced military command. Despite raids on nearby villages and warnings of additional dangers, Colonel Ichabod Alden, an officer sent from Connecticut to manage the strategic town's defense, had prohibited Cherry Valley's residents from moving to the fort. Instead, in an excess of confidence, he had sent them out to their own farms, trusting that his very presence would dissuade Brant or anyone else from attacking the region.

Brant launched a well-planned, many-targeted assault. In little more than an hour, the raid had accomplished its destructive purposes: Only one building, built of brick, remained standing. As volunteer patriot militia faded away in the face of battle, Loyalists and Indians slaughtered the few regulars and the unarmed farmers. Some thirty-two women and children were also killed; many others were taken away as captives. Then the attackers withdrew, as swiftly as they had come. As

for the gentlemanly Joseph Brant, he rejoiced in the precedent-
setting victory and in the message delivered to the Americans,
but said that he "burned with shame" at not having prevented
Walter Butler's slaughter of civilians. Slaughter was not Brant's
style, however strong his hatred.

Ultimately, the Wyoming Valley and Cherry Valley assaults
had a major impact on the American Revolution: They helped
determine the nature of the war. American Protestantism cried
for aid against the Anglican Loyalists and the bloodthirsty Indians. The specter of Brant, the firebrand who was everywhere
at the same time, forced decisions on the highest level of command in America's Continental army. George Washington saw
that he must now "carry the war into the Heart of the Country
of the Six Nations; to cut off their settlements, destroy their
next year's crops, and do them every other mischief of which
time and circumstances will permit."

Washington concluded that only by destroying the corn-
rich Seneca, whose continually impressive harvests kept supplying the British forces with needed grain and game, could he
protect his flank and defeat the British in land campaigns. Yet
the Seneca and their closest Iroquois cousins, the Cayuga and
Onondaga, still comprised a civilian Iroquois population greater
than six thousand—people who were, technically speaking,
blameless. They had spent the first two years of the Revolution
observing the play of forces and determining the wisest course
of action for themselves. They had also quietly maintained
their alliances with the Shawnee and other western people
(most of whom still favored neutrality). Their success in maintaining neutrality could not have been easily achieved.

As Washington designed his strategies against them, he gave insufficient attention to the fact that the Seneca had spiritual resources beyond military strengths with which to fight back—indeed, the inner strengths of an attacked and united people have always been a major problem for an alien force. Additionally, Seneca chiefs were succeeding in efforts to relight the central fire of the Iroquois Confederacy and thus to exert centralized control over all northeastern tribes. This was not only a matter of conducting traditional ceremonies at a new location (Kanadesaga, New York) but of initiating ceaseless diplomatic exchanges among the Six Nations. Thanks to these efforts by the Seneca and to the remaining vigor of their religious leadership, the Iroquois, though now on the defensive, were empowered and energized to endure a punishing war. Washington's handpicked general, John Sullivan of Massachusetts, succeeded in completing an arduous three-pronged campaign against the Iroquois in the autumn of 1779. His united, twenty-three-hundred-man army swept up the Susquehanna and across the Finger Lakes with irresistible power. His victories—particularly the key battle at Newtown (now named Elmira), in which the loyal Stockbridge Indians and Oneida again distinguished themselves (though a number of Oneida withdrew, declining to smite their fellow Iroquois)—were impressive enough to impose peace momentarily on the frontier and to frustrate the provender-starved quartermasters of Great Britain's American armies. But, even though Sullivan razed some forty Indian towns and destroyed vast quantities of corn (an estimated 160,000 bushels), causing thousands of Indian refugees to evacuate the territory for the safety of the

British forts, the war went on even more ferociously the next year.

The Seneca then unstintingly joined the cause of Indian resistance. Quelling internal disputes and uniting behind the war chiefs, they swelled the corps of Brant and the Loyalist leaders. As Brant redoubled his attacks on frontier communities, his band of red and white warriors increased to fifteen hundred, including four hundred Seneca—one of whom was the future prophet Handsome Lake. Indeed, with many towns in trans-Allegheny New York and Pennsylvania torched and abandoned, and with Fort Schuyler itself deserted (Brant having been foremost in that successful siege), the Indians seemed to be avenging Sullivan's campaign by winning the war for the British. Then, suddenly, the French navy changed all by defeating the Royal Navy off Yorktown.

The most telling, most truly revolutionary internal action of the Seneca in their wartime cultural revitalization had been a political shift in favor of nontraditional chiefs within their government. The newly acquired power of these notable warriors, elected as "war chiefs," had strengthened the nation externally while diminishing the internal authority of hereditary sachems. Thus revolutionized, the Seneca would henceforth advance as a more efficient, less elitist, and less village-oriented commonwealth. The distinguished Chief Cornplanter was one of those newly empowered leaders. Yet he, who had stood firm against the Americans at Newtown (where another eminent leader, Red Jacket, had bolted), possessed the intellectual flexibility to work as a spokesman for peace and friendship in the years immediately following British surrender at Yorktown. That was when the cultural creativity of the Seneca could be seen most clearly. There was even a time in this part of God's universe when it looked as if the new breed of leaders among the Indians and the large-souled statesmen among the Americans might try again to build a harmonious future for the two so different people.

At that brief and illusory moment of sunshine, Samuel Kirkland seemed to be one of the American leaders who possessed sufficient breadth of spirit to struggle for biracial brotherhood in the young Republic. During the Revolution he had had no doubts that this was God's army with which he marched, Jehovah at its head. He had served with distinction in the Sullivan campaign and had been promoted for gallantry in action (during which he had observed with horror such brutalities as Americans skinning Indian corpses from the hips down, to make "bootlegs").

Yet though Kirkland's Christian convictions remained strong, he had changed considerably during the war. He had changed also in the type of people with whom he associated. His church at Kanowarohare having been burned to the ground and his property destroyed, he apparently concluded that his time for being an evangelist had come to a halt. Though he informed the Boston Mission Board that the faithful, scattered Oneida and Tuscarora (some eight hundred in number) hoped to return to their home soon, along with the Stockbridgers and other Christian Indians, Kirkland's heart was no longer in that movement. Instead, he, like most veterans with whom he was now personally allied, felt, that victory having been achieved, the day had dawned to lay claim to the worlds thus opened up. With six children to provide for and huge debts to pay, he looked forward to being well compensated in fees and gifts of land for the part he and his fellow nationalists had played and would play in the new peace.

At WAR'S END, the MUTUAL FIGHT for SPIRITUAL SURVIVAL

Significantly, the last battle of the War of Independence was fought not in one of the thirteen about-to-be-liberated colonies but on the Ohio frontier—specifically, near the Shawnee capital of Chillicothe, Ohio, on November 10, 1782. Frontier hero Colonel George Rogers Clark led this action, his fame and rank having resulted from the wintertime campaign of 1778–79 on the rivers of Illinois during which he, aged twenty-five, had won the Northwest Territory for Virginia and thus for the embryonic United States. Also significant was the fact that this trendsetting champion of the frontier, though known for his adoption of Indian dress (hunting shirt and breechcloth), was admired first and foremost for his freewheeling acts of savagery against the Indians, whether combatants or civilians.

Colonel Clark's conclusive action at Chillicothe in 1782 was, in part, a vengeance strike against the Tories and western Indians who had sacked and burned Sandusky the month before. Frontiersmen remembered that year as the "Year of Blood," so grisly were its raids and counterraids. The British victory at Sandusky, terrible enough of itself, had contributed to the further brutalization of the war by attracting many previously uncommitted Shawnee and Miami. Now they were eager to win scalps by joining the king's armies—the apparently victorious and certainly more generous side. Another part of the Sandusky disaster had been the capture and unforgettably hideous torture of George Washington's friend and fellow Virginia speculator, Colonel William Crawford. If ever Washington's policies had favored peace with the Indians (to achieve, of course, his own objectives of gradual assimilation), from now on those policies emphasized reprisal and removal.

Clark's conquests in the Northwest Territory reverberated abroad, amplifying the scope of the American diplomats' treaty talks with the British at Paris in that same year of 1782, so that freedom for America's coastal colonies would no longer be the only issue on the table. Clark's victories also had an intensely psychological, catalyzing effect on the frontiersmen who yearned to grasp the heartland of their continent for themselves. Already in 1779, after Clark's wintertime campaign in Illinois, these irrepressible pioneers had started streaming down the western rivers by the scores and hundreds—some three hundred flatboats being counted at the falls of the Ohio in the summer of that year. By 1785 there were nearly forty-five thousand settlers in Kentucky—rightful heirs of Daniel Boone, as they regarded themselves—and thousands more on the northern side of the Ohio River. As they rushed into the region, they brought with them their disease-bearing animals, with the result that Indian populations were decimated by epidemics, in addition to the losses suffered in battle and by starvation from wartime depletion of game.

Ministering to borderland Indians afflicted by such stresses had been the life goal of Moravian missionary David Zeisberger—a saintly calling to a rather old-fashioned denominational program that had little meaning to most of the newly arrived, rough-hewn westerners. His historic Moravian church—whose members, almost extinguished in the wars of

seventeenth-century Europe and pledged to find new life as
missionaries in the New World—had gained a reputation in the
mid-eighteenth century among Native Americans of the southern and mid-Atlantic territories as the one group of Christians
who would truly live and humbly serve among them. When a
band of militiamen came upon Zeisberger's little community of
Delaware on the banks of the Muskingum River, they assumed
that the foreign-looking place, with its funny name of Gnadenhuetten (meaning Huts of Grace, or Camp Grace), was some
kind of enemy outpost. They therefore readied their arms for
immediate action against no perceptible opposition.

In fact, this community of pacifistic, pietistic German
brethren and destitute Indian refugees—this humble successor
to earlier communities that had been overwhelmed and displaced as the American frontier advanced—had been nearly
wiped out by British raiders during the course of the Revolution (the Indians having complained to their British allies that
the Moravians were "taking over our minds"). Now, when the
militiamen arrived at Gnadenhuetten, it happened that founder
Zeisberger himself was absent. In the distant past, in 1752, he
had been adopted by the Onondaga at the commencement of
his wilderness missionary career. Later, having survived Pontiac's so-called rebellion as well as the Paxton Boys' vigilantism,
he had coped with the uncertainties of the Revolution. At this
moment in 1782, he was off across the Northwest Territory, ex-
ploring chances of building a revitalized community somewhere else.

Those present to greet the arms-readied militiamen were
Indians who had returned to Gnadenhuetten merely to pick up
a few scattered possessions left in the wake of the recent British

raid. But the Americans, perceiving them to be of another color and in the wrong place, paid no attention to protestations of religious neutrality. Striking fast and hard, they clubbed, scalped, and burned a total of ninety Indian victims—a slaughter of harmless people that should not be omitted from American history books. For here, where the Revolution raged on despite the formal treaty, a massacre of minorities helped give that war a new and tragic meaning: freedom for some, persecution for others. Gnadenhuetten stands as one of the worst atrocities committed by either side—a cruel action in a tough time, an action of lasting damage to the word liberty.

Yet there were those men of spirit, both native and white, who continued to believe that American victory in their Revolution would produce good consequences for all, including more opportunities for interracial peace and prosperity. The very next year after Gnadenhuetten, the elderly missionary David Fowler led 420 Stockbridge Indians, many of them veterans of the war against Great Britain, from their homes in what used to be Mahican territory to a new community in Vernon, New York, called Brotherton. In 1784 indefatigable Samson Occom, with George Washington's encouragement, sailed up the Hudson in the ship *Victory*, bent on transporting New England Indians of Christian belief to join the optimistic group in Brotherton. Many of the Oneida who had been forced to flee to Schenectady during the war returned to their homes in Kanowarohare, where the ashes of Samuel Kirkland's church reminded them of good experiments failed and blown away, but of hopes still vibrant.

From their position farther west, the battered but unbowed Seneca (who were definitely not, as Washington thought of them, "destroyed") perceived the post–Revolutionary War era as a time to win a kind of independence from the white man's destructive policies, on their own terms of equality. To the councils of the Six Nations, the strengthened leadership admitted Joseph Brant, that Anglicized Mohawk, only with great suspicion, for he seemed to be playing the old game of collaborating with the whites in some new way. Once the fiery opponent of all Yankees, Brant now let their representatives honor him in his native valley (agents from New York even tried to bribe him with an official commission). This ambivalent Mohawk struck the Seneca as no proper leader—given his lack of rank and his obviously unbroken British allegiances.

Great Britain had, in fact, done great harm to the survival of the Indian nations at the Paris peace talks when it neglected to bargain in any way for the people it had once regarded as its allies. In furtherance of its own imperial image and in defiance of the American victory, the Crown had retained key forts guarding the Great Lakes—at Niagara (where Joseph Brant eventually gathered his people), at Detroit and Michilimackinac, and, ultimately, at Fort Miami. From those forts the British continued to send out contradictory messages to the Indian peoples. Communiqués emphasized that the majesty of the king would always be there to succor the Indian cause (and of course to support British commercial interests). But the Indians were cautioned that no definite guarantees of military backup could be given, if the Indians were to take their case to the point of war. Frustrated by that ambiguity and determined to find out what kind of support he could in fact count on, Brant sailed to England in 1785, ten years after his first trip across the Atlantic. He should have known that the uncertainties of the frontier struggle and the realities of Britain's interests elsewhere would prevent him from obtaining anything like a straight answer at court.

There was also ambiguity about how far American military arms would or could go to back up the settlers who were streaming into the western valleys. Once the 1784 Treaty of Fort Stanwix determined that the Iroquois should be dispossessed of most lands east of the Genesee (except for those retained by the faithful Oneida and Tuscarora) and should be strictly limited within territories to the west of New York and Pennsylvania, government officials dispatched Colonel George Rogers Clark and other high-ranking officers to attempt lecture-style "pacification" of Ohio's restless tribesmen. Though not regarded in treaty language as subjects of the United States, the Indians must respect white American rule.

The western nations, particularly the Shawnee and Miami, were appalled by the report that the Seneca, led by Cornplanter (who had fought valiantly against the Americans in many battles), had submitted to the new Republic's gratuitous dictate that the Iroquois should henceforth do nothing but remain in "peaceful possession of their lands." This seemed a betrayal almost as egregious as Great Britain's abandonment. (Actually, the Seneca declined to sign the Treaty of Fort Stanwix when it was finally reviewed across their council fire.) Yet the Shawnee and Miami recognized that they could no longer count on the supposedly all-mighty Six Nations, with their grand, religion-based confederation and famous Covenant Chain, to defend them with strength and guile against the surging Americans. For a truer defense, they would have to look to their own military leaders—newly made, upstart chiefs such as Little Turtle (son of a Miami chief and Mahican mother) and the Shawnee's

Blue Jacket—who might lack their seniors' cultivated manners around the fire but who had learned how to fight for freedom against the American invaders.

And this they did with astonishing success. During the supposedly peaceful 1780s (with the British continuing to play a sly game of Indian prodding from their forts), between fifteen hundred and two thousand settlers were killed in Gnadenhuetten-like raids and counterraids. Then the frontier war became once more a recognized situation, with Henry Knox (secretary of war under the Articles of Confederation) and the Federalist establishment finally agreeing that the bloody frontier must be brought under control—although Knox only had an army of 672 men under his command. By cobbling together a couple of militia regiments and dredging for volunteers, he managed to send a combined force of 1,453 men into the field under General Josiah Harmar. Little Turtle and Blue Jacket whipped that amateur general so unmercifully in the battle of Kekionga on October 22, 1790, that the people of the United States had reason to question their country's very existence.

President Washington had been inaugurated just the year before. He felt keenly the opposition of external forces to his fledgling nation—Spain, holder of the continental territory to the south and west, had failed to acknowledge the validity of the United States, and the British-Indian alliance still seemed to menace ever more strongly from the north (the British offered fifty dollars for each American scalp). Although Washington's own covetous intentions toward Ohio had been amply demonstrated as far back as the French and Indian Wars, his strong hand now seemed to waver, his policies uncertain and constrained. He warned his generals that "care must be taken neither to yield nor to grasp at too much" in the Ohio campaign. The governor whom Washington had chosen for the territory, the British-born, arch-Federalist Arthur St. Clair (who continued like many of his party to believe in a monarchy), selected himself as commander of the next drive against the Indians—a drive that ignored recently signed treaties. Washington, whose immature government was at that time nearly overwhelmed with debts, could only caution the grandiose general to "beware of surprise."

But surprised was St. Clair, nonetheless, on November 4, 1792. The surprise took the form of an ambush just a few miles short of the general's target destination, what is now Fort Wayne, Indiana. He was shocked not only by the cleverness of the combined Indian assault (their keen eyes having conned his every move) but also by the inadequacy of his arms and the dimensions of his losses. From a corps numbering some two thousand men, he suffered more than nine hundred casualties. With the United States undergoing such a total humiliation in the field, Washington and his cabinet saw that a thorough revision of both the army and the philosophy behind their government would have to be made. For the new nation to survive and expand, it needed to create a new concept of nationhood.

Particularly in the borderlands, St. Clair's defeat induced spasms of fear and self-examination. What might be the meaning of the defeat, and how might Christians best repent to ease God's wrath? Indeed, how might American society be reshaped to better reflect God's will? A resurgence of revivalism indicated that Americans, forced to the wall, tended to find recourse in the evangelistic strain of their Protestantism. Challenged to defend their borders and identify themselves in the process,

Americans waxed simultaneously religious and militaristic. A burgeoning of pacifistic communal sects showed the continual inventiveness of their spiritual lives. At the same time, they realized they must gird themselves to fight, not as amateur soldiers of a small-time state, but as professional legionnaires of a dominant, continental nation. Responding to that call, Revolutionary General "Mad Anthony" Wayne—no politician but a tested soldier—agreed to form the professional army that would complete the United States by securing its western border.

Yet another Revolutionary War hero, Marinus Willet (whose fame had been won in the defense of Fort Schuyler), saw the projected assaults on Indian territories quite differently. He believed that his nation could be whole and entire without the subjugation of the western Indian nations. But history unfortunately gives no clue to what part of the U.S. population shared his more respectful view of Native Americans. "It has been uniformly my opinion," Willet wrote, "that the United States ought to avoid an Indian War. . . . The intercourse I have had with these people, [and] the treatment I have myself received . . . make me an advocate for them. To fight with them would be the last thing I should desire." He urged that the United States should work to effect peace among its western neighbors; throughout his life, this reckonable patriot and robust Christian tried to make room in the new Republic for the Indian tribes as independent nations. Simultaneously, the Indian people were experiencing spiritual awakenings and political disagreements. Many of them had recently been drawn toward Christianity—that triumphant faith seeming to be a logical choice for all religiously inclined folk in the post–Revolutionary

War world. Many others rediscovered their nativist roots, heeding the call of new prophets and joining the armies of the Shawnee generals.

HANDSOME LAKE'S INNER REVOLUTION, TENSKWATAWA'S OPEN DOOR

Among spiritually inclined white Americans, the compulsive return to religion and to God's presumably safe embrace had commenced even before Harmar's and St. Clair's twin defeats. The Fort Stanwix treaty negotiations had seemed an opportunity for religious representatives to weave stronger relationships with the Indian nations (specifically with the Iroquois). Later, when treaty confirmation talks were held in November of 1794 on the order of President Washington's envoy Timothy Pickering at Canandaigua, New York, denominationalists showed up in impressive numbers to help matters along, Quakers being the most numerous. The Canandaigua conference was to be, in fact, the last diplomatic agreement signed between the United States and the Six Nations—last if only because the United States would never again recognize the independent status of the Iroquois.

Not coincidentally, the Canandaigua conference was held just three months after General Anthony Wayne's immense force of legionnaires finally succeeded in defeating the Ohio Indians in the Battle of Fallen Timbers. There, Blue Jacket's men (who had fasted, perhaps excessively, before the battle, this being a holy and ultimate war) fought and died by the hundreds, their deaths being all the more poignant because they occurred in the shadow of the locked gates of the new stronghold built by the Indians' British allies, Fort Miami on the Maumee River. British guns remained silent in accordance with white men's treaties as Blue Jacket's men fell before the advance of Wayne's efficient soldiers.

The Canandaigua conference also occurred just four months after the United States defeated an uprising of Pennsylvania frontiersmen, a potentially ruinous insurrection of nation-defying ruffians that was given a deceptively jocular name, the Whiskey Rebellion. In their challenge to federal tax authorities and to the army command of George Washington and Alexander Hamilton, the whiskey rebels had tested how far yahoo-style, individual liberty could go in the new land spawned by the Revolution. They learned, as had the western Indians, that the Republic was finally organizing itself as a nation defined by laws and tested in battle.

Amid all the diplomatic and religious posturings at Canandaigua at the end of that critical year of 1794, the Seneca chief Red Jacket moved with dignity and credibility. When his turn came, he orated with his usual eloquence, urging the Indian peoples to remain firmly united, "as with the heart of one man." It is to him more than any other man that the success of the conference is owed; one feels his presence in the treaty's strong and avowedly *perpetual* pledge that "peace and friendship are hereby firmly established" between the United States and the Six Nations. Red Jacket also forced the American authorities to admit both Indian and white women to the conference, a truly revolutionary breakthrough. Among the whites admitted was the beautiful Jemima Wilkinson, a revivalist who called herself the Public Universal Friend and who gathered enthusiasts about her in the bosky glens of Penn Yan, New York.*

Jemima Wilkinson saw the Canandaigua proceedings as a God-given occasion for the assembled Indians to confess to all assembled the sinfulness of their wartime deeds and their savage lives. Red Jacket, with customary aplomb, replied this was also an appropriate moment for the whites to repent themselves of their dishonest practice of treaty breaking. But the treaty commissioners, fearing that such spiritual correlations could only lead to an undermining of U.S. domination, instructed the Public Universal Friend to take her good intentions elsewhere. The Quakers, on the other hand, made an impression on Red Jacket—perhaps in the way they offered that their "inner light" would be truly productive of peace.

In order to right old wrongs and establish new ways among the Indians, the Quakers planned to introduce modern agricultural techniques, making impressive gifts of tools and equipment. They directed their particular energies toward the Seneca, with five trained missionaries reaching Cornplanter's flood-ravaged village of Jenuchshadago on the upper Allegheny River in May of 1798. Establishing a demonstration village nearby, the Quakers gradually discovered that the local population of about four hundred people was bitterly divided about the acceptability of their suggested way of life. The radically

---

*It was this peculiar tendency of New York State to initiate enthusiastic communities which flamed and died, flourished and exploded, that prompted historian Carl Carmer to underscore one of the region's nicknames: the Burnt-over District.

different way of farming, the demanding school for youngsters, and, of course, the contemplative religion (with its emphasis on sobriety and book learning) directly challenged traditional Iroquois behaviors.

The main social change required by the imposed economy was that the men, not the women, should work the fields and should also develop mechanical skills. Thus, hunting should be forsaken as counterproductive to the common goal of building an agricultural surplus. The surplus (certainly no new concept to the prudent Seneca) would be accumulated for purposes of sale and trade—though the sale of mother earth's bounty had always seemed inherently immoral to the Iroquois. The school, housed in Jenuchshadago itself, opened on to a yard in which happened to stand an impressive statue of Tarachiawagon, the Good Twin. The brooding statue seemed to distract the children when they came to school—which they did, in fact, without much regularity. The Quakers' religious and social teachings were also constantly put to the test, both by tradition-loving women and by men disinclined to abandon hunting and gambling.

The greatest test of all came in the spring of 1799 when Cornplanter's half-brother, Kanyadaligo (Handsome Lake), emerged from the forests with his companions after a winter of hunting and roistering. Into the sober, disciplined town they burst like a sudden storm from the north, some of them drunk, many of them carrying kegs of whiskey, all of them disposed to disrupt the unnatural order brought to Jenuchshadago by the Quakers. This they did in a weeklong orgy of terror and destructiveness. The only positive result of that dreadful spring was that it led to a new resolve by Cornplanter's people to dedicate themselves, more ardently, to the type of civilization advocated by the Quakers.

Meanwhile, in his tent, Handsome Lake suffered the agonies of hangover and guilt. A woman had been killed in the course of the orgy; his own niece had mysteriously died, possibly from witchcraft. What was his old world coming to? He became so distressed in withdrawal and illness that his family feared he would die. But, as the Iroquois historian Anthony F. C. Wallace points out, Handsome Lake was suffering something beyond the classic cultural syndrome of bereavement; he was undergoing a profound spiritual change. This would ultimately lead to the formation of a new faith. When Handsome Lake's family heard him cry from his tent, *"Niio!"* ("So be it!"), they feared that he was surrendering to death; in fact, he was responding to the call of heavenly messengers.

This was the first of three visions experienced by the fifty-year-old sachem in the course of 1799. The attendant Quakers were profoundly impressed by the importance of the event— not only by the quality of his revelations (in which God was seen as warning his people against the four sins of whiskey, witchcraft, experimenting with love magic, and using abortion and sterility medicine) but also by the genuine enthusiasm with which his people responded. The Quakers reported that they "felt the love of God flowing powerfully among us all." They rejoiced as the Seneca hailed the revelations and set about reforming themselves, with Handsome Lake as their prophet.

The Quakers could not comprehend, however, that this was far more than a momentary response to an inspired leader of that place and time. Indeed, this was simultaneously the rebirth of an ancient religion and the formation of a broad-based religious philosophy, whose code—the *Gawiio,* or gospels—would endure among the Iroquois and other Native Americans for many generations. Nor was the import of the movement fully perceived by President Thomas Jefferson when he acclaimed Handsome Lake's reforms following the prophet's visit to Washington in 1802. What Jefferson saw was primarily an opportunity to advance his own agrarian policies through the new lifestyle of the prophet's communities.

It remained difficult for white society to advance beyond a mere appreciation of the reforming effects of the prophet's teachings to an understanding of the validity of the message and the extent of the revolution. Handsome Lake's teachings included not only profound economic and social changes but also religious and political revelations—that is, his visions included not only heaven and hell but also George Washington and Jesus. This movement was to be an American faith, born of Indian lineage yet open to all who would follow, an American faith on which a free way of life could be based. Obviously this was not a military victory—not the triumph of arms that had been sought by such a man as Joseph Brant—but a triumph of the spirit, providing the even greater gift of inner freedom. It was also a reminder that, in the words of Gregory Dowd (author of *A Spirited Resistance*), Indians tend to live "in a world beyond [their time and] locality."

Crucial to Handsome Lake's faith—the movement that has come to be called the Religion of the Longhouse—are four obligatory rites, practiced to this day by Handsome Lake's followers with great joy and solemnity. These are the Thanksgiving Ceremony; the *adowe,* or individual prayers and thanksgivings; the communal Bowl Game; and the Dance of Worship. These rites, like the majority of Handsome Lake's teachings, are neither inventions nor imitations but evolutions from ancient uses and forms of expression, including most notably the dance. Whereas some critics have pointed out the "borrowing" from the Quakers of certain themes within Handsome Lake's program, believing that program to be but another syncretistic adaptation, more impressive is the program's continuity with beliefs and rites dating from even before Hiawatha's time. That was how the founder saw his creation—not as a new religion but as the return to ancient truths.

It is no small wonder that even within the prophet's lifetime, visiting Quakers moderated their enthusiasm for Handsome Lake's unique and evolved gospel, taking particular exception to his preference for communal living (as opposed to their individual family farms) and his never abandoned delight in the dance. But, if there is reason to credit the concept that traditional beliefs are *advancing* as they evolve, the Longhouse religion gives evidence that that advance may be more internal (meaning individual) and less external (meaning tribal). Whereas in preceding decades the individual's fears and desires might have been dramatized by means of a flaming scene of torture, they are now constrained within that person's soul. The individual asks his god to help him deal with those fears and desires not through revenge or physical action but through the healing devices of religion. Thus did the cultural system practiced by Handsome Lake's converts advance itself from tribal aggression to patriotic pacifism and universal applicability, the third phase of that ancient religion's evolution.

To many of the Seneca and their neighbors, that transition seemed disastrous. Red Jacket, whose colorfully expressed opposition to anything like assimilationist Christianity made popular reading for early nineteenth-century Americans, strove to assert the old ways and to maintain the historic independence of the Seneca. Joseph Brant, in despair at the acceptance by many Iroquois of American materialism, cursed the treaty-breaking conquerors with the memorable words, "Cease, then, to call yourself Christians!" Finding the status quo intolerable, he redoubled his efforts to attract western tribes into a military federation. Even Cornplanter resisted Handsome Lake's ameliorative teachings; he was converted to his brother's religion only on his deathbed. The Shawnee were particularly resistant to Handsome Lake's messages of peace. They, too, had a new prophet— Tenskwatawa, the brother of Tecumseh—and his visions prefigured another working out of the Indian spiritual revolution.

This prophet from the Shawnee nation was a particularly unattractive individual, sources tell us. Originally named Lalawetheka, meaning Noise Maker or Rattle, he only acquired his more famous name, Tenskwatawa, meaning The Open Door (possibly The Open Mouth), after suffering a powerful, epiphanic experience. His brother, the handsome and athletic Tecumseh, had seemed slated for leadership among his Shawnee people from the very beginning of his life. Timid Lalawatheka, the least promising looking of a set of later-born triplets (his twisted body being made uglier by an eye blanked out in a hunting accident), seemed an unlikely candidate for that leader's spiritual advisor. Yet that was the historic role he did indeed take on after his encounter with the Master of Life in 1805, when aged thirty.

To some extent, this was a prototypical Indian spiritual encounter, similar to Handsome Lake's and Hiawatha's, in that a man, sickened by whiskey and depression, had sunk into a coma so profound that funeral preparations had been made. Then, passing through a stage even more awful than death itself, he returned to life with the conviction that he was charged to bring the Master of Life's message to humanity. But whereas this had happened in Handsome Lake's and Hiawatha's cases to a sachem and warrior of whom greatness might naturally be expected, in Lalawatheka's case, the message came to a wretch so cowardly that he had never fought in battle—or if he had, it was at Fallen Timbers, from which he was believed to have run away.

Now, resurrected, this no longer timid voice spoke of heaven and hell, described the behavior that was necessary for a man to enter paradise, and warned of the dreadful things that would happen if a man contaminated himself by associating with the white invaders. The Shawnee flocked to hear him preach his message of reformed and purified behavior (no alcohol or polygamy or witches) and of militant aggression toward the whites. He spoke as Tenskwatawa, The Open Door, who welcomed all to the brightness of his presence but who warned that the surface of the earth could be darkened for days at his command. Before all eyes he functioned as the prophet who guided his brother's course, in keeping with the doom-threatening messages to him from on high.

Tecumseh, who had fought valiantly as a company commander against General Anthony Wayne (called the Black Snake by Indians) at Fallen Timbers, was now asserting himself as the leader of a new pan-Indian alliance. Whereas the Seneca, on behalf of the Iroquois Confederation, had once held the strings that might have pulled such an alliance together—so strongly demonstrated in the Canandaigua conference—they now seemed to collude with the Yankees and to be engaged solely in selling away their own land. The prophet warned that the Seneca had even adopted white-influenced religions, religions that would lead to their corruption and destruction. The Yankees themselves, though pledged by the 1795 Treaty of Greenville (Ohio) to a policy of "Peace and not increase of territory," were pushing inexorably westward into the region that would be known as Indiana. It was clearly vital for Tecumseh to seize this moment, while the American politicians were still professing peace and racial harmony, to pull the nations together and to lead them toward the ultimate battle, the final victory in the Indian revolution.

As more and more believers from a great diversity of tribes came to hear Tecumseh's stirring words and to visit the prophet at Greenville—the number of pilgrims having reached fifteen hundred in the spring of 1807—Governor William Henry Harrison and other government officials worried that the strange combination of the two brothers, one a veteran soldier, the other a trained shaman, might succeed in destabilizing the frontier. More specifically, they worried that the united and resolved tribesmen would wreck the government's money-minting practice of acquiring lands through rock-bottom cessions from the Indians and selling them to eager speculators at far higher prices.

Governor Harrison saw that many of the pilgrims returning from Greenville clutched small and intricately carved sticks that seemed to be sacred. Were these, in fact, signs of enlistment in a vast rebel army? Harrison sent intelligence agents to investigate, among whom were members of the Shaker communities in nearby Kentucky, curious religionists who were eager to investigate the phenomenon of The Open Door.

The visiting Shakers, on coming back from Greenville, reported that the prophet and his converts were perfectly harmless, nothing but pious reformers. "Surely God is in this place!" they said of the Shawnee Prophet's town. Yet Harrison paid little heed to their reassurance. He regarded the Shakers as a pacifistic and irregular group of communalists who, though Christian, might even be suspected of favoring some of the Prophet's irregular beliefs. In those suspicions he was quite correct—for the Shakers, in fact, absorbed much from the Indians (including an increased awareness of native herbs and respect for the voice of women). They remain one of the most interesting religious groups in American history: Their open-mindedness and creative interrelationship with Native American culture have been matched by no other sect.

Founded in England in the previous generation as the United Society of Believers in Christ's Second Coming, these millennialists won their nickname of "Shaking Quakers" because of the severe agitations they experienced during times of worship. One of their earliest converts, Ann Lee, became leader upon the death of the movement's founders; she led the group to America on the strength of her personal, strongly feminist vision. The Shakers arrived in Watervliet, New York, in 1776, just as the Revolutionary War burst upon the colonies. Despite, or perhaps because of, the stresses of the war, Mother Ann (as she came to be called) was able to attract many storm-tossed people to the quiet, celibate, agricultural community she founded at Mount Lebanon, New York, in 1787.

Even after Mother Ann's death in 1784, the society continued to grow, with eighteen more communities establishing
themselves in New England and the mid-Atlantic states by the
mid-1820s (when a total of sixteen thousand members could be
counted). Shedding most traces of their origins in England, the
Shakers published their "Bible," the *Testimony of Christ's Second
Coming*, in 1808. Produced as a straightforward guide for communities on the frontier, it was a thoroughly American document. With their ardent belief in the dance plus singing and
marching as rites of worship, the Shakers were predisposed to
be sympathetic to the observances they witnessed at Greenville.

Yet, while the Shakers believed strongly in public confession as another valid rite, they were troubled to find that
confession to a minister was regarded as proper among the
prophet's worshipers. Hearing their question about whether or
not this was a papist practice, Tenskwatawa graciously agreed
in the winter of 1806 to sit down with the Shakers and discuss
such matters. He admitted that he had first learned of this
priestly form of confession from a Wyandot schooled by the
French in Detroit, but he explained (without irony) that his
people were different from the Roman Catholics in that they,
having made their confessions, were truly repentant and never
returned to the sinful activity.

As for Tecumseh, he, too, seemed willing to spend time
with and offer friendship to the Shakers; he scorned other
Americans who held these dancing Christians in such low regard. He remarked to Governor Harrison: "You have shaken
[sic] among you and make light of their worship!" It seemed
impossible for the white Americans, with their monotheistic,
monochromatic, self-righteous history, to make any room in

their society for people, including co-religionists, who lived and moved to different music. Even President Jefferson, who was still urging the Indians to become profitable agriculturists, with each family individually clinging to its little prescribed acreage, could not imagine the communally managed Indian way of life as being a productive and acceptable alternative.

Reassured by what they had witnessed among Tecumseh's friendly people, the Shaker scouts returned to Kentucky to write the report that Harrison scorned—a report altogether favorable to the prophet's followers. "We felt as if we were among the tribes of Israel on their march to Canaan," they had acknowledged. "Their simplicity and unaffected zeal for the increase of the work of the Good Spirit...were considerations truly affecting." Subsequently they wrote to Tecumseh that they had been "profoundly moved by the hard-working character of [your] people" and that "the same Good Spirit is working in you and in us."

But it was not to Canaan, in truth, that Tenskwatawa and Tecumseh planned to march. In the spring of 1808, having perceived that the Greenville area was becoming too crowded, that their activities were too much under the eyes of the American observers, and that a possible renewal of war between Great Britain and the United States made it healthier for them to be out of the line of fire, the Shawnee brothers concluded that they should move their center farther into the native forests. Accepting the invitation of certain Kickapoo and Potawatomi chiefs, they moved about 150 miles farther west to the Wabash River. The name of the new site was Tippecanoe, located as it was near the mouth of that fateful creek.

CHAPTER 8

The IMMINENT APOCALYPSE and the ULTIMATE REMOVAL

ON JUNE 16, 1806, precisely the day predicted by the Shawnee Prophet, the heavens grew dark and all life hushed under a gradually imposed reign of utter blackness. This was the convincing moment, stark proof to many that the Prophet did command extraordinary powers—scientists' forecasts of the solar eclipse having been but scantily available on the frontier. From now on few of the assembled followers would doubt his apocalyptic revelations of the world to come or his perceptions of good and evil; both those followers and their prophet belonged to a pivotal place and time in American history.

In response to Tenskwatawa's call, a host of men and women from a variety of tribes in the Great Lakes region flocked to the new center on the Wabash. These were the loosely confederated people judged by Governor Arthur St. Clair to have been "utterly destroyed" by the threat of American armies. Yet with admirable resiliency they had regrouped themselves after the military traumas preceding the 1795 Treaty of Greenville. Now their spirits alternately soared at the Shawnee Prophet's words, then plummeted because of food shortages and international confusions. In the year immediately preceding the move to Prophetstown (as the new center came to be called), the British warship *Shannon* had forced the submission of the U.S. frigate *Chesapeake* off the Virginia capes. With war prompting rougher moralities, it seemed only a matter of time before the Americans would forsake all previous treaties and resume their attacks on the western tribes—again in the name of liberty from Great Britain.

Simultaneously, in that same singular time when Indians of the northwest were responding to the Shawnee Prophet's call, Americans of the young and fragile Republic were being stirred by another religious awakening. Although Deism and rationalism ruled in the eastern capitals—Harvard succumbing to Unitarianism in 1805—there burned, even in those liberal precincts, some remnants of the old Puritan fire. When Timothy Dwight, grandson of Jonathan Edwards, took over the presidency of Yale in 1795, an intellectual force seemed to combine with the spirit of revivalism for the empowerment of a new generation of teachers and writers. But it was on the frontier that revivalism once again truly prospered—a camp-meeting-style phenomenon witnessed joyfully by Samuel Kirkland before his death in 1808. And it was on the frontier, where Methodism and such magnetic speakers as James McCready and Charles Grandison Finney came into their own, that American history was jolted once again by a spiritual force of profound consequence.

There, on the frontier, in response to the needs of the people, arose a new breed of millennium-hailing preachers. Though they may not have had the rigorous intellectual training of the preceding generation's Puritans, they knew how to speak the language of the people. What came to be called the Second Great Awakening was their creation, for good and ill. On the one hand, it inspired emotional outpourings of religious enthusiasm and apocalyptic expectation;* on the other, it created institutions of reform—schools, hospitals, and benevolent societies, the marks of newly disciplined communities. Yet, with all this benevolence, the most impressive product of the Second Great Awakening was the democratic, religious spirit that imbued America's early nineteenth-century nationalism. And this was the force that, gloved in godly intentions and sheathed in Christian rhetoric, delivered the most crippling blow to the Indian peoples—that is, failure to prevent their removal from the land that gave them their cultural identity.

The wonder remains: Why did that upsurge of Christian feeling and deep-seated patriotism not extend itself to include those other Americans, the ones to whom the land belonged by virtue of primary and direct inheritance? In the name of humanity, if nothing else, one might have expected that those democrats/republicans who had been stirred by Jefferson's all-inclusive agrarian message, those who were now once again renewed by an antiaristocratic religion, would have found the means to make the Republic work for everyone within its

---

*Most passionate of all the millennialists may have been the Millerites (Second Adventists), whose leader, William Miller, predicted in 1831 that Christ would reappear on earth in 1843. Huge crowds responded by garbing themselves in white and ascending to barn roofs in anticipation of the heaven-sent event. When nothing much happened, the Bible was consulted again and a later date set.

bounds—white, red, and black as well. In the 1820s and 1830s, sensing that some sort of mob license lurked behind the democratic, Bible-thumping rallies of the new Jacksonian westerners, the more Calvinistic of the eastern preachers warned religious America against pursuing "liberty without virtue" (that is, without moral discipline). The Indians, whose cause the godly congregations supported with more enthusiasm than success, might have asked, "What liberty, what virtue?"

"Civilizing" the Indians for the security of the frontier (and for "the honor of the nation," as some romanticists preached) was becoming an increasingly fraught and suspect concept. Seasoned toilers for harmony between the races, specifically those professionals who sought to supply the tribesmen with goods by means of a 1796 system of fur-trading posts called "factories," found themselves deprived of federal funds and outmaneuvered by private entrepreneurs. Missionaries were pushed aside by the rough-and-tumble frontiersmen, as well as by the government and its armies. Ultimately, the War of 1812—with its unleashing of interracial horror on the northwestern and southeastern frontiers, its justification of indiscriminate conquest in the name of patriotism, and its bringing forth of opposed prophets and apostles—ended all practical hopes for a mutual brotherhood and a shared nationality.

William Henry Harrison, appointed by Jefferson as governor of the Indiana Territory in 1800, saw little chance that civilizing the Indians would work. He recognized that the American frontiersmen—the people who would open their hearts to the white itinerant preachers and would create new citadels of Christian charity for other whites—were a hard lot when it came to interracial relations. "A great many of the inhabitants of the Fronteers [sic]," he wrote, "consider the murdering of the Indians in the highest degree meritorious."

Yet it was Harrison's assignment in the first decade of the nineteenth century not only to acquire whatever acreage he could from the tribesmen for the pauperized government to sell to wealthy speculators (a job at which he was stupendously good, succeeding in persuading a succession of chiefs to cede their lands), but also to conciliate the Indians and control them by all means short of war. He took comfort from the fact that Blue Jacket, defeated at the Battle of Fallen Timbers, had been given a government pension and now counseled peace to all who would listen. Harrison gave as much credence as possible to the Shakers' reports of harmless, prayerful dancing at Prophetstown. He even went so far as to provide food for the followers who flocked from the west to the ceremonies on the Wabash. If he went beyond common sense to be so charitable, how could the tribesmen possibly turn to the British?

"The MASTER of LIFE KNOWS NO BOUNDARIES"

While William Henry Harrison was known for possessing an extreme form of patriotism, Tecumseh tapped into an extreme form of nativism when he sought to create a continental alliance of tribesmen against the Americans. As Tecumseh saw it, the test now at hand was one of fundamental faiths: one religion-based culture against another. The Americans prayed to an exclusive, biblical god who strengthened the arms of the (supposedly) righteous in their push for more and more land; the Indians prayed to variegated and ancient spirits who could be experienced through rites and heard through prophecies. Tecumseh utilized the apocalyptic message of his brother the Shawnee Prophet (which said, essentially, "Come now and join our pan-Indian movement against the Americans or you will be over-whelmed by blackness and swallowed by the earth") as a unifying gospel for people of immense diversity.

At first Tecumseh had sought to evade the public eye, stay-ing out of the light that danced about his strange, charismatic brother. This was not merely to hide his strategies from Harri-son and the generals in Washington but also to avoid an appear-ance of pushing his pan-Indian message down the throats of the highly sensitive local chiefs. For the brothers were Shawnee— and therefore not closely related to these Algonquian people of the northwest. Their invitation to move into Ohio had come from the Kickapoo and Potawatomi. It surely did not entitle them to assume a dominant role—particularly in the face of the Miami who had dwelled along the Wabash and other regional rivers for centuries.

On their side, these two Shawnee did let it be known that they were the special people of Waasha Maneto, the Great Spirit. While they called the Delaware their grandfathers and the Wyandot (and the Iroquois!) their uncles, the Shawnee ad-dressed other tribesmen of the region as little brothers. Early al-lies of the French, and displaced from their eastward homelands by treaties written by the victorious Anglo-Americans, they ex-isted in the early 1800s as a battered and peculiarly vengeful people. So Tecumseh (whose father had been killed in Governor Dunmore's War) cautiously bided his time and cooled hotter heads. He could not, however, bring himself to sign the humili-ating 1795 Treaty of Greenville. And Tenskwatawa (who, to the horror of some, urged his followers to throw away their old magic-filled medicine bags and went so far as to declare himself the reincarnation of the first man on earth) seemed not so much interested in militancy as in reform. He directed the assembled tribesmen to practice rites and dances reclaimed from past days of greatness and to build up the new town as a ceremonial space.

Shawnee representatives had often visited with the Iroquois—where they heard with fascination the religious preachings and assimilationist teachings of the Seneca prophet Handsome Lake. Not for the Shawnee would there be any such leaning toward the white men's ways. On the contrary, Tecumseh and Tenskwatawa impressed on their audiences at Prophetstown the concepts of racial purity and of national unity, difficult concepts that drew from the Prophet's nativistic faith. Their broad ambitions for their cause extended beyond the related peoples of the Great Lakes region (of whom the Ojibwa and Chippewa, intimately related to the Ottawa and Potawatomi, were the most numerous) to the far more wealthy and populous southern tribes.

Among all those very different people of the southeast (whose numbers approached four hundred thousand), Shawnee pioneers had been establishing settlements and family connections during the past century. If Tecumseh could attract the southern tribesmen into his confederation (an essential if), he might hope to establish a sufficiently large population base for the creation of an all-conquering army. Because of the connections made by the Shawnee pioneers, Tecumseh dared hope he could win a friendly reception in villages down the southern valleys. Along with his plea for pan-Indianism, he would take the message that all land should be held in common, not in the individualistic American way—that is, not by self-seeking cap-italists—but in the communal Indian way, by all tribesmen and women. The key passage in Tecumseh's planned addresses was that "the Master of Life knows no boundaries . . . nor will his red people acknowledge any."

A year before Tecumseh took action and headed south, Governor Harrison commenced his land-acquisition program throughout the newly established Indiana Territory. Climax of this strategy was the so-called Treaty of Fort Wayne; and Harrison invited Tecumseh and a few of his councilmen to the signing of this treaty at Vincennes in the summer of 1809. Te-cumseh saw the invitation for what it was: a grand opportunity for the governor and his gold-trimmed officers to legitimize the government's acquisition of former Indian lands. By gathering signatures and marks on the treaty, Harrison would not only se-cure the lands his president had ordered him to deliver (which totaled nearly six million acres), he would also deny the Indians any right to struggle further against his imperial methods of dis-possession. Tecumseh knew that something had to be done to tip over the governor's wagon.

Paddling down the Wabash to the treaty conference in a flotilla of eighty canoes containing four hundred warriors, Te-cumseh made sure that his force was mighty enough to make an impression. His initial attitude was so uncompromising—he declined to enter the white man's house, insisting that the open-ing session be moved to a nearby grove—and so dramatic that he succeeded in unnerving the solemnly gathered and formally seated officials. At one point, the confrontation between gover-nor and chief became so hot that soldiers leaped up to defend

Harrison against equally agitated warriors. The next day Tecumseh, having shown his muscle, revealed his moral superiority. In a lengthy address, he reviewed the wrongs of the Americans, emphasizing their repeated violation of the Treaty of Greenville (which had supposedly guaranteed the integrity of Indian lands). "You are constantly driving the red people," he told Harrison. "[You will] at last drive them into the great lake where they can't either stand or work."

He then focused his anger on the wickedness of Harrison and the Americans in tricking the red people (as he is reported to have called them) by first dividing and then conquering them. Tecumseh stated that, in opposition to this destructive strategy, he and his brother were organizing a great coalition of the northwestern tribes. They were putting aside former national "distinctions" and were establishing themselves as one nation.

When Tecumseh and Harrison parted some days later—having each taken the other's measure and having developed a degree of mutual respect—the governor vowed that he would forward Tecumseh's objections to President Madison. By this time he acknowledged that the Shawnee chief, as well as being physically commanding and militarily daunting, was truly the leader of the northwest's Native Americans. Harrison went beyond Tecumseh's own boast that he was "alone the acknowledged chief of all the Indians" to report (with some astonishment) that the chief was "really an efficient man, the Moses of the family—and capable of any undertaking." But, for all that respect, he was compelled to tell Tecumseh that he could not back away from the terms of the Treaty of Fort Wayne and that the United States could not countenance the principle of commonly held lands.

Historian Bill Gilbert reports the reply that Tecumseh gave to the official position:

As the great chief [Madison] is to determine the matter, I hope the great Spirit will put sense enough into his head to induce him to give up this land; it is true, he is so far off he will not be injured by the war; he may sit still in his town and drink his wine, while you and I have to fight it out.

If ever Tecumseh had favored a peaceful acceptance of the white man's incursions, the tricky Treaty of Fort Wayne convinced him that now war was the only path to follow. No longer would he merely cause unease by threats against American settlements or by vague warnings that the British were about to join the federation in an all-out campaign to reclaim the lost territories. He would plan a definite campaign, meticulously timed and carefully targeted. Soon after the Vincennes confrontation, Tecumseh was on the move, seeking to solidify alliances with other tribes and to clarify the intentions of the continuously polite but ambiguous British. Despite recognition that he now drew from a far smaller population base than did the U.S. government—Indians of the northwest numbering only 70,000, as against the 170,000 white settlers who had thronged into the region—his hopes of attracting many of the far more numerous warriors from the southern nations to his pan-Indian cause seemed well founded. Furthermore, he had every expectation of being able to convince England's hesitant rulers to supplement the goods they already supplied so generously with superior weapons and seasoned troops. Meanwhile, Tenskwatawa, with the skills of a master propagandist, was urging the British to regard Prophetstown as successful demonstration of capital building and as a strategically important site.

To all visitors (including Harrison's spies, who came disguised as traders) the town did indeed seem impressive proof that, under the brothers' leadership, the allied Indians had sufficient skills and unity to cast aside old differences and build a center that would act as a catalyst for Indian unity. Although modern archaeology has not yet produced evidence of its exact location or design, historic reports indicate that the town was laid out, atypically, in a symmetrical pattern. As demonstrated in a large-scale model now visible at the Museum at Prophetstown near Battle Ground, Indiana, the commodious community on the north bank of the Wabash was divided into quadrants for the various assembled people. Above the orderly rows of bark wigwams rose the roofs of three larger structures: the Council House (now approximately reconstructed), the Prophet's medicine lodge, and a "House of the Stranger" for visiting tribesmen. In addition, the occasional cabins of traders and sutlers mark the town as a vibrant, commercial center, with a total population approaching three thousand.

The Prophet made every effort to give a spiritual heart to the community through his cosmological and ritual instructions. While never ceasing to proclaim his doom-filled, apocalyptic message, he tutored believers and visitors alike in the dances and songs of the new deliverance. Although most of the Shawnee and Delaware in the community followed his precepts faithfully, other tribesmen scorned his antialcohol rules and his ban of the Anglo-Americans' bread and tools. The Prophet's witchcraft trials were particularly contentious and divisive issues. Yet a famed Potawatomi prophet named Main Poc—who

confirmed his birth relationship with the Great Spirit by showing the lack of thumb or fingers on his left hand—supported
Tenskwatawa's religious drive (even while continuing to drink
whiskey).

Adding to the Shawnee brothers' difficulties were the constant problems of obtaining enough food for the assembled
peoples and of persuading the allies to accept Tecumseh as the
single leader and war as the only logical action. Not far from
them in Ohio, another Shawnee chief named Black Hoof was
demonstrating that his peaceful people, living and working in a
"civilized" agricultural community, could actually fulfill the
Jeffersonian ideal by producing bumper harvests. The brothers
saw that their traditional Indian pattern of working the land
might be less efficient than the one that American agricultural-
ists favored. Prophetstown's harvest was initially so low that
new appeals to the British and the Shakers had to be pressed; in
the first winter of 1808–09 horses and dogs were sacrificed to
the stew pot. By the fall of 1810, however, the crop yield looked
somewhat more promising. Tecumseh, who had been given a
great belt of war by the enthusiastic Wyandot, went off on his
recruitment drive to the southern tribes the next spring, desperate for more warriors and convinced that he had a successful
cause to sell.

The brothers' mother had been Creek, one of the most important tribes west of the Appalachians in present-day Tennessee and Alabama, a tribe that had already absorbed many
Shawnee into its cosmopolitan embrace. Perhaps more important than that blood connection, the populous southern tribes—
including, besides the Creek and mountain-dwelling Cherokee,
the Choctaw and Chickasaw—shared similar messianic beliefs

(though the Choctaw and the Creek had long been hostile to each other). As observed by the earliest white visitors, the Four Civilized Nations, as these tribes came to be called, had a common tradition of religious dance and a system of kinship that, for all the changing alliances and trade-induced rivalries, provided a kind of unity. Indeed, in 1803 on the banks of Alabama's Coosa River, these four nations had agreed to hold firm and oppose further cessions to the newly victorious, ever pressing Americans. To that interrelated and strongly ruled confederacy Tecumseh attempted to speak, with a message powerful enough to command attention.

According to contemporary sources, Tecumseh, whose powerful physique and rhetorical talents prompted him to come on stage with all the larger-than-life effects of a theater star, chose to preach on this occasion clad only in breechcloth and moccasins (shades of Samoset!). He was here, after all, facing a rhetorical challenge that might be likened to that of Puritan-descended Sam Adams at the First Continental Congress in 1775, or, more accurately, to that of Presbyterian-trained Patrick Henry on the same occasion. The divinities had to be invoked; with the birth of a nation at issue, this was a time for transcendence, a time for men to stand in for gods.

Meeting first with the Choctaw and Chickasaw, Tecumseh urged these adaptive people to forsake the white man's ways and to prepare themselves for the coming battle: all Indians united against the Americans. He then turned to the Cherokee and Creek, addressing more than five thousand of these intermixed people at the capital of Tallapoosa in September 1811. Still split between the forces that had favored the British or the

American sides in the Revolution, the Creek* were only in part responsive to Tecumseh. Many had married into and thoroughly accustomed themselves to the new American economy and disdained to heed the Shawnee's call; many others (particularly the Lower Creek of southern Alabama) considered themselves pacifists, or White Sticks—displaying poles tipped by that color in their villages to indicate a commitment to peace.

The more radical chiefs of the Upper Creek towns were championed by a young half-Scottish warrior named William Weatherford, whose Creek name (Lumhe Chati) means Red Eagle. Related to the famous and recently deceased Alexander McGillivray who had struggled to bolster Creek autonomy against Spanish, British, and American thrusts, Weatherford saw that he must now seize this opportunity to become a part of Tecumseh's campaign. His people, some of whom were called Red Sticks, tended to be intensely religious, known for their enthusiastic dancing under the direction of shamans brandishing vermilion-tipped batons. Now they could blend that piety with the fiery message brought south by Tecumseh and by Seekabo, the Shawnee Prophet's agent who had accompanied Tecumseh.

The naturalist William Bartram, when he passed this way a few decades earlier, had remarked on how the religion-prone Creek should be seen as a "culture of the sacred," demonstrating

---

*Given this name historically by Anglo-American frontiersmen, the Creek are more properly called by their linguistic designation, Muskogee. The Upper Creek had generally occupied the hilly reaches of upland northern Georgia and Alabama, and had tended to be pro-British in the eighteenth century.

the ability to transform both natural events and present-day circumstances into religious experiences. In 1811, uplifted by the Shawnee Prophet's exciting pan-Indian gospel, these accomplished liturgists performed what came to be called the Dance of the Lakes. They danced it all together, the Muskogee traditionalists, the neighboring people from east and west, and the Shawnee visitors; it helped them feel spiritually and culturally one, whether or not they were united politically.

Of the purposely mixed force that had marched south with Tecumseh, two individuals were hotheaded Sioux who, like the more fanatical Red Sticks, favored immediate attacks on the Americans. Yet Tecumseh recognized that the wiser course was the one urged by the British: to do nothing more at this point than to galvanize the people, to gather as many warriors as possible, and to get them ready for an attack the next year. Thus, it was a complex, hurry-up-and-wait message he had to deliver to variegated audiences throughout the lands of the Four Civilized Nations. To Cherokee objections that they had already lost thousands in the French and Indian wars, had benefited from having not joined Pontiac in his "rebellion," and now had a secure (1790) treaty with the United States, Tecumseh replied passionately that their sedentary ways were destroying them and that American policies were demonstrably treacherous. Heatedly, he warned them that his prophet brother had predicted that the earth would shake and swallow them if they declined to take up arms and join the campaign. Moved by neither his political nor his religious messages, they declined to abandon neutrality. In a discouraged mood, Tecumseh left the southern tribes behind and moved on across the Mississippi to attempt recruitment among the Osage of Missouri.

GOD-INSPIRED WARS for a PAN-INDIAN NATION

Governor Harrison, who had heard of Tecumseh's boasts that the Indian armies now numbered more than two thousand, was thoroughly alarmed. Pulling every string at his command, he managed by late summer, 1811, to collect a supportive force of perhaps eight hundred men, many of whom were untried in combat. Then, informing Madison's secretary of war, William Eustis, of his intentions to make a move against Prophetstown at this favorable time when Tecumseh was absent, he moved northward. The secretary responded that with the British still officially neutral, the situation on the frontier was delicate; maximum force should be employed only as a last resort. With that cautious approval, Harrison marched up the Wabash valley. Some hundred miles downstream from Prophetstown (near present-day Terre Haute), he paused to erect a small fort (Fort Harrison) and waited through October in hopes of receiving more troops. Eventually a total of one thousand men made up his army, a small band of Delaware and Miami agreeing to function as scouts.

Nervous and mindful of the recent defeats of Harmar and St. Clair, Harrison could only take some comfort from knowing that the enemy commander was neither Blue Jacket nor Tecumseh himself. Tenskwatawa temporarily held all the power at Prophetstown; and although Harrison had received mixed messages from the Prophet—bellicose threats alternating with suggestions of parleys—he had learned that Tenskwatawa had been ordered by his brother to maintain the peace under all circumstances. On November 6, when Harrison had marched far enough north to bring the Indian village into view, messages came suggesting a truce conference the next day. Harrison's spies informed him, however, that that very night the Prophet in a wild mood had called his warriors to assemble around the fire in his council house. There he boasted that the Great Spirit would protect his warriors with a magical rod and that they must fight a pitched battle against the Big Knives forthwith, before dawn of the next day.

Thus the elements for the Battle of Tippecanoe—the key battle in the epic of the woodland Indians' attempt to win sovereignty for all Native Americans—fell into place. The plan devised by the Shawnee war chief, White Loon (perhaps aided by British military advisors), seemed crafty enough to succeed. His warriors would surround Harrison's force where it lay all unsuspecting and attack it from all sides even before dawn. Special efforts would be made to hit Harrison himself early in the battle. It was known that the general rode a white horse—that would be the target. What White Loon and Tenskwatawa had not paid sufficient heed to, however, was the fact that Harrison's officers in charge (Majors Marston Clark and Walter Taylor) had situated the army's encampment with great care: It was located on an oak-timbered ridge about a mile west of Prophetstown. To reach it, the Indians would have to crawl through wetlands on both sides and then up a steep bank through heavy bushes. There they would meet a watchful enemy. As one of Harrison's volunteer riflemen (Virginian Isaac Naylor) wrote: "A strong guard was placed around the encampment.... The troops were ordered to sleep on their arms."

Harrison retired with the uneasy assurance that a parley was scheduled for the next day. Having informed the Indians that he would not attack if they would agree to the terms set forth in the Treaty of Fort Wayne, he hoped no shots would be fired until he and Tenskwatawa (in whom he now had small confidence, concluding he was a "scoundrel") had attempted to come to terms. But suddenly, shortly before 4:00 A.M., Harrison heard a shot. A nervous sentry had detected a stirring in the leaves and fired at the spot through the darkness. His bullet hit the mark: One of the scouts specially chosen by the Prophet to "crawl through the grass like snakes and strike the sentinels" was severely wounded. Hearing that howl of pain, other Indians commenced to attack prematurely, firing at shapes seen by the camp's watch fires. All at once, the battle raged in full fury.

Harrison, who had been caught when just rising, wasted no time in dressing and mounting the first available horse (black, not white). The militiamen, though giving way at several points and suffering many losses, held most positions, and the officers, some of whom had urged rash counterattacks but had been restrained by Harrison, eventually organized defensive lines. Thereafter it was a matter, from the Indians' perspective, not of continuing the attack but of trying to save their own lives in the face of heavy fire. The Prophet's magic and promises of invulnerability seemed to avail them of nothing, as they fell in increasing numbers beneath the Americans' bullets and as their own ammunition ran short. Perhaps the embattled braves heard Tenskwatawa's war cries; legend has it that he prayed and called out to his troops from a place known as Prophet's Rock—but as visitors can see today, the nominated rock is nowhere near the ridge-top battleground.

Fortunately for history, one of the Native Americans who fought in the Prophet's cause, an Ottawa named Shabonee (thought to be Pontiac's grandnephew), survived to write a stirring account of the event. As well as confirming that there had indeed been redcoat advisors in Tenskwatawa's councils, he reported that, though he had been close enough to see General Harrison riding through the battle on a dark horse, he had not been able to raise his gun to shoot the American leader. "The Great Spirit held it down," he recalled. "I knew then that the great white chief was not to be killed, and I knew that the redmen were doomed."

The battle lasted little more than two hours; when the sun finally rose, the corpses of men and horses littered the ground, lying amid the smoking remnants of the extinguished campfires. The Americans suffered 180 casualties, including 50 men killed. Scouring the field, they found the bodies of forty Indians, though they knew that many more of the attackers had been carried off with severe wounds. On one side of the lofty marble monument that marks the battleground today, one reads the dismissive words: INDIAN LOSS UNKNOWN.

In the days following the battle, Prophetstown was largely destroyed on Harrison's orders. Tenskwatawa, fleeing and hiding even from his own people (particularly the incensed Winnebago), felt himself thoroughly disgraced, his visions discredited, and his religion seemingly demolished. Yet not all were willing to abandon either his philosophy of Indian blood brotherhood or his concepts of heaven and hell. When the earth next rocked—torn wide open by what came to be called the New Madrid Earthquake of December 1811—many remembered his apocalyptic predictions.

But when Tecumseh returned from the west and caught up with him early in January 1812, Tenskwatawa cowered before his brother's wrath. His plea that the Great Spirit's proper commands had not reached him (because of his wife's menstruation) convinced no one, least of all his older brother. Defrocked and demoted, he left religion behind him and became, according to his biographer David Edmunds, exactly what he had previously despised most: a conservative village chief, unwilling to move with the new and exciting spiritual currents of the future.

Gradually and inevitably, the Battle of Tippecanoe assumed mythic proportions: "Tippecanoe and Tyler too!" (Harrison's presidential campaign catchphrase of 1840) rang in harmony with "Don't Give up the Ship," the salty slogan of the War of 1812. A linking of the wars in the Old Northwest with the next war against Great Britain seemed unavoidable when Tecumseh, who had gone north to Canada after Tippecanoe, rode into Detroit with British troops early in 1812. In Detroit he joined the triumphant celebration of that city's surrender. But he took north with him only a tattered remnant of his former army.

Though Tecumseh had momentarily been dealt with, the annihilation of the American population of the Old Northwest seemed far more likely in the disastrous summer of 1812 than the ultimate defeat of the native population. The surrender of General Hull's two-thousand-man army at Detroit gave heart to the Indians, particularly the Potawatomi, who seized Fort Dearborn and then moved on to Fort Wayne. Responding to Tecumseh's triumphant call, war parties including Shawnee and Miami attacked Fort Madison near St. Louis as well as the abominated Fort Harrison on the Wabash. By summer's end, the red warriors controlled most of the original Northwest Territory, except for the part of Ohio south of the Maumee. Huddled behind palisades, the Americans trembled at news of successive slaughters (particularly that of soldiers captured at the Raisin River) and prayed that the nation would respond to their pleas for aid.

Tecumseh himself earned a deserved reputation for noble behavior on the battlefield, though the basis for his lifesaving actions, unlike that of the recently deceased Joseph Brant, stemmed from basic humanity and not from learned courtliness. Both among British forces at Detroit, where he told the permissive General Brock that his troops would always be sober and would not participate in massacres, and at Fort Meigs, where he castigated the British for their own toleration of prisoner abuse, he demonstrated a deep-seated, Brant-like chivalry that outclassed other commanders.

Fort Meigs, the American post near the mouth of the Maumee River, which had at first seemed so ripe for the taking by combined British and Indian forces in the spring of 1813, proved a more difficult objective as the summer matured. Indeed, with the failure of Tecumseh's and General Proctor's attacks against General Harrison's strengthened forces in July, Fort Meigs gained fame as the "Gibraltar of the West." By then Americans had not only recognized that the war had to be won by combined land and sea assaults on the Great Lakes front, but they had also acknowledged that successful generals needed well-trained men and ample resources. When the British forces were finally driven back into Canada, their high command faced with dismay the prospect of another costly war on the continent of North America for no perceptible purposes—except possibly support of the Indians. The trumpets sounded the call for retreat.

As the British moved back along the Thames River after defeats on Lake Erie and the abandonment of Fort Malden (opposite Detroit), Tecumseh, then at the height of his military
renown, hurled the wrath of God upon the king's officers. "You
have got the arms and ammunition which our great father [King
George] sent for his red children," he reminded them. "If you
have an idea of going away, give them to us, and you may go
and welcome for it. Our lives are in the hands of the Great
Spirit. We are determined to defend our lands, and if it is his
will, we wish to leave our bones upon them."

According to Tecumseh's biographer John Sugdon, the
Shawnee chief's warriors (who still numbered more than a thousand) thrilled to this message and rallied. They would carry on
the great struggle for a pan-Indian nation by themselves; they
had by no means lost the war to the entrenched American
"groundhogs." They would be able to continue their victories
in the field and to reclaim their sacred lands. But that dream was
not to be realized. On the morning of October 4, 1813, Tecumseh was cut down in a hail of fire by Harrison's dragoons as they
charged through the swamps surrounding Moraviantown, Ontario. Many times during that climactic battle the Shawnee chief
had been heard to cry out, "Be brave, be brave!" (recalling the
battlefield leadership of Cornstalk during the long-ago Governor Dunmore's War). Finally that voice was heard no more—
though the spirit would continue to echo.

Indeed, the consequences of Indian successes and failures
during the War of 1812 would continue to shape their relationship with the young Republic's emboldened victors. When Harrison's reinforced troops marched north into Canada in 1813,
they spurred themselves on with the strange cry, "Remember

the Raisin!" For the slaughter of American captives by Indians after that riverside battle had already been scorched into the popular mind—another part of the emerging national myth of necessary conquest. As they continued their march up the Thames, they sang this rousingly patriotic, if ill-metered song:

> Freemen, no longer bear such slaughters;
> Avenge your country's cruel woe;
> Arouse, and save your wives and daughters!
> Arouse, and smite the faithless foe!

Faithless, not at all. Faith was a part of the Indians' living and dying. Not long before Tecumseh's last stand on the Thames, Red Eagle and the Creek Red Stick leadership arose in religious fury and committed their followers to a campaign that (unfortunately) helped determine the destiny of all the people of the Four Civilized Nations. Although the Red Sticks had once long ago devoted themselves only to rites and dances, they had become the party of war, identifying Americans plus all Indians allied with them as their just foes. In keeping with the spirit of Tecumseh, they would rise in a great revolution and unify the Muskogee people, then drive the amoral Great Serpent from their holy land.

In August 1813, Red Eagle's forces attacked Fort Mims, a poorly guarded U.S. stockade that at that time was providing refuge for about five hundred settlers including many assimilated Creek. Since they had performed their Dance of the Lakes and purified themselves before battle, they believed that they could not be harmed. But although their attack succeeded in a horrible and bloody way, with some 250 women and children slaughtered, the attackers also fell in great numbers (an estimated 300). Furthermore, this commencement of the so-called Red Stick Rebellion triggered a remorseless campaign by the U.S. government against both native and mixed peoples of the southern nations that would not cease until they had been removed from the scene.

The first retaliation occurred at the Red Stick town of Eccanachacca just before Christmas 1813. Laid out according to the cosmological concepts of the Muskogee prophets, the town was supposed to be inviolable, protected by the Great Spirit's gift of an "impenetrable barrier." Yet, with only a quarter of the defenders armed with muskets, the town fell easily to an American brigade aided by Choctaw and Cherokee ancillaries.

Then the full might of the U.S. military establishment fell upon the rebellious Red Sticks. Andrew Jackson, commander of western volunteers, took full advantage of those loyal Creek and other Indians who, throughout the Revolution and subsequently, had favored the American cause. Led by William MacIntosh (son of a Scotch trader and Creek mother) who had risen to the office of head chief of the Lower Creek, these pro-Americans were regarded as little better than outlaws by the more traditional Upper Creek. MacIntosh's personal rival was another mixed-blood warrior named Menewa, or Hothlepoya (Crazy War Hunter), who captained a division of Red Eagle's anti-American Red Sticks. MacIntosh's and Menewa's bitter struggle for leadership underlay the Creek's brief but important contribution to America's victory in the War of 1812.*

---

*Ultimately, when the war ended in surrender, Menewa was ceremonially executed by MacIntosh for selling off tribal lands against common agreement. Red Eagle raised the white flag and received a warrior's pardon from Jackson.

Having raised the cry "Remember Fort Mims!" and promising death to the "cowardly dogs," Jackson mobilized a combined force of fourteen hundred Tennessee militiamen plus a greater number of volunteers who rushed to join from other states. They were aided by several hundred of MacIntosh's warriors and six hundred Cherokee allies. In the midst of the Cherokee force might have been seen the tall figure of their adopted son, Sam Houston. They struck the Red Sticks in March 1814 at Horseshoe Bend on the Tallapoosa River in Alabama. At that strategic point the defenders had gathered a thousand poorly equipped warriors; of them more than eight hundred died in the fray. Though Menewa, badly wounded, managed to escape, Jackson could content himself with the thought that never before had so many Indians died in a single battle.

Hearing these results, the South's renowned diplomat, General Thomas Pinckney (who had recently won from Spain free passage on the Mississippi for the United States), crowed that "Almighty God has blessed the arms of the United States." He chose to forget, as did most other Americans, how much more difficult it would have been for them to achieve a kind of victory in 1816—and thus finally to achieve independence for the nation from Great Britain—if Tenskwatawa had won the battle at Tippecanoe and if many more Indian warriors had hastened to join the British-Indian cause. As Americans rejoiced in their forgetful victory, Jackson—over the objections of federal authorities and friendly Creek—demanded fourteen million acres of Indian land, the largest single cession in that region. He and Governor Harrison seemed to be engaged in a kind of immoral rivalry to determine who could gain more dispossessed territory.

Meanwhile, to religion-minded Americans, particularly those caught up in the enthusiasms of the Second Great Awakening, the long-dreaded War of 1812 had seemed a call for a national regeneration. As the war ended, the moralists' question of whether the Republic could achieve true liberty without the virtue of disciplined faith and all-embracing brotherhood became increasingly focused on the embarrassing question of the Indians. Could a Christian nation dispossess its native populations in pretended peace or annihilate those people in war while claiming any sort of religious identification? Both in the camp meetings of the frontier and in the eastern pulpits, that guilt-shrouded issue struggled for resolution. Yet that was one challenge for the saints of America's Second Great Awakening that they failed to meet.

Very few official structures existed that might have helped the remaining Indians of north and south stay on their feet; outstanding among them were the government's fur-trade houses (the "factories"), which had been set up for the economic benefit of the cooperating Indian nations. Here the hunters could bring their furs and exchange them for much needed (slightly subsidized) supplies to assist survival. By this means they might continue to function as a supply-side feature of the American trading economy—and that function might serve as a practical argument against removing the Indians altogether from their ancestral lands. But the diligent federal workers who had been attempting to keep this marginal system in place also found themselves dispossessed by the War of 1812.

Of the ten posts in operation when hostilities began, the British and their allied Indians had destroyed or forced the

abandonment of five; two others were forced to close temporarily. Although an honest and energetic Quaker named
Thomas McKenney was named to head the system immediately
after the war's end (1816), the doom of the factory system was
already visible. In that very same year, Congress encouraged
American enterprise into the fur trade by decreeing that foreigners should be barred from the potentially huge western
source of supply. Responding swiftly, the entrepreneurs made it
clear that the business was too risky for them to undertake unless the government's monopolistic factories were abolished.
McKenney, believing ardently in the charitable purpose of the
money-losing factory system, struggled in vain against such
horizon-glimpsing merchants as John Jacob Astor.

As energizing as victory in the War of 1812 may have been
for Americans of the new American Republic, with their new
myths and their self-centered revivalistic religion, it was crushing for the Native Americans. Their visionary plans and powerful dance prayers for a pan-Indian confederation had not been
fulfilled; also canceled was the grand old game of playing various timorous white men off against each other. With the stars
and stripes flying high—that is, with the psychic identification
and territorial solidification of the United States—that time-
tested strategy could never be employed again.

AROUSED CHRISTIANS FIGHT INDIAN REMOVAL

With the extension of U.S. boundaries to the Pacific and the ad-
mission to the union of states on both sides of the Mississippi
River (Illinois in 1818, Missouri in the famous Compromise of
1821), the hope of a secured Indian homeland in the Northwest
Territory dimmed considerably. Nonetheless, faithful people

of both races kept high expectations for brotherhood in both this world and the next. The editor of Boston's influential *Panoplist* hailed the advent of peace as the "herald of millennial expectations."

Thomas McKenney, backed by both established and evangelical religious groups, went so far as to call for the "sanctification" of the remaining Indian land. The headquarters for much of this salvationist enthusiasm was Boston, where the American Board of Commissioners for Foreign Missions (ABCFM) had been established just before the War of 1812. Transparently, the strategy of the ABCFM (successor to so many missionary groups in preceding generations) was to serve not one but two purposes: first, the evangelical cause of missionary work in foreign lands, including that among the Indians, and second, a consequential revival of Christianity in white communities near at hand. In the ABCFM's own language: "The most efficacious method of promoting religion at home, is for Christians to exert themselves and to send it abroad." The Indians would yet be useful.

Boston continued to consider itself the "City upon a Hill," the inspiration and moral arbiter of the nation; Christian editor Jeremiah Evans referred to Boston as the "irradiating point" for the reform movement. But in fact New England no longer called the tune financially, politically, or spiritually. Though Massachusetts' John Quincy Adams managed to win the presidency in 1825, his was the last of New England's dynasts. Andrew Jackson's personality and politics had begun to get a grip on the popular mind—indeed, he had won more votes than any of the four other candidates in the 1824 presidential campaign. Cheated, as he saw it, of the prize itself, he commenced a self-promoting campaign against the still resistant Creek of Georgia that had lasting consequences for the nation.

The Creek's southern neighbors and relations, the formerly isolated Seminole, whose numbers had nearly trebled as a result of the inpouring refugees, found themselves active participants in a new war, the so-called First Seminole War. Because Florida had been returned to Spanish rule by the British at the Revolution's end via the Treaty of Paris, the Seminole had regarded themselves at the century's beginning as removed from America's Indian tumults (and as providing something of a safe haven for escaped blacks and Indians of varying nationalities). But in 1817, Jackson's three-thousand-man army struck south in a whirlwind invasion under the pretext of recapturing escaped slaves but with the real hope of winning more acreage for the expanding cotton plantations. Spain soon entered into high-level diplomatic negotiations on the subject of Florida, with the clear objective of yielding the contested territory to the United States at a good price. Claiming that some of the hostile Creek were Red Sticks who had participated in the massacre at Fort Mims, Jackson pursued them with a special passion and with public support, even when he stormed beyond the Georgia border. But there, to Old Hickory's surprise, Florida's Seminole fought back with unimagined fury (though they had inadequate arms and little military training). Prominent in their leadership was a cadre of fundamentalist prophets. Though they were aware that the Shawnee Prophet's religion and Tecumseh's dream had collapsed, they respected the beliefs of the Red Sticks and lent spiritual strength to the combined Indians' defense. Upon Jackson's ultimate victories at Fort Negro (Apalachicola) and Old Town on the Suwanee and the seeming defeat of the

Seminole, three of these prophets were among the first Native Americans to be hanged.

Unsubdued Seminole continued to evade the grasp of the American forces—a problem Jackson would try to solve by his soon-to-be-introduced policy of Indian removal. As a result of their struggle with the United States, the Seminole gained a certain renown. Portraits of their splendidly attired women and drawings of their high-stilted houses appeared in contemporary lithographs. They came to be regarded as the fifth civilized nation. But as they entered into a series of constricting treaties with the conquering Americans, their survival as an independent nation seemed doubtful. Old Hickory (Sharp Knife, as he was known among the Indians) had declared it was "an absurdity" to make treaties with the Seminole or any other Indians, for these were not members of regular nations but merely U.S. subjects.

Whatever rationalizations he employed to explain his actions against the Five Civilized Nations, Jackson's very self-serving desire to free up land for his constituents' cotton plantations in Alabama and Mississippi was clearly the leading motive. Through his military conquests and notorious Indian-removal actions, it was Andrew Jackson,* as general and as

---

*By his cruel wars and unfair treaties against Indians, Jackson gained a deserved reputation for being their worst enemy, en masse. But by his adoption of and love for a Creek boy whose parents had been killed by the general's forces, he deserves also to be known for his respect of them, individually. Named Lincoyer and called "son" by Jackson, the promising young Creek was raised in Jackson's house and apprenticed to a harness maker; tragically, he died of tuberculosis when aged sixteen. Would any one of the contemporary New England mass moralists have demonstrated such individual affection?

president, who put muscle behind the eradicationist policies that had been favored more quietly by preceding presidents Monroe and Adams. And it was Jackson, as plantation owner and member of the South's new elite, who fed the hunger for Alabama land, called "Alabama fever," that would infect the entire South, to the uncalculable harm of the red peoples as well as of the black. Yet while the North experienced a slowly growing sense of outrage at the South's slavery policies, Indian removal from southern (and northern) territories never quite aroused the same militant passion.

Fighting the southern elite's desire for Indian removal were, first and foremost, the missionaries who continually sought to "civilize" the Indians, hoping thereby to save their territories. Curiously, that ancient hope, born in the era of John Eliot but frustrated repeatedly by wars and real estate realities, had not yet died—in spite of its lack of financial supporters and its two built-in philosophical flaws. The first of these flaws revealed itself in the frightful words of missionary leader Samuel Worcester, the philanthropist who said that "We propose to destroy the culture to save the people." The second and more important flaw was the desire and ability of the Indians still to fight back. This is also what Native American spokesman Vine Deloria refers to the "uncompromising ideology of Indian nationalism." Most Indians refused to be divided and conquered or adopted; they preferred to obey the call of the prophets to some new kind of unity. The missionaries' proposed solution of destroying the culture was seen for the horror it was by most Indians who survived the white men's plagues and wars. Yet the genuine conversion to Christianity of certain noteworthy people as well as the conversion to Native American ideals of

increasing numbers of wilderness-inclined Americans continued to mark the not quite separate cultures of the un-unified
nation.

Having recognized that the most crucial battleground in this
struggle to "save" the Indians now lay in the south, if only because that was where the greatest number of survivors remained,
the missionaries moved swiftly to establish themselves among
the Cherokee. That nation of particularly vigorous people traditionally occupied the areas of North Carolina and Tennessee,
where the settlers now streamed through on their way to the
west and south; it was therefore coveted and vulnerable. The
ABCFM strategists trusted that they could help the Cherokee
cling to their own land by demonstrating that the people were
both Christian and economically productive. Toward that end,
they established a mission school at Chickamauga in 1816, immediately upon the end of the War of 1812. They named the
school for David Brainerd, the well-remembered saint of America's first Great Awakening. They also established a school in
Cornwall, Connecticut (1817), to which eastern glade they
shipped off a number of Cherokee youths. All of this was done
hastily, while there was a chance of success, in the face of the
perceived enemy, Andrew Jackson. For he had decreed, "The
people of the [new] West will never suffer any Indian people to
inhabit this country again."

Strangely, these salvation efforts by the missionaries had
only a slight connection with the evangelical fervor that was
sweeping through the frontier communities at this time or with
the benevolent societies spawned by that movement. The more
radical Presbyterians, heirs of the Tennents, rejoiced that in
those regions beyond the mountains, "God is shaking the dry

bones on the frontier." Methodist preachers rode forth on underfed nags to visit the squalid communities where pious people from rocky, abandoned New England farms had found reinvigoration in ecstatic camp meetings. New denominations sprang up like blazes in dry forests struck by wildfire sparks. But the Indians, viewed as a problem of nature related to the unsettled and unfarmed wilderness, seemed irrelevant to these expressions of individual and small-town piety.

For God appeared to have blessed America as it moved west from the Appalachians toward the Mississippi. This new America perceived itself, theologically, as a cosmic occurrence. Millennialist Alexander Campbell, editor of the *Christian Baptist* (1830) and founder of the Disciples of Christ, urged both that Christians should "restore the ancient order of things" and that July Fourth should be celebrated as a religious event of equal rank with the Jewish Passover. An equation was made between American democracy and the fundamentalist religions that arose within America's newly settled and churched territories from Michigan and Indiana down through Tennessee and Alabama. Nor were these frontier churches, with their independent-minded and not necessarily well-educated clergy, demonstrations of what eastern, rationalistic Christians dreaded. That is, they were not individualistic breakaways contributing to the license and the opportunism of the Jackson era. On the contrary, the frontier churches proved to be strongholds of morality and citadels of conformity. Historian William Warren Sweet recently discovered that "the Elkhorn Baptist Association of forty churches . . . expelled 183 out of 2,442 members in 1803 for lack of discipline."

Yet small-town revivalism and Jacksonian populism seemed to be about other things than aiding the Indians. Indeed, when Andrew Jackson assumed the presidency in 1829, he immediately introduced to Congress his favorite piece of legislation, the Indian removal bill. During the process of the bill's consideration, he took the opportunity to ride out from his Hermitage home and meet with Chickasaw chieftains at present-day Franklin, Tennessee. There he urged them and other Indians to abandon all land they occupied within the southern states, presuming to admonish them in spiritual terms:

> Old Men! Lead your children to a land of peace and promise before the Great Spirit shall call you to die. Young chiefs! Forget the prejudices you feel for the soil of your birth. . . . You must submit—there is no alternative.

Also early in his administration Jackson fired from office Thomas McKenney, even though this recently appointed director of the Bureau of Indian Affairs and opponent to Indian removal had concluded that that cause was hopeless. Having once inveighed against the illegal sale of tribal lands as the "principal curse" of the Indians and having called Jackson's bill a "mockery" of humanity, McKenney reluctantly agreed that removal would be "satisfactory to them [the Indians] and honorable to the United States."

This was far from the opinion of the still feisty Foreign Missions Board, however. They resolved to do everything possible, to ring the bells from all church towers across the land, in order to defeat the removal bill. The good citizens of Hartford, Connecticut, stated that Indian removal was indeed an issue involving national honor: Such action would violate Christian morality. New Haven echoed the cry. Daniel Webster was brought into the congressional debate, adding thunder to the cause of righteousness. Edward Everett of Massachusetts—viewed by the press as the Apollo of Politics—declaimed against the bill in the public halls as ladies swooned in the galleries.

Even Congressman Davy Crockett—who had done his share of Indian killing—went on record as opposing the bill (and lost his seat as a result). Jackson cohort Lewis Cass, victor of the Battle of the Thames in which Tecumseh had died and soon to be appointed secretary of war, explained to the country's soft hearts that the purpose of the bill was to save the Indians from "utter extinction." Remove them to the wilds of Oklahoma, he and Jackson urged; there they would no longer be harassed by white neighbors and could rediscover their wilderness skills. That clever bit of upside-down morality, along with southern militancy, was sufficient to block many congressmen's ears from hearing the pro-Indian message of the religious zealots.

The debate was extraordinarily hot, even for those hot-tempered times. Senator Theodore Frelinghuysen of New Jersey, descendant of one of the earliest New Lights and a member of the ABCFM as well as the Bible, Tract, Sunday School, and Temperance Societies, lectured the Senate on behalf of the Cherokee for six unbroken hours. His brilliant defense notwithstanding, the upper house approved the bill early in 1830. It went immediately on to the House of Representatives, which initially declined to pass it (ninety-nine to ninety-three). But after numerous attempts to table the measure, a series of quorum calls, and efforts at adjournment, the House agreed to reconsider it in a third reading. It squeaked through on May 24, one hundred to ninety-seven. Exhausted, the representatives voted to adjourn for the day.

Defeated churchmen saw the vote as but another aspect of the devilishness of Jackson's election: the rejection of Christian republicanism and the triumph of unbridled opportunism. In protest, missionaries chose to be imprisoned in support of the Cherokee—the largest and most important of the southeastern tribes—who then went on to defy Georgia's removal laws. The devout Good Samaritan missionaries found it difficult to accept that, in the United States, religion (meaning Protestant Christianity) was no longer a public imperative—a fact that had already been implied in the administration's defeat of laws to ban business on Sundays. Henceforth in America, religion, if it were visible at all, would be a private matter—though modern scholars, in probing the American soul and associated political structures, have found an undergirding spiritual consensus that they call a "civil religion."

Of all the eloquent speakers against Indian removal, none was more moving than the Cherokee leader John Ross. Born in 1790 of mixed parentage, this Christian chief (named Kooweskeewe in Cherokee) had been educated in Kingston, Kentucky, and had served meritoriously in the War of 1812 as adjutant officer with Jackson against the Creek. His words to the U.S. Congress rise above the contests of this time, ringing with transcendent power and undying faith:

We are indeed an afflicted people! Our spirits are subdued! Despair has well nigh seized upon our energies! But we speak to the representatives of a Christian country; the friends of justice, the patrons of the oppressed. And our hopes revive, and our prospects brighten, as we indulge the thought. On your sentence, our fate is suspended; prosperity or desolation depends on your word. To you, therefore, we look! Before your august assembly we present ourselves, in the attitude of deprecation, and of entreaty. On your kindness, on your humanity, on your compassion, on your benevolence, we rest our hopes, To you we address our reiterated prayers, Spare our people! Spare the wreck of our prosperity! Let not our deserted homes become the monuments of our desolation! But we forbeare! We suppress the agonies which wring our hearts, when we look at our wives, our children, and our venerable sires! We restrain the foreboding of anguish and distress, of misery and devastation and death, which must be the attendants on the execution of this ruinous compact.

While the Congress turned deaf ears to Ross's fervent plea, the U.S. Supreme Court seemed equally incapable of halting the tragedy of Indian removal. The seventy-five-year-old Chief Justice John Marshall, ruled in favor of the appellant Cherokee and against the state of Georgia, which, in his view, had acted in haste to remove the Indians in denial of all previous treaties to the contrary. He wrote that Georgia's actions were "repugnant to the constitution, treaties, and laws of the United States and ought, therefore to be reversed and annulled." When he heard about the court's judgment, President Jackson is reputed to have scoffed, famously: "John Marshall has made his decision; now let him enforce it."

At one point it appeared that Ross and other Indian Christian leaders might do more themselves to secure their cherished territory than would any white Christians or even any variety of Tecumseh-inspired pan-Indianism. At the end of his service with Jackson in the War of 1812, Ross had devoted himself to the development of democratic government for his Iroquois-related Cherokee people. The prime feature of that grand effort was the writing of a constitution that mirrored in large part the foundation document of the United States. Its preamble—which might rightly apply to any Native American nation—reads (in part): "We, the Cherokee People, constituting one of the sovereign and independent nations of the earth, and having complete jurisdiction over its territory . . ."

What made the Cherokee government's 1827 code of law all the more historically remarkable was that, in its inspired unification of a number of constituencies through a system of checks and balances, it mirrored Deganawidah and Hiawatha's Great Law of Peace, the Kaianerekowa. Having been cited by Franklin at Philadelphia in the eighteenth century, that ancient law now inspired yet a new nation—or perhaps a nation within a nation.

Demonstrating their capacity to be reckonable nation builders, the Cherokee had striven to make their republic as successful physically and economically as it was theoretically. They had built an infrastructure of roads and irrigation ditches, they had constructed schools and churches at central points, and they had opened a training location for artisans. In this, the prime mover had been Ross, supported by a heterogeneous group of people, many of them fractionally white or black, all determined to become parts of a Cherokee unity. Ross ran a three-hundred-acre cotton plantation on the Coosa River (the farm being called Head of Coosa) as well as a ferry, while also serving as federal postmaster to the region. He understood the need for a religious base to underlie his new nation and accepted the missionaries' plan to introduce Christian schools within Cherokee territories. Yet he devoted most of his time to energizing his political faction. Having been elected one of the two constitutional chiefs, he had championed the two revolutionary causes of modernizing the Cherokee nation and keeping the seat of the Cherokee population and government on its mountainous ancestral land. The former cause had brought him into direct opposition with the traditional chiefs, one of whom (White Path) had staged a brief and unsuccessful rebellion against the new authority in 1827. The latter cause had brought him into opposition with his former commander, Andrew Jackson, who, unfortunately, no longer had need of Indian ancillaries, the tribes of the southeast having been essentially subdued and the Spanish empire having retired to Mexico.

Besides John Ross, another freedom-minded Cherokee who represented everything Jackson had disliked most—half-breed Indians with "extravagant pretensions" toward civilization—is known to history as Sequoyah. His white name, George Guess, indicated that his trader father may have been a member of the Gist family, scouts for both George Washington and Daniel Boone. A trader himself as well as a silversmith, he lacked education and knew little English. But, after twelve years of intense study and creative experiments, he had produced a workable Cherokee alphabet of eighty-five distinctive characters. Having taken some letters from English workbooks, he modified them and invented others to represent Cherokee sounds. In 1822 he had visited the part of the Cherokee tribe that had already departed for the Oklahoma Territory and taught thousands of schoolchildren there to read and write in their own language. How joyous and approving John Eliot and Richard Bourne would have been to observe that parts of the Bible would soon start appearing in this new orthography!

A printing press having been obtained, Sequoyah's alphabet had proved useful in the production of a weekly newspaper, the *Cherokee Phoenix*. Published in both Cherokee and English and immediately popular, this extraordinary journal of news and opinion had served, in addition to the Cherokee's constitution, as a unifying element for the new nation. Appearing first in 1828, the *Phoenix* lasted for more than a decade. Yet, threatened by Jackson's policies and uncertain about many of the Ross-induced innovations, many Cherokee had lost heart and had decided to join their cousins in the west. By the end of the nineteenth century's second decade, some six thousand had departed from the hills of Georgia.

With the passage of the Indian Removal Act in 1830 and the failure of the Supreme Court to support Native Americans' efforts to remain on their own lands, Georgia, Alabama (created in 1819 mainly from Creek and Cherokee country), and Mississippi (created in 1817 mainly from Choctaw and Chickasaw country) passed legislation placing the Indian nations under the jurisdiction of state laws and outlawing tribal governments. The U.S. Army, ordered to "inaugurate an operation of war" against the Creek in 1836, then staged a roundup with the aid of those Creek warriors who had always followed army commands. Manacling and chaining the "hostiles" in double-file processions, they started them out on the long march to Oklahoma.

The unsubdued Cherokee, who had momentarily taken heart when hearing of Chief Justice Marshall's decision, soon saw all their hopes dashed. They finally realized that—even with their proofs of peacefulness and of economic productivity, even with all the right on their side—further resistance would be met only by greater force. In a desperate move to carry on their age-old religious beliefs even after being removed to another land, they dug up and packed up with them their ancient copper plates as well as the coals from their sacred fires. Their death-dealing march along the infamous Trail of Tears then began.

BLOOD and TEARS on the TRAIL to OKLAHOMA

In the Choctaw's Muskogean language, *houma* means red and *Okla* means people. Thus the territory to which the Choctaw and their wealthy Chickasaw cousins (plus many other tribesmen) were forced to move in the 1830s earned the name Oklahoma. As the Chickasaw with all their wagons and baggage and horses prepared to move, observing whites were amazed to see men and women wandering about their luxuriant and revered landscape in mournful farewell, touching these trees and plants, those rocks and streams. They were departing from the mother earth that had nourished them. One is reminded of Tecumseh's son who, when finally removed from his beloved native valleys, refused to become a plow-pushing farmer, saying that he would not scar his mother's face.

For an emigrating group of Christian Choctaw, which numbered more than one thousand (many of them women and children) and which was led by two missionaries, the trail was particularly disastrous. Starting west ahead of others in the fall of 1830, they struggled through unfamiliar country during the coldest winter on record. Only eighty-eight of them succeeded in reaching the intended settlement on the Kiamichi River in the extreme southeastern corner of the designated Choctaw portion of Oklahoma. Though the missionaries spent all their available money to buy food for the survivors from white settlers in Arkansas, no government help reached them until late in the spring. A few other survivors straggled in to join them later, a grim remnant of a still proud nation.

Some of the tribes attempted resistance, including the ever obdurate Creek, who were not forced into complete submission until 1836. Then sixteen hundred of them were shackled together like a great slave procession and bundled aboard steamboats, first downriver to Mobile then on to Memphis and the west. More than three hundred Creek drowned when the unfit steamer to which they had been assigned by the prodding government forces blew up on the Mississippi River. Additionally, the nation's early side-wheelers, many of them cheaply made and primed for disaster, harbored cholera and malaria germs that claimed many emigrant victims. The Seneca gathered in Ohio—first of the Indian tribes to be removed by force—seemed to be particularly plagued by decrepit canal boats that swamped or sank on their way west, with additional hundreds lost.

Other members of the old Iroquois Confederation were dispossessed of their lands by increasingly crooked land deals—though the heirs of Handsome Lake managed to cling to a sizable reservation. The trustworthy Oneida, grandchildren of the patriot warriors who had aided Americans at Valley Forge and Saratoga, were persuaded by a possibly well-intentioned but at best naive Episcopal catechist named Eleazer Williams that they would find an "empire in the West." One consenting Oneida, contemplating the arranged move to Winnebago country, expressed the hope that, "Surely in emigration westward lies our escape from the grog shops." But, after the arduous move to Green Bay, Wisconsin, he and his fellow tribesmen found themselves restricted to an unpromising-looking patch of land that took decades for the people to turn into a worthy home.

Elsewhere in the Midwest, the fires of independence lit by Tenskwatawa continued to burn. One of his successors, called the Winnebago Prophet, inspired a warrior chief named Black Hawk with nativist preachings and divine warnings against removal. Black Hawk, a chief of the Illinois Sac and Fox nations who had fought alongside Tecumseh in the final days of the War of 1812, had vowed to stop illegal incursions of white settlers into his lands. After initial strikes against the squatters in 1832, he succeeded in routing the hastily called-up Illinois militia. Then he and his band of nearly a thousand people fled north, attempting to evade further pursuit by crossing the Mississippi. But they were slaughtered at the crossing by fire from steamboats even as they raised the white flag; survivors who reached the western bank were hunted down by U.S. Army–allied Sioux warriors.

Black Hawk managed to live through the engagement, was eventually freed, and won popularity in well-publicized appearances. His widely read autobiography, with its attempts to explain the Indian singularity, contains the famous affirmation, "I am a man!" Other midwestern Indians were not so fortunate in their attempts to survive. The Miami people—what remained of them after the defeat of Tecumseh's confederacy—obstinately resisted attempts to remove them from their Ohio river valleys. Stalling against orders to move to Indian Territory within five years, they were finally rounded up by army units in 1846. In company with their Potawatomi and Ottawa cousins, and with their chiefs chained and crammed into a carriage so that all tribesmen would follow obediently behind, they were forced to march past the blood-soaked Tippecanoe battleground on their so-called Trail of Death westward. Miraculously, a few escaped and managed eventually to reestablish themselves in their home valleys.

The rich and well-governed Cherokee of Georgia perhaps suffered the greatest humiliation of all. In their one-thousand-mile-long Trail of Tears to Oklahoma, this historic trek of some seventeen thousand people witnessed more than three thousand deaths from exposure, disease, and harsh treatment in virtual concentration camps. They had resisted removal as long as possible (until 1838), facing increasingly fierce treatment from the military under the command of General Winfield Scott. Anthropologist Anthony F. C. Wallace, a student of the Cherokee tribulations, describes the climactic event of May 23: "Detachments of soldiers arrived at every Cherokee house, often without warning, and drove the inhabitants out at bayonet point, with only the clothes on their back." A young army private who watched the wagon train pull out recalled that he had seen the Cherokee "loaded like cattle or sheep into six hundred and forty-five wagons...When the bugle sounded and the wagons started rolling, many of the children waved their little hands good-bye to their mountain homes."

The extraordinary Cherokee leader John Ross, evicted from his mansion on the Coosa, was forced at first to live in a dirt-floored log cabin in Tennessee. Finally, he consented to march west with his people, reaching Oklahoma after a year's journey—but not before the anguish of his wife's death from hardships endured on the trail. Yet, Christian faith firm, he trusted that some kind of benign future might be possible for him and his surviving people.

Even more fiercely than the Creek and Black Hawk's warriors, the Seminole fought back against removal. Land dispossession treaties having been forced upon them in 1832 and 1833, the people determined to heed the leadership of a warrior named Osceola. From his English father he had received the last name of Powell; from his Creek (Mikasuki) mother and her family in Georgia, he had learned the spiritual strengths and militant stance of the Red Sticks. Moving into Florida, he seized the opportunity to head up a group of Seminole willing to hold the line. Backed by these so-called fanatics, Osceola declared to the U.S. agent, General Wiley Thompson, that they were resolved to assassinate any chief who signed up for removal. Echoing the assertions of the Red Sticks, Osceola told his followers that "the Great Spirit will protect us!" Though briefly imprisoned and forced to sign treaty papers in order to gain his freedom, he continued to preach resistance.

In demonstration of his determination to prevent any Seminole migration, he ambushed and killed a chief named Charley Emathla who had been preparing to move out with his people. Soon thereafter, Osceola and his companions attacked and killed General Thompson himself. Thus began the frustrating, $20 million Second Seminole War (1836-1838), during which a succession of army generals waged ineffectual war against Osceola's wily but ever retreating forces. At the war's height, when the Seminole had been driven as far south as the Everglades, General Thomas Sidney Jessup had eight thousand troops committed to the dragged-out struggle. In all, the war demanded the deployment of more than thirty thousand soldiers.

As the press belabored the inefficiencies of the army and touted the wisdom of Osceola, it appeared to both sides that the time for peace talks had perhaps arrived. But when certain less militant chiefs agreed to remove westward and gave hostages to insure their sincerity, Osceola stormed into camp with two hundred warriors and liberated all the Indians involved. Finally, however, Osceola himself agreed to talks. Tricked into captivity, he was taken to Fort Moultrie, South Carolina. There he succumbed to illness in January 1838. Soon after calling for and donning his battle dress and lying down, he died, battle hatchet in hand.

Hailed by historians as one of the Indians' greatest heroes, Osceola, like Tecumseh, often appears on the printed page as a martial genius, a figure of romantic myth. In fact, Osceola's greatness lay not so much in his military brilliance as in the spirited heritage of resistance he bestowed on all Indians and particularly on his Mikasuki tribesmen in the Everglades. They continued the struggle for many years, never formally surrendering. Though his domain and perhaps his dream were smaller than Tecumseh's, Osceola's resolute defiance of impertinent American constraints deserves an equal regard.

While the nation's press featured stories about Black Hawk and Osceola, highlighting their bravery and otherworldly nobility but de-emphasizing the theft of their property, the organs of the Protestant churches conscientiously continued to press for Indian missions, for frontier schools, and for agricultural assistance (meaning support for the cultural shift to an American agrarian lifestyle). But one extraordinary group of awakened

Christians, sprung from the misty soil of New York State's "Burnt-over District," took a totally different approach to the deeply troubling issue of how Americans should explain their cruel wars against and cultural difficulties with the Indians. These were the Mormons, Joseph Smith's Church of Latter Day Saints, whose fundamental scriptures explained how the Indians ("Lamanites") would be restored to their rights and lands, come Judgment Day.

For the FINAL DAYS, a WHITE PROPHET and a NATIVE SAINT

Many commentators on the Mormons have been distracted from that faith's religious worthiness by the folkloric character of its origins—including Joseph Smith's own scalawag character and youthful experiments with up-country magic. Yet none can doubt either that faith's relevance to the American experience or its enduring vibrancy as a movement. It stands as the indigenous religious sect that has sustained the most rapid growth in U.S. history; if current trends hold, demographers say Latter Day Saints could number 265 million worldwide by 2080, second only to Roman Catholics among Christian bodies. The church's mission work among and relationship with the Indian nations has been particularly intense—though too little, too late, and too imposed.

This intensity stems in large part from *The Book of Mormon*, the scriptures discovered by seventeen-year-old Joseph Smith near his family's farm in Palmyra, New York. According to his account, in 1823 he was visited by the angel Moroni, who told him of the existence of gold plates on which the scriptures were inscribed. When he discovered and transcribed them, the plates

would give to all the world a true (and astonishing) account of
the former inhabitants of North America, whose origins had
been in Israel. Indeed, according to Moroni, if one would read
this translation—which recounted the ancient warfare in Pales-
tine between the Nephites (led by a general named Mormon)
and the Lamanites (ancestors of the Indians)—one might dis-
cover the totality of the Bible. Further, by a study of this complete Bible, both God's redemptive purpose and the risen
Christ's latter-day mission could be grasped.

Joseph Smith succeeded in discovering the plates in 1827;
they were of gold, not of copper like those sacred to the
Cherokee. They seemed to him a true gift from heaven; with
their guidance and God's help, he could confidently build a
church and avoid the rampant denominationalism then swirling
through New York (and setting his mother and father at odds).
Significantly, the 1820s were the beginnings of a religious revival in central New York and also the years when lawyer
Charles Grandison Finney rose to sudden prominence as a li-
censed minister. As mentioned earlier, Finney attained the reputation as the greatest preacher of America's Second Great
Awakening. He had grown to manhood and mounted his first
pulpit in the very town where Samuel Kirkland had worked
among the Iroquois—Oneida, New York. There his fiery sermons earned him the title, Madman of Oneida. Ranging around
the state to stage revivals among the poorest and least lucky
frontiersfolk, he adopted such techniques as installing an "anxious seat," on which an about-to-confess sinner could ponder
his peccadilloes. His crowd-packed Rochester revivals of 1830-
1831 were so productive that Lyman Beecher referred to them as
"the greatest work of God and the greatest revival of religion

the world has ever seen in so short a time." Finney's self-absorbed, American-style religion had no room for such catholic issues as the banished Indians; in booming Rochester, the Indians were already a thing of the past.

Although Joseph Smith, a latter-day messiah, and Charles Grandison Finney, a master revivalist, were contemporaries, their versions of Christianity were largely dissimilar. Both God-struck men had family roots in New England Calvinism. Both shared with other innovative preachers of the day a healthy disrespect for overeducated clergy ("hireling priests"), and both were resolved, like John the Baptist, to restore "the ancient order of things." But whereas Charles Grandison Finney attempted to bring wandering sheep into the welcoming fold of an existing Christian church,* and whereas he eventually moved among the rich and the newly affluent members of the middle class to advance his philanthropic causes, Joseph Smith (believing as he did in direct revelation and in the advent of the Second Coming) called for the creation of an entirely new church. When he and his disciple Oliver Cowdery baptized each other in the Susquehanna River, they took the first step in founding the Church of Christ (formally established in 1830).

Very soon after the creation of their church, Joseph Smith sent Oliver Cowdery out to preach among the Indians. They prayed that the Indians would see the Book of Mormon as the

---

*Despite his social acceptability, staid Presbyterians were bothered by Finney's "new measure" techniques. Thus when the more enthusiastic citizens of Brooklyn, New York, sought to attract him to their pulpit, they had to leave their old church and build a special tabernacle as home for Finney's preachings.

good news they had been waiting for, a revelation from their ancestors, and would thereby trust in God's eventual purpose of restoring them. And one of the most encouraging reports that Joseph Smith received back from the field in those early, tumultuous years of the church's growth was that Cowdery had had "initial success among the Delawares" of Pennsylvania. Cowdery stated that he had told the Indians that they "should be restored to all their rights and privileges; should cease to fight and kill one another; should become one people; should cultivate the earth in peace, in common with the pale faces."

They listened with more curiosity than conviction to Cowdery's gospel. Such a sympathetic message was certainly not what the land speculators and the government agents who supported them wanted to have preached to the Indians. The Mormons' exceptional attitude toward the Indians and toward the communal ownership of land was, indeed, one of the prime reasons for opposition to these tightly banded people as they moved west to Missouri and then on to Nauvoo, Illinois, where they arrived in 1839. From the splendid temple and burgeoning residences they built at Nauvoo, a crowd of violent neighbors hauled away Joseph Smith and his brother, Hyrum, on June 21, 1846. Imprisoned in Carthage, Illinois, under the charge of treason to the United States, the brothers were wrenched from jail three days later. Then the mob murdered them.

At that desperate point began the extraordinary experience of the Mormons' own transcontinental removal—that is, their trek to Salt Lake City, Utah, under the leadership of Brigham Young. Whether it was a matter of divine inspiration or organizational genius, the Mormons triumphed in that westward migration and in the making of a garden out of a mountainous desert. They also recommenced their missionary work among the Indians, those other Americans who had found not a Jerusalem in their western allotments, but only another place and time for persecution and repression. Some Mormons, admitting that missionary work among North American Indians has not been a runaway success, point to the tremendous growth of their church among native populations in South America. Perhaps, they surmise, the tablets were Mayan. And thus the revelation continues to evolve, to temporize, and to deal with new tomorrows.

Although the spiritually exciting years of the Second Great Awakening might appear to have brought more misery than sustenance to the Indians of the United States, one man stands forth as a legitimate product of that time and a true if modest herald of Indian independence. Without the peculiar, inspirational power of the Awakening, he might not have found his voice. His name was William Apess, a Pequot and thus an heir of that famous nation. Once his ancestors had dominated the Connecticut River valley with their trading and diplomatic skills. But they were finally confronted and defeated by the combined might of the New England colonies in the Pequot War of 1637. The revolt that Apess stirred up was of another kind, a successful, religion-based revolt of tribesmen in Mashpee, Massachusetts (home of some of New England's earliest missionary work). Yet the revolt should be seen not as a victory beacon flashing eternally against the dark but as a light blinking from near obscurity for future inquirers into Indian nationalism.

Fortunately for later knowledge, Apess wrote an autobiography, published as *Son of the Forest* in 1831, the first such work in American literature. It explains, rather quaintly, that he was born in 1798 in Colrain, Massachusetts, "where my father pitched his tent in the woods." But he was raised in his early years by his Pequot grandmother, and it was among those people that he subsequently found his true identity. Indeed, as his biographer, Barry O'Connell, points out, William Apess enjoyed two kinds of baptism: one as a convert to Methodism (in Bozrah, Connecticut, in 1818) and another as he gradually came to understand his position in the dynamic culture of Native Americans.

His first introduction to the liberating side of Christianity occurred in 1809, the dawning of the Second Great Awakening, when he was living as an indentured servant in the home of the William Williams family in New London, Connecticut. When the Williamses, proud members of that haughty clan and strict Congregationalists, learned that the boy had been sneaking out to the Methodist revival meetings, they forbade him from attending any other such sessions. When he disobeyed them in that regard, they beat him severely. Apess reacted in the standard American way: He ran away to the west, eventually ending up as a U.S. Army infantryman among other reluctant warriors in the War of 1812.

Finally separated from that service, he spent some time among the Mohawk and other northern Indian groups; he referred to them as "my brethren, who ornamented the wood with their camps and chanted the wild beasts of prey with their songs." At last, in 1818, he returned to southeastern Connecticut, was reunited with his family, and again experienced the quickening joy of worship at Methodist meetings. The meetings led to his conversion, to his baptism, and to his marriage in 1822. Though working as a shoemaker and bookseller, he obeyed God's pressing call to be a preacher. He began that service by moving around the countryside as a prayer leader and Methodist exhorter, and in 1829 he was ordained as a Protestant Methodist minister.

By then he had completed his biography and was gaining a reputation as a writer and public speaker. Sent out by the American Conference of Protestant Methodists to be a missionary among his own Pequot, he was soon invited (1833) to Mashpee. This Cape Cod town, a remarkable survivor from the vibrant days of the praying villages, happened to be caught up then in a struggle for the survival of its governmental and spiritual life. Apess was just the man to take them through that uprising into independence.

Immediately after arrival on Cape Cod, he had found, to his horror, that Massachusetts authorities had determined that the Mashpee were ripe for Jackson-style removal. Posting sentries to make sure that no official forces could take them by surprise, Apess and the Mashpee leadership erected barricades and prepared to fight it out. When the expected wagons arrived, the contracted teamsters, surrounded by protesting Mashpee, went bullishly ahead to load up their carts with wood, hay, and the townsmen's other possessions. But following Apess's commands, the Mashpee surged in to unload whatever had been collected. As it was reported at the time: "While two of [Apess's] number stood near him as aides, with clubs in their hands, six others, in defiance of the laws of the land, proceeded forthwith to execute his orders and to drive the whole concern from the territory."

Having won the battle to retain their land and their goods (in what came to be called the Mashpee Revolt of 1833), Apess and his enlivened community went on to secure their basic freedoms. In this effort, they struggled against both the overseers who had been imposed on the Mashpee by the Commonwealth of Massachusetts and against the established church's installation of a white minister in the pulpit of the Old Indian Meeting House. Because Apess had been adopted by the community, he felt that he acted on the strength of local authority as well as in the righteousness of his own ordination. Drafting petitions to the governor as well as to the Harvard Corporation, and contending with innumerable delays (as well as Apess's arrest and imprisonment), the Mashpee finally accomplished both their political and their religious objectives. In March 1834 the state legislature granted to the community the same rights of township self-governance as other citizens possessed, and in 1840 the legislature endowed the district of Mashpee "with all the powers and privileges . . . which [all other] parishes or religious societies possess." Apess took charge of the pulpit of the Old Indian Meeting House. For the moment, equality had been achieved.

In winning these victories, Apess was aided by such New England luminaries of the day as William Lloyd Garrison and Benjamin Hallett. Apess became something of a hero in the liberal Puritan capital, delivering there a lengthy and remarkably popular speech, entitled the "Eulogy on King Philip, as Pronounced at the Odeon, in Federal Street, Boston" (1836). While making this dramatic, flowery address, he took the occasion to lambaste the supposedly democratic United States government for having enacted the cruel Indian Removal Act. Identifying himself with King Philip by lineage and by cause, he parodied what the government's removal agents had so recently told the Indians: "You need not cry, you must go, even if the lions devour you . . . for we promised the land you have to somebody else long ago, perhaps twenty or thirty years [ago]; and we did it without your consent, it is true, but this has been the way our fathers first brought us up."

Apess also made the more far-reaching point in this speech and in his autobiography that, just as he now regarded himself not as a Pequot but as an American Indian, belonging to a national family with all other Indians, so, too, did he regard himself as a universal Christian. That is, he was a convert not to the white man's religion but to the worldwide religion that Christ had intended. Speaking of his Christian mother as well as himself, he wrote: "For a Pequot to convert to Christianity is not . . . to take on white ways but to claim one of her rights as a human being." Revealing the process by which he had arrived at that all-encompassing conclusion, he added: "I felt convinced that Christ had died for all mankind—that age, sect, color, country, or situation made no difference. I felt an assurance that I was included in the plan of redemption with all my brethren."

In the vitally important act of conversion, he saw missionaries as unfortunately more often dangerous than helpful. He put that sentiment in the form of a question: "But must I say, and shall I say it, that missionaries have injured us more than they have done us good—by degrading us as people, in breaking up our governments, and leaving us without any suffrages whatever, or a legal right among men?" He then added, "Oh, what a cursed doctrine is this!"

He tried through the spiritual theatricality of the Second Great Awakening to demonstrate to all sorts and conditions of people (including blacks)—to any people whom the majority culture sought to repress—that they had no need to accept Anglo-Americans as possessing a divinely ordained superiority.

It was through the concept of "civilizing the heathen" that they had attempted to justify their conquests as an aspect of that superiority. No, America's true Christian people needed nothing of that sort. Instead, they needed faith and a vision. These he and others would hope to supply for the future, just as King Philip had supplied it almost two hundred years earlier.

In another revolutionary passage that echoed the Mormons' racial view in an unintended way, Apess made a cultural statement followed by a biblical question: "America has utterly failed to amalgamate the red man of the woods into the artificial, cultivated ranks of social life. Has not one reason been that it was not the purpose of God that it should be done—for lo, the blood of Israel flowed in the veins of these unshackled, freeborn men?"

Yet the passage that he and his Mashpee community inscribed as the first article in their declaration of independence may be the most memorable statement of his religious and political beliefs. It may also be the most important precept to keep in mind as Americans face a new century in which concepts of Indian sovereignty are being reconsidered. The passage resolves:

> That we as a tribe will rule ourselves,
> and have the right so to do
> for all men are born free and Equal
> says the Constitution of the Country.

Beyond the Constitution, this precept finds justification and authority in the spirit of the Iroquois's Guswenta—the Two-row Wampum Belt—which envisioned Native Americans and the United States as forever pursuing related but differentiated courses. That anciently founded and spiritually blessed concept, confirmed not only for the Iroquois but for all Native Americans in the 1794 Treaty of Canandaigua (ratified by George Washington in 1795), deserves enshrining in any thoughtful book of American history.

Yet at the time of the Indian Removal Act and the Mashpee Revolt, an end of sorts came to the possibility of thoughtful or creative interaction among the peoples. It was then that the confrontation with Native Americans shifted largely from the eastern woodlands to the western plains and also when a decrease of tensions seemed to make for a diminishing of divine revelations. Euro-Americans having asserted their claim to the eastern half of the continent, a change of vast consequences occurred in the national culture: Americans devoted themselves to sectors other than the mysterious borderlands, and history followed along behind.

Nonetheless, many historic and theological themes remained in place. Certainly the work done in peace and in war on the opening western frontier by a fresh (if less magnetic) breed of apostolic missionaries and by new native prophets echoed (if dimly) the work of their eastern predecessors. Joseph Brant's cry that Indians, including his own Mohawk, were "all of one mind, one heart!" can still be heard ringing within the Lakota chant that "we [Indians] are all related!" Similarly, Jonathan Edwards's 1742 holy argument that we are "two armies, separated and drawn up in battle array" can be heard today whenever churchmen clash with secularists.

But the time for regarding such prophetic voices, such specially empowered men, as national saviors passed many generations ago. After the 1830s it became much less clear to most Americans of all origins through whom the gods of peace might ever work their purposes out.

BIBLIOGRAPHY

Ahlstrom, Sydney E. *A Religious History of the American People.* New Haven: Yale University Press, 1972.

Aldridge, Alfred O. *Jonathan Edwards.* New York: Washington Square Press, 1966.

Anderson, Fred. *Crucible of War: The Seven Years' War and the Fate of Empire in British North America, 1754–1766.* New York: Knopf, 2000.

Andrew, John A., III. *From Revivals to Removal: Jeremiah Evarts, the Cherokee Nation, and the Search for the Soul of America.* Athens, Ga.: University of Georgia Press, 1992.

Axtell, James. *The European and the Indian: Essays in the Ethnohistory of Colonial North America.* New York: Oxford University Press, 1981.

————. *The Invasion Within: The Contest of Cultures in Colonial North America.* New York: Oxford University Press, 1985.

Bellah, Robert N. *The Broken Covenant: American Civil Religion in Time of Trial.* New York: Seabury Press, 1975.

Benn, Carl. *The Iroquois in the War of 1812.* Toronto: University of Toronto Press, 1998.

Billington, Ray Allen. *America's Frontier Heritage*. New York: Holt, 1966.

Bloch, Maurice. *Prey into Hunter: The Politics of Religious Experience*. New York: Cambridge University Press, 1992.

Bordeur, Paul. *Restitution: The Land Claims of the Mashpee, Passmaquoddy, and Penobscot Indians of New England*. Boston: Northeastern University Press, 1985.

Bourne, Russell. *The Red King's Rebellion: Racial Politics in New England, 1675–1678*. New York: Atheneum, 1990.

Bowden, Henry W. *American Indians and Christian Missions: Studies in Cultural Conflict*. Chicago: University of Chicago Press, 1981.

Brabiner, J. Bartlet. *Canada: A Modern History*. Ann Arbor, Mich.: University of Michigan Press, 1960.

Bragdon, Kathleen J. *Native People of New England, 1500–1650*. Norman, Okla.: University of Oklahoma Press, 1996.

Brodie, Fawn. *No Man Knows My History: The Life of Joseph Smith, the Mormon Prophet*. New York: Knopf, 1971.

Brown, Joseph Epes. *The Spiritual Legacy of the American Indian*. New York: Crossroad, 1982.

Bushman, Richard L. *From Puritan to Yankee: Character and the Social Order in Connecticut, 1690–1765*. Cambridge, Mass.: Harvard University Press, 1967.

———. *Joseph Smith and the Beginnings of Mormonism*. Urbana, Ill.: University of Illinois Press, 1984.

Butler, Jon. *Becoming America: The Revolution before 1776*. Cambridge, Mass.: Harvard University Press, 2000.

Calloway, Colin G. *The American Revolution in Indian Country*. New York: Cambridge University Press, 1995.

Campisi, Jack. *The Mashpee Indians: Tribe on Trial.* Syracuse, N.Y.: Syracuse University Press, 1991.

Carmody, Denise. *The Republic of Many Mansions.* New York: Paragon, 1990.

———. *Native American Religions, An Introduction.* New York: Paulist Press, 1993.

Carroll, Peter N. *Puritanism and the Wilderness: The Intellectual Significance of the New England Frontier, 1629–1700.* New York: Columbia University Press, 1969.

Cashin, Edward J. *William Bartram and the American Revolution on the Southern Frontier.* Columbia, S.C.: University of South Carolina Press, 2000.

Cave, Alfred A. *The Pequot War.* Amherst, Mass.: University of Massachusetts Press, 1996.

Chalmers, Harvey. *Joseph Brant: Mohawk.* East Lansing, Mich.: Michigan State University Press, 1955.

Cherry, Conrad. *The Theology of Jonathan Edwards: A Reappraisal.* Garden City, N.Y.: Doubleday, 1966.

Cogley, Richard W. *John Eliot's Mission to the Indians before King Philip's War.* Cambridge, Mass.: Harvard University Press, 1999.

Cohen, Ralph, ed. *History And . . . : Histories within the Human Sciences.* Charlottesville, Va.: University Press of Virginia, 1995.

Cornelius, Carol. "The Thanksgiving Address: An Expression of Haudenosaunee Worldview." *Akwe:kon Journal,* Fall 1992.

Costain, Thomas B. *The White and the Gold.* Garden City, N.Y.: Doubleday, 1954.

Covey, Cyclone. *The Gentle Radical: Roger Williams.* New York: Macmillan, 1966.

Cowing, Cedric B. *The Great Awakening and the American Revolution: Colonial Thought in the Eighteenth Century.* Chicago: Rand McNally, 1971.

Cronon, William. *Changes in the Land: Indians, Colonists, and the Ecology of New England.* New York: Hill & Wang, 1983.

Debo, Angie. *A History of the Indians of the United States.* Norman, Okla.: University of Oklahoma Press, 1970.

Delbanco, Andrew. *The Puritan Ordeal.* Cambridge, Mass.: Harvard University Press, 1989.

————. *The Real American Dream: A Meditation on Hope.* Cambridge, Mass.: Harvard University Press, 1999.

Deloria, Vine, Jr. *Behind the Trail of Broken Treaties.* Austin, Tex.: University of Texas Press, 1974.

————. *God Is Red: A Native View of Religion.* Golden, Colo.: Fulcrum, 1994.

Densmore, Christopher. *Red Jacket: Iroquois Diplomat and Orator.* Syracuse, N.Y.: Syracuse University Press, 1999.

Dodds, Elizabeth D. *Marriage to a Difficult Man: The Uncommon Union of Jonathan and Sarah Edwards.* Philadelphia: Westminster Press, 1973.

Dowd, Gregory Evans. *A Spirited Resistance: The North American Indian Struggle for Unity, 1745–1815.* Baltimore: Johns Hopkins University Press, 1992.

Eckert, Allen W. *A Sorrow in Our Heart: The Life of Tecumseh.* New York: Bantam Books, 1992.

Edmonds, Walter D. *The Musket and the Cross.* Boston: Little, Brown, 1968.

Edmunds, R. David. *The Shawnee Prophet.* Lincoln, Nebr.: University of Nebraska Press, 1983.

————. *Tecumseh and the Quest for Indian Leadership.* Boston: Little, Brown, 1984.

Ehle, John. *Trail of Tears: The Rise and Fall of the Cherokee Nation.* New York: Anchor Books, 1988.

Eliade, Mircea. *The Quest: History and Meaning in Religion.* New York: Meridian, 1963.

Fantel, Hans. *William Penn: Apostle of Dissent.* New York: Morrow, 1974.

Fenton, William N., ed. *Parker on the Iroquois.* Syracuse, N.Y.: Syracuse University Press, 1968.

Fiske, John. *The Beginnings of New England, or the Puritan Theocracy in its Relations to Civil Religious Liberty.* Boston: Houghton Mifflin, 1891.

Fitzhugh, William W. *Cultures in Contact: The Impact of European Contacts on Native American Cultural Institutions, AD 1000–1800.* Washington, D.C.: Smithsonian Institution Press, 1985.

Flexner, James T. *Lord of the Mohawks: A Biography of Sir William Johnson.* Boston: Little, Brown, 1959.

Francis, Convers. *Life of John Eliot, the Apostle to the Indians.* Boston: Hiliard, Gray, 1836.

Frazier, Patrick. *The Mohicans of Stockbridge.* Lincoln, Nebr.: University of Nebraska Press, 1975.

Gilbert, Bill. *God Gave Us This Country: Tekamthi and the First American Civil War.* New York: Atheneum, 1989.

Graymont, Barbara. *The Iroquois in the American Revolution.* Syracuse, N.Y.: Syracuse University Press, 1972.

Grumet, Robert S. *Historic Contact: Indian People and Colonists in Today's Northeastern United States in the Sixteenth through Eighteenth Centuries.* Norman, Okla.: University of Oklahoma Press, 1995.

Gura, Philip F. *A Glimpse of Zion's Glory: Puritan Radicalism in New England, 1620–1660.* Middletown, Conn.: Wesleyan University Press, 1984.

Hardman, Keith J. *The Spiritual Awakers: American Revivalists from Solomon Stoddard to D. L. Moody.* Chicago: Moody Press, 1983.

Hauptman, Laurence M. *The Iroquois Nations and the Rise of the Empire State: Ditches, Defense, and Dispossession.* Cooperstown, N.Y.: New York State Historical Society, 1998.

Heimert, Alan. *Religion and the American Mind: From the Great Awakening to the Revolution.* Cambridge, Mass.: Harvard University Press, 1966.

Henry, Thomas R. *Wilderness Messiah: The Story of Hiawatha and the Iroquois.* New York: Sloan, 1955.

Hertzberg, Hazel. *The Search for an American Indian Identity: Modern Pan-Indian Movements.* Syracuse, N.Y.: Syracuse University Press, 1971.

Herzberg, Will. *Protestant, Catholic, Jew: An Essay in American Religious Sociology.* Chicago: University of Chicago Press, 1960.

Holly, Marilyn. "Handsome Lake's Teachings: The Shift from Female to Male Agriculture in Iroquois Culture. An Essay in Ethnophilosophy." *Agriculture and Human Values,* vol. vii, Number 3&4, Summer–Fall, 1992.

Horowitz, David. *The First Frontier: The Indian Wars and America's Origins, 1607–1776.* New York: Simon & Schuster, 1976.

Hoxie, Frederick E. (ed.). *Encyclopedia of North American Indians.* Boston: Houghton Mifflin, 1996.

Humphreys, Mary G. *Missionary Explorers among the American Indians.* New York: Scribners, 1913.

Jahoda, Gloria. *The Trail of Tears: The Story of the American Indian Removals, 1813–1855.* New York: Holt, 1975.

James, William. *The Varieties of Religious Experience.* New York: Longmans Green, 1912.

Jennings, Francis. *The Invasion of America: Indians, Colonialism, and the Cant of Conquest.* Chapel Hill, N.C.: University of North Carolina Press, 1975.

———. *The History and Culture of Iroquois Diplomacy.* Syracuse, N.Y.: Syracuse Unversity Press, 1985.

———. *Empire of Fortune: Crowns, Colonies, and Tribes in the Seven Years' War in America.* New York: W. W. Norton, 1988.

———. *The Ambiguous Iroquois Empire: The Covenant Chain Confederation of Indian Tribes with English Colonies.* New York: W. W. Norton, 1990.

Josephy, Alvin M., Jr., *The Patriot Chiefs.* New York: Viking, 1961.

———. *Now That the Buffalo's Gone.* New York: Knopf, 1982.

Kelsay, Isabel Thompson. *Joseph Brant, 1743–1807: Two Worlds.* Syracuse, N.Y.: Syracuse University Press, 1984.

Krickeberg, Walter, ed. *Pre-Columbian American Religions.* New York: Holt, 1970.

Kupperman, Karen. *Settling with the Indians: The Meeting of English and Indian Cultures in America, 1580–1640.* Totowa, N.J.: Rowman and Littlefield, 1980.

Lambert, Frank. *Inventing the Great Awakening.* Princeton, N.J.: Princeton University Press, 1999.

Lennox, Herbert John. *Samuel Kirkland's Mission to the Indians.* Chicago: University of Chicago Libraries, 1935.

Lepore, Jill. *King Philip's War and the Origins of American Identity.* New York: Random House, 1998.

Levin, David (ed.) *Jonathan Edwards: A Profile.* New York: Hill & Wang, 1969.

Love, W. deLoss. *Samson Occom and the Christian Indians of New England.* Boston: Pilgrim Press, 1899.

Martin, Joel. *Sacred Revolt: The Muskogees Struggle for a New World.* Boston: Beacon Press, 1991.

McDermott, Gerald R. "Jonathan Edwards and the American Indians: The Devil Sucks Their Blood." *The New England Quarterly,* Vol. LXXII, no. 4, December 1999.

Miller, Perry. *The New England Mind in the Seventeenth Century.* Cambridge, Mass.: Belknap Press, 1939.

Morgan, Edmund S. *Visible Saints: The History of a Puritan Idea.* New York: New York University Press, 1963.

Niebuhr, Richard. *The Kingdom of God in America.* New York: Harper, 1937.

Nobles, Gregory H. *American Frontiers: Cultural Encounters and Continental Conquest.* New York: Hill & Wang, 1997.

O'Brien, Jean. *Dispossession by Degrees: Indian Land and Identity in Natick, MA, 1650–1790.* New York: Cambridge University Press, 1997.

O'Connell, Barry, ed. *On Our Own Ground: The Complete Writings of William Apess, a Pequot.* Amherst, Mass.: University of Massachusetts Press, 1992.

Parkman, Francis. *The Battle for North America* (Abridged and edited by John Tebbel). Garden City, N.Y.: Doubleday, 1948.

————. *The Conspiracy of Pontiac and the Indian War after the Conquest of Canada* (2 vols.). Boston: Little, Brown, 1901.

Parrington, Vernon Louis. *The Colonial Mind, 1620–1800.* New York: Harcourt Brace, 1927.

Patrick, Christine S. *The Life and Times of Samuel Kirkland: Missionary to the Oneida Indians, 1741–1808.* Buffalo, N.Y.: SUNY Buffalo Press, 1993.

Pilkington, Walter, ed. *The Journal of Samuel Kirkland: 18th Century Missionary to the Iroquois, Government Agent, Father of Hamilton College.* Clinton, N.Y.: Hamilton College Press, 1980.

Richter, Daniel K. *The Ordeal of the Longhouse: The People of the Iroquois League in the Era of European Colonization.* Williamsburg, Va.: University of North Carolina Press, 1992.

Ruland, Richard, and Malcolm Bradbury. *From Puritanism to Post Modernism: A History of American Literature.* New York: Viking, 1991.

Salisbury, Neal. *Manitou and Providence: Indians, Europeans, and the Making of New England.* New York: Oxford University Press, 1982.

Schaaf, Gregory. *Wampum Belts & Peace Trees: George Morgan, Native Americans, and Revolutionary Diplomacy.* Golden, Colo.: Fulcrum, 1990.

Schwartz, Regina M. *The Curse of Cain: The Violent Legacy of Monotheism.* Chicago: University of Chicago Press, 1997.

Sedgwick, Sarah Cabot. *Stockbridge, 1739–1974.* Stockbridge, Mass.: Berkshire Traveller Press, 1974.

Segal, Charles M., and David C. Stineback. *Puritans, Indians, and Manifest Destiny.* New York: Putnam, 1977.

Simmons, William S. *Spirit of the New England Tribes: Indian*

History and Folklore, 1620–1984. Hanover, N.H.: University Press of New England, 1986.

Smith, Huston. *The Religions of Man*. New York: Harper, 1958.

Smithline, Arnold. *Natural Religion in American Literature*. New Haven, Conn.: Yale University Press, 1966.

Stone, William L. *The Life and Times of Red Jacket*. New York: Putnam, 1841.

Strout, Cushing. *The New Heavens and New Earth: Political Religion in America*. New York: Harper, 1974.

Stubbs, Denise C. *A Burning Shining Light: The Life and Ministry of the Rev. David Brainerd*. Morgan, Pa.: Soli Dei Gloria, 1997.

Sugdon, John. *Tecumseh, A Life*. New York: Holt, 1997.

Sweet, Leonard I., ed. *The Evangelical Tradition in America*. Macon, Ga.: Mercer University Press, 1984.

Sword, Wiley. *President Washington's Indian War: The Struggle for the Old Northwest, 1790–1795*. Norman, Okla.: University of Oklahoma Press, 1985.

Tinker, George E. *Missionary Conquest: The Gospel and Native American Cultural Genocide*. Minneapolis: Fortress Press, 1993.

Trelease, Allen W. *Indian Affairs in Colonial New York: The Seventeenth Century*. Ithaca, N.Y.: Cornell University Press, 1960.

Turner, Frederick Jackson. *The Frontier in American History*. New York: Holt, 1920.

Van Doren, Carl. *Benjamin Franklin*. New York: Viking, 1938.

Van Dusen, Albert E. *Puritans against the Wilderness: Connecticut History to 1763*. Bridgeport, Conn.: Eastern Connecticut State College, 1975.

Vaughn, Alden T. *New England Frontier: Puritans and Indians, 1620–1675*. Boston: Little, Brown, 1965.

————. *William Wood's "New England's Prospect," 1634.* Amherst, Mass.: University of Massachusetts Press, 1977.

Viola, Herman J. *Thomas McKenney: Architect of America's Early Indian Policy, 1816–1830.* Chicago: Swallow Press, 1974.

Wallace, Anthony, F. C. *The Death and Rebirth of the Seneca.* New York: Vintage, 1972.

————. *The Long, Bitter Trail: Andrew Jackson and the American Indians.* New York: Hill & Wang, 1993.

Ward, W. Reginald. *The Protestant Evangelical Awakening.* New York: Cambridge University Press, 1992.

Washburn, Wilcombe E. *The Indian and the Whiteman.* New York: New York University Press, 1964.

————. *The Indian in America.* New York: Harper, 1975.

Weisberger, Bernard A. *They Gathered at the River: The Story of the Great Revivalists and their Impact upon Religion in America.* Boston: Little, Brown, 1958.

Wells, David A. *God, Man, and the Thinker.* New York: Random House, 1962.

Wheeler, Rachel M. "Living upon Hope: Mahicans and Missionaries, 1730–1760." Unpublished dissertation. Yale University, New Haven, Conn., 1999.

Wilkins, Thurman. *Cherokee Tragedy: The Story of the Ridge Family and the Decimation of a People.* New York: Macmillan, 1970.

Willison, George F. *Saints and Strangers.* New York: Reynal & Hitchcock, 1945.

Wilson, Edmund. *Apologies to the Iroquois.* Syracuse, N.Y.: Syracuse University Press, 1992.

Winslow, Ola Elizabeth. *John Eliot: Apostle to the Indians.* Boston: Houghton Mifflin, 1968.

————. *Master Roger Williams: A Biography.* New York: Macmillan, 1957.

Wright, Ronald. *Stolen Continents: The New World through Indian Eyes since 1942.* New York: Viking, 1942.

Wright, Wyllis E. *Colonel Ephraim Williams: A Documentary Life.* Pittsfield, Mass.: Berkshire County Historical Society, 1970.

Wynbeek, David. *Beloved Yankee.* Grand Rapids, Mich.: Erdmans, 1961.

Young, Alexander. *Chronicles of the Pilgrim Fathers of the Colony of Plymouth, 1602–1625.* Boston: Little, Brown, 1841.

ACKNOWLEDGMENTS

THANKS TO THE cooperation and friendship of many Native Americans from a variety of tribes and to the guidance and encouragement of many historians and archivists from a variety of institutions, I was able to carry out the research for this book sustained by a strong sense of intellectual comradeship and spiritual support. However, each meeting with these chiefs and professors, librarians and theologians, curators and Park Service personnel left me with the professional misgiving that not even my most scrupulous attention to detail would do justice to their meticulous concern for materials and sites in their charge. That said, I retain the hope that there may be certain sections of my text that will reward them in part for the care they so generously devoted to my concerns.

Although this is primarily a book of American history, it also delves into such sensitive subjects as evolving Indian beliefs and European Christianity as it was altered by indigenous American factors. In these fraught subject areas, interpretation is risky and legends are to be respected; also, in these areas where angels have traditionally feared to tread, not even the most helpful guides could always succeed in steering me clear from error. I can only trust that, in naming a number of the men and women who did attempt to assist me, they will not be held accountable in any way for blunders that are mine and mine alone.

I should also explain that, living as I do within the range of Cornell University's beckoning bell tower, I am profoundly grateful for the services provided by that university's welcoming libraries. The Director of Cornell's American Indian Program (AIP), Professor Daniel Usner, rendered extraordinary assistance by reading and commenting on the manuscript. Both Dan and his predecessor at AIP, Jane Mt. Pleasant, were essential in introducing me to present-day sources and leading figures within Iroquoia.

John Mohawk, a Seneca and assistant professor of American Studies at the Buffalo campus of the State University of New York, rendered great service by pointing out the differences between the role played by Christianity in the course of western civilization and the role of Native American religions in the history of the American tribes. In his interpretation, native religions, until the time of contact with the white invaders, were "reasonably sane"—meaning that they dealt with real matters, not abstractions and miracles. Subsequent conversations with Tom Porter, spiritual head of the Mohawk Center near Fonda, New York, helped me understand that, along with faith, two other issues have been fundamental to Indian survival: land and language.

That fact was also emphasized by Jean O'Brien, an Ojibway and associate professor of American History at the University of Minnesota. Her book on Indian dispossession and her talk at the American Antiquarian Association in Worcester, Massachusetts, in April 1999 brought me to an over-due appreciation of the strategies Indian tribes have pursued in their increasingly successful struggle for survival and identity.

The research for this book began, appropriately, with Plymouth. There, at Plimouth Foundation, the library staff, led by Carolyn Traverse, steered me directly to original materials. Although I felt the lack of my late friend, the deceased and revered Nanapashamet, educators Linda Combs and Joan Tavares rendered kind assistance in introducing me to the most authoritative spokesperson for their tribe—Russell M. Peters of the Mashpee Tribal Council. My subsequent conversation with Mr. Peters, author of *The Wampanoags of Massachusetts: An Indian Perspective on American History* (Boston: Nimrod, 1987), provided primary intelligence for both chapters 2 and 8 as well as many leads to additional sources.

At the Mashpee Historical Commission, I was graciously welcomed and given rich helpings of information by Jim Morony and Rosemary Burns. Through their kindness, I made a memorable visit to the Old Indian Meeting House, as reported in chapter 4. Some months later, I enjoyed an equally meaningful visit to the Eliot Church in Natick, Massachusetts. Thanks to Anne K. Schaller, director of the Natick Historical Society and Museum, I also viewed many materials relating to John Eliot. These included both the illustration of Eliot preaching which appears in this book and a view of the grand mural in the Massachusetts State House which shows Eliot and his Native American audience.

In the course of researching chapter 3, I was privileged to have several conversations with the staff of the Huronia Museum in Midland, Ontario. Canada's first re-created Native

village, called "Saint-Marie among the Hurons (1639–1649)."
The village presents not only a view of life among the Hurons
during the years of St. Jean de Brébeuf's mission, featuring activities in the longhouse and native games, but also displays
many artifacts reaching back through ten thousand years of
pre-contact culture. I am especially grateful for input from the
museum's director/curator, James Hunter, who explained the
relationship between the Jesuits' mission stations and the existing native villages.

For closer knowledge of Jonathan Edwards's Stockbridge
(chapter 5), I am greatly indebted to curator Barbara Allen and
the staff of the Stockbridge Library.

I am also in the debt of Professor Kevin Sweeney of
Amherst College's Department of American Studies, for it was
he who introduced me to the exciting new scholarship that exists
on both the Williams family and the so-called Housatonic Indians. It was also he who allowed me to comprehend that the religious-political affairs of Stockbridge were impelled equally by
Algonquian-Iroquois strategies and by colonialist expansionism.

Just as Fort Stanwix was the most strategic point on the
northern frontier as Great Britain's colonial empire triumphed
and faded and as religion-inspired revolutions burst forth, so
does Fort Stanwix National Monument continue to play a leading role today in scholarship and interpretation of these historic
decades. For assistance in locating that re-created fort in the
bustling city of Rome, New York, I must give thanks to our fellow family member and long-time Rome resident, Mary Salerno.
I am also profoundly grateful to Michael R. Kusch, chief of
Visitors' Services at the Fort, for his introduction both to materials specifically related to the site's battles and treaties and to

broader scholarship on Native American and colonial strategies. Similarly, I owe warm thanks to Tony Wonderly, historian at the nearby Oneida Nation's Schao:wi cultural center, for his interpretation of events and personalities. His explanation of the variability of the Oneida's religious experience and of the enduring importance of their patriotism were extremely helpful for part 2 of the book.

Two other central New York sites also provided rich yields of pertinent materials. I refer to Cherry Valley, whose historical society houses a masterful diorama of the Massacre of 1778 and the Indian Castle Church of 1769, which so handsomely evokes the chapels beloved by Joseph Brant. To the friendly curators of those institutions, I would like to extend many thanks.

Ranging farther afield for this book's part 3, I had the immensely gratifying experience of meeting Daryl Baldwin, director of the Native American Complex at the Museum at Prophetstown, near West Lafayette, Indiana. Daryl, a Miami and a noted proponent of the rediscovery of his and other Native American languages, is part of a team creating a center for Woodland Indians which will explore their respective histories and strengthen their mutual ties. He was extremely kind in explaining that program and in showing me around the sites associated with the Battle of Tippecanoe on a day when the Indiana prairie grasses positively glowed. In nearby Battle Ground, I had the additional pleasure of being guided through the Tippecanoe Battlefield Museum by helpful and knowledgeable staff members.

Returning to New York State, and in great need of an on-location introduction to Mormonism, I journeyed to the Hill Cumorah Visitors' Center and Historical Site near Palmyra.

There, on what had been Joseph Smith's farm, I learned much about the founding and history of the Church of Latter Day Saints from Elder Jerry Hess, director of the center. Particularly valuable in this introduction was Elder Hess's insistence on tracing the evolutions and characteristics of the church (including its hopeful message of restoration for the Native Americans) back to chapter and verse in the Mormon scriptures. For that and other courtesies, I am much obliged.

In the final phases of preparing the book for publication, I benefitted from the efficiency and patience of numerous curators and archivists whose knowledge of their institutions' collections enabled me to gather the illustrations for this book as well as to write accurate captions. Some of these contributors have already been named. Others are: Barbara Katus of the Pennsylvania Academy of Art, Peggy Baker of the Pilgrim Society, Vernon Nelson at the Moravian Archives, Shelley Stocking of the New York State Historical Association, Suzanne Warner of the Yale University Art Gallery, Anne Slater of the Buffalo & Erie County Historical Society's library, Kirsten Kertsos of the Smithsonian's American Art Museum, Duryea Kemp at the Ohio Historical Center's archives, Lisa Anderson of the New York State Museum's Cultural Education Center, Nicole Wells of the New York Historical Society, and Laura Latman at Bowdoin College

In the search for and identification of the remarkable George Washington Covenant Belt which is included in the book's illustrations, I am particularly grateful to Chief Irving Powless, Jr., of the Onondaga Nation. I would also like to express thanks to G. Peter Jemison, editor of the seminal volume, *Treaty of Canandaigua, 1794.* He not only facilitated my picture research but also prevented me from making several grave textual errors. He then wished me and this project "Skannoh," Peace, a blessing which I return.

Because of his personal concern and continuing, professional enthusiasm for this project, Clyde Taylor—my friend and literary agent—ends up having this book dedicated to him. How I wish he had lived to see it completed. Other friends at Harcourt and elsewhere have also played key roles in the book's completion. These include Frank Bonamie, a Pine Tree chief of the Cayuga Nation, who gave me both hearty encouragement for the work and seasoned advise about Iroquois affairs. They also include the Rev. Richard Fenn, professor of Christianity and Society at the Princeton Theological Seminary. He helped me figure out what it was I was trying to say about religion in American history, then gently implied that I must have read certain traditional and fresh sources, which I had not.

For the tact as well as the expertise of my manuscript's prime editor, my wife Dora Flash Bourne, I remain eternally grateful. As companion and commentator on many of the book's research jaunts, she also provided invaluable services. Taken altogether, her support has been such that I cannot wait to get started on our next project.

INDEX